The Forward-Focused Organization

The Forward-Focused Organization

Visionary Thinking and Breakthrough Leadership to Create Your Company's Future

Stephen C. Harper

AMACOM
American Management Association

New York • Atlanta • Boston • Chicago • Kansas City • San Francisco • Washington, D. C.
Brussels • Mexico City • Tokyo • Toronto

ALEXANDRIA LIBRARY
ALEXANDRIA, VA 22304

Special discounts on bulk quantities of AMACOM books are available to corporations, professional associations, and other organizations. For details, contact Special Sales Department, AMACOM, a division of American Management Association, 1601 Broadway, New York, NY 10019.
Tel.: 212-903-8316   Fax: 212-903-8083
Web site: www.amacombooks.org

This publication is designed to provide accurate and authoritative information in regard to the subject matter covered. It is sold with the understanding that the publisher is not engaged in rendering legal, accounting, or other professional service. If legal advice or other expert assistance is required, the services of a competent professional person should be sought.

Library of Congress Cataloging-in-Publication Data

Harper, Stephen C.
    The forward-focused organization : visionary thinking and breakthrough leadership to create your company's future / Stephen C. Harper.
        p.   cm.
    Includes bibliographical references and index.
    ISBN 0-8144-0603-3
    1. Leadership.   2. Strategic planning.   3. Organizational effectiveness.   I. Title.
    HD57.7.H368   2001
    658.4'092—dc21   2001022381

© 2001 Stephen C. Harper.
All rights reserved.
Printed in the United States of America.

This publication may not be reproduced,
stored in a retrieval system,
or transmitted in whole or in part,
in any form or by any means, electronic,
mechanical, photocopying, recording, or otherwise,
without the prior written permission of AMACOM,
a division of American Management Association,
1601 Broadway, New York, NY 10019.

Printing number

10   9   8   7   6   5   4   3   2   1

Contents

Acknowledgments

I want to thank Professor Robert Keating, who has been a friend and colleague since 1985. He is the best-read person who I have ever known. He has provided me with dozens of articles to read over the years. I doubt that I would have written this book without Bob's cross-pollination of ideas, management discussions, and reading assignments.

I want to thank all my students. My undergraduate students remind me what it is like to be young and excited about what tomorrow will bring. My graduate students have been a fountain of ideas and differing perceptions. Their questions about why organizations are so slow to change challenge me during every encounter.

I particularly want to acknowledge my father, the late H. Mitchell Harper, Jr. He opened my eyes when I was growing up to the dynamics of business and the development of people. On numerous occasions, he stepped aside so that I could feel the excitement of having my hands on the throttle. My father and Jim Clarkson, a coach in my formative years, showed me that exciting things happen when you are challenged in a supportive and caring environment.

I want to thank a number of executives who provided interesting leadership role models: Thomas Watson, Jr. of IBM, who sent me a copy of his book, *A Business and Its Beliefs,* when I was a graduate student. His emphasis on having a few core values, especially superiority in everything you do, left a lasting impression on me. Jack Welch of General Electric came along at a time when there were no role models. He showed the way for U.S. companies to reestablish world leadership. Herb Kelleher of Southwest Airlines showed how to shake up an established industry and create a company where work can be fun.

I want to thank the following management writers who have

provided considerable food for thought: Peter Drucker, who is the father of management education; John Gardner, who provided insights into the nature of organizations; Warren Bennis, who has taken leadership to a new level; Rosabeth Moss Kanter, who has provided insights into the dynamics of change; Bob Townsend, who in his book *Up the Organization* was the first author to show irreverence to management practices; Tom Peters, who has taken irreverence, candor, and high-energy presentations to a whole new level; H. Igor Ansoff, who wrote the first book on planning and strategy that I ever read; Gary Hamel, who combines Drucker-type insights with Peters-type candor to provide the most interesting reading and presentations today on business strategy; and Stephen Covey, who has championed the crusade to reestablish human values in organizations. I would also like to thank the people who put together *Fast Company,* which has provided a never-ending stream of ideas and examples of the new breed of managers and the companies that are boldly going where no companies have gone before.

    Last, but not least, I want to thank my wife, Marshall; my son, Taylor; my daughter, Allison; my son-in-law, John; my mother, Ellen, and her husband, Giff; my mother-in-law, Buzz; and her husband, Bunny. They are the best things that have ever happened to me. Their love, candor, support, and sense of humor have kept me going over the years.

Introduction

Good-bye and Good Riddance to the *Comfort Zone*!

"We have to release this death grip on the past and deal with the future."[1]

—John Naisbitt, author of *Megatrends*

This book is based on the following five premises:

1. What worked well yesterday will be less effective today, ineffective tomorrow, and obsolete the day after tomorrow.
2. Change is no longer an exceptional occurrence but the rule. Change can be either evolutionary or revolutionary, depending on how executives approach the future.
3. Executives need to focus more of their attention on creating a forward-focused company than on improving its present.
4. Breakthrough leadership will be required if the company is to thrive in the ever-evolving marketplace. Traditional leadership techniques that served companies well in times of continuous improvement will not be sufficient to allow the company to break away from the pack.
5. Breakthrough leadership should not be the chief executive

officer's exclusive domain. To excel, companies need to have visionary leaders at all levels and in every unit. Every person has the potential to make a difference and every person should play an integral role in moving the company forward and in creating its future.

IT'S A WHOLE NEW BALL GAME

The past twenty years have seen incredible change. Things that people thought could never happen did happen. Things that were supposed to take decades took only a few years. Things that were supposed to take years took place in only a few months. We live in a world where products and services that didn't exist ten years ago are common in most households, offices, or automobiles. We also live in a world where what was common is now a thing of the past.

The new economy is a place where the rules have changed so radically that one wonders if there still are any rules. Power is now equalized between buyers and sellers. A start-up's revolutionary product can make the market's leading product obsolete. It is an economy where there are no time-outs and no commercial breaks. In fact, change itself is changing in this new economy as it increases in speed and complexity. Change can strike a company like a relentless and merciless series of waves. It is an economy where change comes at a company from all sides and where change makes it difficult to catch your breath and stay on your feet. Sometimes, change can be so unanticipated, so radical, so comprehensive that it sucks the air right out of your lungs!

The new economy presents new challenges. So many changes have occurred on so many fronts in such a short period of time that many companies have been caught off guard. Their executives appear to be frozen in time, much like deer caught in the headlights of an oncoming truck. The new economy is catching both large and small companies in its headlights. Even successful companies have been stunned by the speed at which revolutionary technology has been developed, new products have been introduced, and existing markets have been reconfigured.

The new economy operates at the speed of the Internet. The concept of a product having only a one-day shelf life is not that far-fetched. In the new economy, companies need to develop products that will cannibalize their own products. Instead of focusing on beating their competitors' products, companies need to move forward and create new products that make their own existing products obsolete.

The rules of business have not only changed; they are being rewritten each day. The premise "If it ain't broke, don't fix it" has been replaced with "Break it before your competitors do." The premise that the company will succeed if it incorporates continuous improvement processes has been replaced by the premise that only the innovative will survive. Incremental and linear change used to be sufficient for making a company competitive. Today, the market beckons for bold initiatives and breakthrough innovations.

The new economy is based on ideas. It beckons new ways to do things and new things to do. An economy of ideas is also an economy of insights and revelations. Executives who are savvy about market dynamics will be in a position to prevent potential problems and to capitalize on emerging opportunities. When Jeff Bezos learned about the projected increase in the use of the Internet, he quit his job and headed west in search of the best opportunity to pursue. Bezos's perceptiveness was an epiphany. It was a sudden realization that electronic commerce would be like a tsunami hitting the business world. He dropped everything he was doing so that he could ride the wave of change, which eventually made him one of the richest people in the world. The lack of perceptiveness and flexibility of established book, music, and video retailers caused them to be blindsided by the electronic commerce wave.

CREATING YOUR COMPANY'S FUTURE BY DEVELOPING A FORWARD-FOCUSED ORGANIZATION

Change can be dramatic or it can be traumatic. Executives who want to move their company forward and create its future must embrace the prelude to *Star Trek*. They must be willing to take their companies "where no company has gone before." They must be able to take their companies forward to the next level, and to levels beyond that one. Their people must be able to think thoughts they have never thought before, and to do things they have never done—or no one else has ever done! They must be able to develop new technology, and then use it to create significant competitive advantages. They must know their customers better than their customers know themselves. Companies that can anticipate where the market is going will be in a position to create their future.

The forward-focused organization is like a magnet. It attracts customers, employees, investors, and allies who want to be partners in its journey into tomorrow. Developing a forward-focused organization involves doing everything that is possible to be the employer of choice, the supplier of choice, the investment of choice, and the customer of choice. It means creating a company where highly talented people will stand in the rain for the opportunity to be considered for a position. A forward-focused organization creates a corporate culture that unleashes people and enables them to surprise themselves with what they can think and do. In this environment, people are committed to making possible what the marketplace considers impossible. It means having the answers before anyone else even knows the questions by developing products, services, and processes that leapfrog the competition.

Developing a forward-focused organization is not about maintaining a competitive position; rather it is about launching preemptive strikes. Creating the company's future goes well beyond preserving market share and keeping existing customers; it involves searching for emerging markets and attracting new customers. When creating a company's future, the goal shouldn't be to merely satisfy customers but to delight them instead.

Developing a forward-focused organization requires irreverence for almost everything that exists. It takes vision and the guts to do what needs to be done today to create a better tomorrow. Creating the company's future involves developing an environment where change is the way of life, where repetition is abhorred, and where maintaining the status quo is sinful. It involves slaughtering sacred cows and encouraging everyone to blow a whistle when they run across any form of "b.s." Robert Townsend, who helped turn around Avis, aptly phrased the need for challenging things when he recommended that companies establish the position of Vice President in Charge of Killing Things![2]

HELP WANTED: ONLY BREAKTHROUGH LEADERS NEED APPLY

Developing a forward-focused organization requires breakthrough leaders. Creating a company's future requires bold thinking and bold action. These leaders don't sit and talk about their dreams; they lead revolutions. Instead of spending their time pushing data, they recognize that revolutions start with ideas. They don't expect ideas to implement themselves because they realize that ideas succeed only to the extent to which they are well executed. Instead of waiting for their turn, they stick their necks out. They don't dwell on finding fault or rationalizing; instead they provide solutions. They take the initiative rather than waiting for someone else in the company to take the lead. They don't wait to be asked; they volunteer. Instead of waiting for opportunity to knock, they find the door and kick it open.

Breakthrough leaders don't seize *the* moment; they seize *every* moment. They don't wait until the time is right, that is, when they have all the necessary resources, time, information, authority, talent, and support from above. They make things happen in spite of the odds. They know leadership is not given to you; instead you must seize the opportunity to lead.

Dynamic leaders have the guts to approach things in a real-time manner, to commit resources, to take a stand, and to say "We can do it!" They have the guts to eliminate the word *someday* and to squash anything that resembles procrastination. They also have the guts to start what should have already been started and to drop what should have been dropped years ago.

Innovative leaders know they must have a sense of urgency, a tolerance for turbulence, and a bias for action. They know creating the company's future is more like exploring than navigating, because when you go where no one has gone before there are no maps or signs to guide you. They recognize you have to make judgment calls and that you cannot be correct 100 percent of the time. If you want to be at the leading edge, you don't have the luxury of spare time and complete information. They know that for the company to be more entrepreneurial you cannot succumb to paralysis by analysis. They also know that for companies to go the distance, they must avoid quick-fix management fads and being seduced by short-lived opportunities.

Innovative leaders see reality and attempt to create a whole new one. They have the courage to ask the questions that need to be asked, to challenge the ways things have been done, and to take the company where other companies fear to tread. They have the ability to create an environment where people can make a difference. They recognize that for the company to thrive in the years ahead, people at all levels in the company must come up with the answers to tomorrow's questions today.

Moving your company forward and creating its future involves more than taking the road less traveled—it involves creating the road yet to be traveled. It is not about taking the company to the next rung on the ladder, but about creating a whole new ladder to climb where there are no other climbers. Breakthrough leadership is not about creating a better tomorrow, but rather an entirely different tomorrow. Visionary leaders know that evolutionary change may be too slow. They also know that radical change may backfire if the company is not ready for it. Innovative leaders recognize that creating their company's future will require revolutionary evolution.

THE MODEL FOR CREATING YOUR COMPANY'S FUTURE

Executives who want to create a forward-focused company must become venture catalysts. They must be committed to building a great company rather than acting like venture capitalists, who are preoccupied with cashing out for considerable personal gain in a relatively short period of time. Unlike venture capitalists, who are almost solely concerned with generating wealth for investors, venture catalysts take pride in what their companies offer, care about their company's employees, and foster mutually beneficial relationships with the company's other stakeholders.

The ever-changing marketplace will reward companies that have their acts together and trample companies that are out of sync. Companies that are able to develop and sustain competitive advantages on multiple fronts will have a higher probability of success than those that stand out in only one area. The competitive bar has been raised. Excellence in only one competitive facet may not be sufficient to win in the marketplace.

A few years ago, companies that provided excellent quality stood out in the crowd. Today, anything less than excellence and the company is out of the game. Yet, in a world where excellence is becoming the standard, companies must be more than excellent. They must be exceptional if they want to win in the marketplace. The model depicted in Figure I-1 reflects the various dimensions that executives need to keep in mind if they want to transform their companies into exceptional enterprises.

If a company is to excel in the marketplace and thrive in the years ahead, it must develop and sustain numerous competitive advantages. These advantages include the company's ability to keep pace with—if not be ahead of—changing conditions; be either first-to-market or to have such superiority as a fast follower that it blows its competitors out of the market; meet its target market's needs so well that its customers do not even consider other companies; and create an environment where employees identify with the company to the point that they cannot imagine working for any other company.

The model depicted in Figure I-1, which serves as the foundation for this book, reflects a causal flow from left to right. Certain prerequisite conditions must exist before the company can gain these competitive advantages. These prerequisites need to be in place before the drivers of change can emerge, which, in turn, facilitate the emergent factors that foster the development of the company's competitive advantages.

Figure I-1. Creating a forward-focused organization.

Prerequisite Conditions →	Drivers of Change →	Emergent Factors →	Competitive Advantages
Breakthrough Leadership	Talent	Leaders at All Levels	Ever-Evolving Enterprise
Anticipatory Management	Insights	Lucrative Opportunities	Temporary Legal Monopolies
Innovative Systems	Ideas	Innovative Products/Services	Delighted Customers/Addicts
Revolutionary Culture	Commitment	Inspired Employees	Champions/Fanatics

Creating an Ever-Evolving Enterprise

For your company to move forward, it must be an ever-evolving enterprise. Rising customer expectations and the real-time speed of the Internet have created a Darwinian world where only the "smartest and swiftest" will survive. Bonnie Robertson, director of leadership development at Great Plains, captured the challenges of the new economy when she observed, "The Internet has triggered what is referred to as a business revolution, and we intend to provide our customers and partners what they need to win in this revolution. Being part of a revolution can be chaotic and unsettling. We are continually evolving, changing every day, and we rely on constant input from customers, partners, and other team members across the organization. This requires high-performing world-class leadership in all areas of the organization."[3]

Creating Temporary Legal Monopolies

Companies must seek opportunities where they can own the market. While U.S. executives may have been taught to avoid having their companies considered a monopoly by the protectors of free enterprise in the Justice Department, they should strive to be the only company customers seek in the marketplace. Executives should make every effort for their company to be so superior that other companies think twice before they consider competing against it. They also need to anticipate emerging markets so they have the necessary lead time for developing products and services that meet their needs when the "window of opportunity" opens. Being first-to-market provides the company with a *temporary* legal monopoly.

Forward-focused organizations rely on "corpreneurial" strategies to gain temporary legal monopolies. Corpreneurial strategies focus on emerging market opportunities and developing innovative products and services rather than on making minor modifications to existing products in established markets. Forward-focused companies, through their corpreneurial strategies, resemble entrepreneurs in their efforts to change the way the game is played. The spirit of corpreneurship is emphasized throughout this book. Five different corpreneurial strategies are presented in Chapter 7.

Creating Delighted Customers and Addicts

Marketing has been defined as the process by which a company tries to create and maintain customers for a profit. When the marketing concept was first developed, it was believed that corporate success was contingent on the company's ability to serve the market. At that time, serving the market meant providing products and services that were in tune with market expectations. With the passage of time, however, customer expectations and the availability of competitive alternatives increased. Customers wanted to be more than merely served; they wanted to have their needs and desires *satisfied*. Companies that were designed to satisfy their customers trampled companies that were designed only to serve their customers.

Today's marketplace is experiencing the emergence of a whole new level of consumer expectations. Every minute of every day is a moment of truth for companies. The days of "Let the buyer beware" and mass marketing are over. Today, serving and satisfying customers will not cut it because they expect customized solutions. Customers expect to be wowed. If companies want to create and maintain customers and to gain temporary legal monopolies, then they must be designed to delight their customers.

Creating Champions and Fanatics

Executives need to pay as much attention to the people within the company as they do to targeted customers. All products, processes, patents, and profits come from people. The company's future is tied directly to the quality of its human resources and the extent to which they are committed to creating the company's future. No company will ever have all the best people. Companies will succeed only to the extent that they are able to bring out the best in their people. Ordinary people can do truly extraordinary things under the right conditions.

CHANGE NEEDS TO BE APPROACHED WITH THE PROPER MENTAL FRAMEWORK

Change efforts are rarely simple. Executives who want to initiate change need to recognize that change must be seen in a contextual manner. They will succeed only to the extent they take into consideration the uniqueness of their corresponding situations. The greater the complexity, the greater the likelihood that factors and relationships will be missed, thereby affecting which change effort is selected as well as its effectiveness.

The Contextual Change Model, depicted in Figure I-2, identifies the five stages associated with initiating effective change. The Contextual Change Model begins and ends with stage five. Organizations are created to achieve certain results. This notion is captured in Stephen Covey's principle that executives need to "begin with the end in mind." Management must have a results orientation in everything it does. Change should never be initiated for the sake of change, but rather to achieve specific results.

Executives should identify their company's key result areas and set specific objectives for each area. Once the desired results are identified, attention needs to be directed to the awareness stage. Management must take the company's unique situation into consideration to achieve the desired results. Stage one encourages management to identify all factors and forces that are relevant to the company's situation, and that may have some bearing on the change effort. Every relevant factor and force is listed in stage one. These factors include the nature of competition, economic conditions, the rate of technological change, and the company's available resources.

Stage two encourages management to analyze how the factors and forces may be interrelated. We live in a world of cause-and-effect relationships where few things exist in isolation. The understanding stage can be seen as an attempt to build a model that reflects the whole situation, its parts, and the relationships among the parts. The model is then used to capture the expected sensitivi-

Figure I-2. Contextual change model.

Awareness → Understanding → Management → Change → Results

Stage One: Awareness of the factors that can affect performance
  Stage Two: Understanding of the relationships among the factors.
    Stage Three: Management (making key decisions and developing action plans)
      Stage Four: Initiating **Change** (implementing the action plans)
        Stage Five: Achieving the desired **Results**

ties among various factors and forces. Scenarios and simulations are helpful in identifying possible relationships and their relative sensitivities.

The first two stages are critical in the management of change. Too often, managers enter the decision-making process prematurely. They either go in with too little understanding of the unique situation they are facing or they approach today's decisions with yesterday's information. A decision can only be as good as the information that was used to make it. Managers need to recognize that in times of change every situation is unique. This is what happened to many first-generation dot-coms. While their founders may have seen the potential for e-commence and put together flashy Web sites and clever advertising campaigns, they did not recognize the importance of the back end of their businesses. The ability to attract hits was not matched with the ability to deliver the goods on time. Ventures like Pets.com crashed when they failed to develop significant competitive advantages, positive cash flow, and profitability.

Stage three represents the decision-making side of change management. When management is satisfied that it has a true understanding of the unique situation, it can direct its attention to generating and evaluating possible change strategies. Alternative solutions for achieving the desired results given the unique situation at hand must also be generated. The alternatives then need to be evaluated in terms of their ability to effectively and efficiently achieve results. The availability of resources and the degree of risk also affect which alternative is selected.

Once the change strategies under consideration are ranked, management can select the change effort that best fits the company's unique situation. Management then makes all the corresponding decisions for implementing the decision. The decisions include: What is to be done? How will it be done? Who will do it? What resources will be needed? and When will it need to be done? Contingency plans may also be developed during this stage.

Stage four represents initiating change to achieve desired results. This stage recognizes that decisions do not implement themselves. Management needs to recognize that every plan is based on a set of assumptions about reality. If the assumptions do not hold up, then the plans may need to be modified. Implementation includes monitoring the change effort's success on a periodic or on-going basis.

Monitoring frequency is contingent on the volatility of the situation, the likelihood of error, the consequences of an error, and the length of time it takes to address an error. The greater the sensitivity, the greater the need for frequent monitoring. Life is full of surprises and few things go as planned, so this stage may involve adjusting the change effort or launching a contingency plan to get the company back on track.

Stage five is a reality check. It involves ensuring that the change effort fulfilled original performance expectations. If the company was unsuccessful in its efforts, then management needs to recognize that its decisions for the change effort were probably built on a weak foundation.

TO MOVE A COMPANY FORWARD, CHANGE NEEDS TO BE EMBRACED, NOT FEARED

Leading organizational change begins with the recognition that companies are entering uncharted waters. Peter Drucker noted, "A time of turbulence is a dangerous time, but its greatest danger is the temptation to deny reality."[4] Change is no longer an option. The status quo is not a safe haven.

Michael Eisner, as CEO of Disney, captured the nature of change when he stated, "We as a company will continue to change and evolve and take risks and blaze new trails as we move forward. It may seem easier for our life to remain constant. But change, really, is the only constant. We cannot stop it and we cannot escape it. We can let it destroy us or we can embrace it. For an organization like ours, change is the engine of growth and the muse of creativity."[5]

While initiating change may seem risky, executives who are reluctant to change place their companies at even greater risk. John Walter, as president of AT&T, stated, "When the pace of change outside an organization becomes greater than the pace of change inside the organization, the end is near."

NEW REALITIES CALL FOR NEW APPROACHES TO LEADERSHIP

The ever-accelerating nature and ever-increasing magnitude of change call for a completely new perspective in viewing the change process. Breakthrough leadership begins by noting the following realities:

Principles of Change for Breakthrough Leadership

- Change isn't merely a set of tools and techniques, it's a state of mind.
- Change isn't about fixing yesterday's mistakes, it's about preparing for a new tomorrow.
- Change isn't about surviving, it's about thriving.
- Change isn't only about the bottom line, it's about focusing on the "top line."
- Change isn't only about putting out fires, it's about blazing new trails.
- Change isn't the enemy, it's about making change an ally.
- Change isn't about creating fuzzy mission statements, it's about creating a compelling vision.
- Change isn't about developing detailed and inflexible plans, it's about "futuring."
- Change isn't about competing in the future, it's about creating the future.
- Change isn't about incrementalism, it's about breakthrough innovation.
- Change isn't about isolated tweaks, it's about multifaceted change efforts.
- Change isn't about coping, it's about making change a way of life.

Change Isn't Merely a Set of Tools and Techniques, It's a State of Mind

Breakthrough leadership is an attitude. It is the way you approach situations, challenges, and change. It is about how you see the future, technology, risk, and people. Executives who understand the complexities of innovative leadership will be able to break away from the pack. Executives who continue approaching the world around them with the same mental models and approaches they used in the past will be left behind.

Change Isn't about Fixing Yesterday's Mistakes, It's about Preparing for a New Tomorrow

There is a story about two managers supervising teams of workers who were cutting their way through a forest. While one manager is busy measuring the group's progress, the other manager climbs a tree and yells down, "We're in the wrong forest!" New realities call for a new breed of leader. Albert Einstein once noted, "You cannot solve the problem with the same kind of thinking that created the problem." Hopefully, the days that were once devoted to "stopping the bleeding" can be replaced with a commitment to building strength.

Change Isn't about Surviving, It's about Thriving

Leading change involves gaining temporary legal monopolies in target markets by outthinking and outdoing your competition. It is about sensing change before others do so that you have a mental head start over your competitors. It is about being the first to see opportunities so that you can develop competencies to help your company thrive . . . while other companies desperately try to survive.

Change Isn't Only about the Bottom Line, It's about Focusing on the "Top Line"

Top-line management encourages a company to seek new revenue opportunities. It encourages executives to scan the horizon for emerging opportunities and to be more entrepreneurial. It also encourages the company to do exploratory marketing to find new markets to serve and new ways to serve existing markets. Top-line management embraces being first to market and making preemptive strikes because the companies that are first to market often have the opportunity to establish brand identity and to set the rules for how the competitive game will be played.

Change Isn't Only about Putting Out Fires, It's about Blazing New Trails

Few things capture people's excitement more than being part of a vibrant entity and exploring new possibilities. Capitalizing on growth opportunities and developing innovative approaches capture the human spirit far more than efforts geared to downsizing and outsourcing. Executives will serve their companies well if they direct their attention toward looking at the world ahead of them through new eyes—and at their companies as if they were a fresh sheet of paper—because they will then find opportunities for their companies to excel.

Change Isn't the Enemy, It's about Making Change an Ally

Leading change means being the initiator and beneficiary of change rather than the recipient and victim of change. Rosabeth Moss Kanter, author of *The Change Masters*, noted, "Change can either be friend or foe, depending on the resources available to cope with it and master it by innovating. It is disturbing when it is done to us, exhilarating when it is done by us."[6] According to Kanter, "Change can be exhilarating, refreshing—a chance to meet new challenges, a chance to clean house. . . . Change brings opportunities when people have been planning for it, are ready for it, and have just the thing in mind to do when a new state comes into being."[7]

Change Isn't about Creating Fuzzy Mission Statements, It's about Creating a Compelling Vision

Breakthrough leadership can only occur if executives have a strong future orientation and if they can develop a vision for where their companies should be in that future. Jack Welch noted the importance of having a vision for the future when he began his transformation of GE. Welch stated, "If you can't articulate your business vision, if you can't get people to buy in, forget it."[8] In a sense, the vision is the call to arms that empowers people at all levels and mobilizes the company's resources to make exciting things happen.

Change Isn't about Developing Detailed and Inflexible Plans, It's about "Futuring"

Although a vision may help clarify the direction in which a company should be headed, a clear vision statement cannot be developed unless executives scan the horizon for what may be ahead. The real challenge of breakthrough leadership may be in ensuring that the company keeps its eyes on the horizon. Karl Albrecht, author of *The Northbound Train*, emphasizes the need for executives to do "futuring." He defined futuring as a "constantly active mental process that generates action strategies for capitalizing on the unfolding environment."[9] Plans that are inflexible and too formal are like quicksand. They can elicit a degree of organizational rigidity that impedes a company's ability to adjust to an ever-changing world. Executives who recognize future discontinuities will prevent their company's tomorrow from becoming a linear extension of its past. They are also in a better position to steer their companies through the whitewater that lies ahead.

Change Isn't about Competing in the Future, It's about Creating the Future

Breakthrough leadership in its purest form is not about preparing for the future, but rather creating the company's future. These leaders break the rules, make new rules, and then change the rules again. Visionary leadership goes beyond managing in a world of change; it means leading the change. It is about being proactive and entrepreneurial. Innovative leaders have the ability to change the probabilities, payoffs, and states of nature. They ponder what opportunities may exist and then position their companies to create their futures by capitalizing on these opportunities. Breakthrough leaders embrace Alan Kay's philosophy that "the best way to predict the future is to invent it!"

Change Isn't about Incrementalism, It's about Breakthrough Innovation

Creating a world-class company involves more than merely making minor changes to existing products. When he was vice president of research and engineering at Pillsbury, Philip D. Aines noted, "It's much more difficult to come up with a synthetic meat product than a lemon-lime cake mix because you know exactly what the return is going to be. A synthetic steak is going to take a lot longer, require a much larger investment, and the risk of failure will be much greater."[10] For far too many companies, the tendency to spend the company's resources on making a new lemon-lime cake mix is greater than the courage to develop breakthrough products and services.

Change Isn't about Isolated Tweaks, It's about Multifaceted Change Efforts

Organizational contexts are as multifaceted as a diamond. Executives need to approach change from a holistic or systems perspective. Executives need to recognize that a company is part of an ecosystem. Change efforts need to recognize that a company is actually a web of relationships. Executives need to be able to differentiate between causes of problems and symptoms of problems. Changing one component of the system will affect other components. Some effects will be obvious; others will be subtle. Some effects will be immediate; others may not appear for quite some time. Executives need to view change as if they were throwing a stone into a pond. They need to anticipate the ripple effect and make certain that the overall effect is what they desire before they throw the stone.

Change Isn't about Coping, It's about Making Change a Way of Life

Coping has become a way of life for most companies. Too many executives only focus on making it through the day. They spend too much time and energy trying to make certain things do not fall through the cracks. They also spend too much time bracing themselves for the next wave of change. An organization has only a limited amount of energy. The energy can be spent defending its borders and maintaining its present position, or it can be directed toward initiating change and moving forward to the high ground. Carl Wallenda, the great high-wire performer, captured the inherent energizing force of change when he stated, "Being on the tight-rope is living . . . everything else is waiting!"[11] Breakthrough leadership creates opportunities for everyone in the company to feel alive by providing them with opportunities to make a difference.

CONCLUSION: LEAD OR GET BLOWN OUT OF THE WAY!

The business world is not a touchy-feely world. It is a world where competitors don't take prisoners and where being a day late means going out of business. However, it is also a world full of opportunities for the initiators of change because they will thrive. Conversely, it is a world full of threats for companies that are out of touch because they will not survive.

The marketplace shows no mercy for companies that are out of sync. There used to be room in the marketplace for good companies and good managers. As long as companies offered something within reason and at a price that was acceptable, they could make a reasonable profit. The classic twentieth-century saying of "Lead, follow, or get out of the way" is being replaced with the reality that you either lead or get blown out of the way. In times of rapid change, there is little room for companies that follow. If you are not markedly better, then you are dead.

IN THE FOLLOWING CHAPTERS . . .

This book shows you how to blend corporate culture and leadership style with business strategy and essential business processes to achieve exceptional results. It helps you to develop a mental framework for creating a forward-focused company. It demonstrates how visionary thinking and planning "two markets ahead" will help you to spot emerging opportunities. It shows how breakthrough leadership and corpreneurial strategies can help you catch the waves of change so that your company can continue moving forward while other companies fall by the wayside. It helps you frame a compelling vision and monitor performance so that there will be fewer surprises. It also offers two appendices, which provide cautions so that you and your company will not drive off your employees and customers.

This book offers hundreds of ideas, insights, and examples. It also provides insights from the new breed of entrepreneurs and the emerging dot-coms. We can learn from the irreverent attitudes embraced by entrepreneurial companies that live at the edge. We can learn from the new business models used by e-commerce companies that are blazing new trails even though they may be light years away from generating the level of profit needed to justify their capitalization.

This book is not intended only for people who are already at the helms of their companies but for people at all levels in the company. It will help those who want to get to the helm as well as those who want to make a difference in their current positions.

ONE LAST THING . . . CAVEAT EMPTOR!

Most books about leading change focus on how leaders can get the other people in the company to change. They focus on how to get other people to follow the leader. This book focuses on how people need to change themselves so that they can become visionary leaders. Rather than waiting for someone else to save the day, this book encourages you to seize immediate challenges and take the initiative in creating your company's future.

This book is like a mirror and a coach. It encourages you to identify your strengths, shortcomings, and blind spots. Breakthrough leadership means saying good-bye and good riddance to what you have done and how you have done it. It means leaving your comfort zone and not creating a new one, unless the process of initiating change and embarking on new journeys is what you consider to be your *new* comfort zone. Innovative leadership occurs only when the anxiety of doing the same things the same way is far greater than the anxiety associated with doing things you have never done before!

> "All problems become smaller when you don't dodge them but confront them. Touch a thistle timidly and it pricks you; grasp it boldly, and its spines crumble."
>
> William S. Halsey,
> World War II admiral

NOTES

Portions of the material in the introduction originally appeared in the article "Leading Organizational Change" by the author in *Industrial Management,* May–June 1998, pp. 25–31. Reprinted with the permission of the Institute of Industrial Engineers, 25 Technology Place, Norcross, Georgia 30092.

1. John Naisbitt, *Megatrends* (New York: Warner Books, 1984), p. 13.
2. Robert Townsend, *Up the Organization* (New York: Alfred A. Knopf, 1970), p. 93.
3. "Strategic Leadership," *Fortune,* March 6, 2000, p. S5.
4. Peter F. Drucker, *Managing in Turbulent Times* (New York: Harper & Row, 1980), p. 4.
5. *Disney Annual Report,* December 2, 1994, p. 4.
6. Rosabeth Moss Kanter, *The Change Masters* (New York: Simon & Schuster, 1984), p. 64.
7. Ibid.
8. Noel Tichy and Stratford Sherman, *Control Your Destiny or Someone Else Will* (New York: HarperCollins, 1994), p. 410.
9. Karl Albrecht, *The Northbound Train* (New York: AMACOM, 1994), p. 62.
10. "The Breakdown of U.S. Innovation," *Business Week,* February 16, 1976, p. 57.
11. Warren Bennis, *Leaders* (New York: Harper & Row, 1985), p. 69.

Part I

The Role of Leadership in Creating a Forward-Focused Organization

Part I indicates how breakthrough leaders provide the electricity needed to transform companies into exceptional enterprises. It profiles how leaders need to set the example for how things should be done, to create a culture where change is a way of life, and where learning—and learning quickly—enables the company to keep pace with, if not ahead of, change. This section highlights how ideas and innovation need to percolate from every level and every person. It also highlights how the ability to turn on a dime can make the difference between success and failure.

Breakthrough leadership is not about playing it safe. It involves having the courage to make a commitment, take the initiative, and leap into the unknown. Only then will you be able to create your company's future.

1

Twelve Guidelines for Leading Change

"There is nothing more difficult to take in hand, more perilous to conduct, or more uncertain in its success, than to take the lead in the introduction of a new order of things."

Niccolo Machiavelli, *The Prince*

The ability to lead change will be more important in the years ahead than at any time in the past. The accelerating rate of change and multifaceted nature of change will challenge even the most gifted leaders. The twenty-first century will place demands on companies that will make today seem like the good old days. Although the future may be uncertain, one thing is clear: Without breakthrough leaders to guide them into the future, companies will have no future.

New challenges call for new approaches to leading change. The following guidelines should help you lead your company through the minefield of new realities:

- Leading change must be a way of life.
- Leading change is as multifaceted as a diamond.
- Leading change requires commitment from all involved.
- Leading change means sloughing off yesterday and today.
- Leading change involves avoiding the "boiled frog" syndrome.

- Leading change must establish relevance.
- Leading change means asking the right questions.
- Leading change means creating early victories.
- Leading change means recognizing the paradox of success.
- Leading change involves creating a learning organization.
- Leading change means competing against oneself.
- Leading change means building coalitions.

LEADING CHANGE MUST BE A WAY OF LIFE

Managers must recognize the risks of continuing the present. Years ago, Thomas Watson, Jr., as chairman of IBM, noted, "There has never been any future in the status quo."[1] While most people recognize that change is a fact of life, a number of people share the philosophy of management held by Bert Lance, who served as a member of Jimmy Carter's cabinet. Lance was fond of the statement "If it ain't broke, don't fix it!" which echoes in the halls of many organizations today. This sentiment needs to be replaced with the attitude of "Change or be changed."

Breakthrough leaders have contempt for the status quo. They constantly look for gaps and ask, "Are we doing what we should be doing?" or "Should we still be doing this?" Innovative leaders know that being good enough is not good enough anymore. They also know that if you are merely trying to be competitive you will always be eating someone else's dust.

Change must go well beyond rhetoric—it must be internalized and operationalized. Change cannot be done on a virtual organization basis and it cannot be outsourced to consultants who are prone to use generic approaches. Charles Fishman stressed that for change to be effective, it must be led by people who know the business.[2]

Change takes time and hard work. Since it requires a commitment to go the distance, change should not be expected to produce overnight successes. Transforming a company into an exceptional enterprise could take years. Change must be seen as a never-ending journey. Since change takes commitment from everyone in the company, it must be encouraged, enabled, reviewed, and rewarded at every level.

Executives who want to be innovative leaders must recognize

that change is not an occasional proposition. There are no short-cuts, time-outs, or commercial breaks. They must recognize that no facet of the organization is immune, that nothing will go un-touched, and that nothing is sacred. Change cannot be ignored or postponed; rather it must be substantive and continuous. It must involve bold initiatives as well as continuous fine-tuning. Change is not something that is done only when it is convenient.

LEADING CHANGE IS AS MULTIFACETED AS A DIAMOND

Leading change is not a simple process. Numerous factors need to be considered. The more frequently that these factors are incorpo-rated into the change process, the more likely that it will produce beneficial results. Change cannot be engineered and managed with the same precision that an assembly line can be designed and man-aged. It takes perceptiveness and finesse. The following sample of insights may prove beneficial before embarking on a change effort:

Corporate Change Facts of Life

- Change is a fact of corporate life. Most people resist change, especially if they are not prepared for it. Create an environment where people embrace change, rather than brace themselves to resist it.
- Change is occurring at an ever-accelerating pace. Improve the company's ability to sense change while it is still on the horizon—when people can see it coming and prepare for it.
- Change is more acceptable when people see it as beneficial to them rather than as a threat. Show that it is relevant and worth the effort.
- Change will be implemented better if the people who must make it happen are coarchitects of the change.
- Change is more acceptable when it is prompted by a sense of reality than when it is imposed from above as a "Just do it!" edict.
- Change is more likely to be accepted if it follows a success-ful change effort. Capitalize on the momentum.

- Change is more likely to be accepted if it is initiated after a previous change has been assimilated, rather than if it is initiated while a major change is under way. Let employees catch their breath for a brief moment before moving on.
- Change is more likely to be accepted if it is the result of deliberate analysis rather than a knee-jerk response to an unanticipated event or crisis.
- Change is more likely to be accepted by people who have limited experience than by people who are accustomed to doing things in a particular way.
- Change is more likely to be accepted if the people in the company are familiar with change models and change processes.
- Change is more likely to occur if executives set the proper example for others to follow.

LEADING CHANGE REQUIRES COMMITMENT FROM ALL INVOLVED

Leading change calls for more than going through the motions the way most companies did in the 1990s by using total quality management and business process reengineering. Leading change is not for people looking for quick fixes. Change calls for total commitment, not merely participation. Innovative leaders know the difference between commitment and participation. When they are asked to describe the difference they say, "It's the difference between eggs and bacon. While the chicken participated in making the breakfast possible, the pig was truly committed!"

Dynamic leaders recognize that change efforts will succeed only to the extent they are able to create an environment where people want to get on board. Change efforts may encounter varying levels of commitment. Some change efforts are expedited because they start with a high level of commitment. Other change efforts are destined to fail because they face stiff resistance. The following levels of commitment may be encountered in a change effort:

The Seven Levels of Commitment

champions—those who are the architects or initiators of the change

> **committed**—those who embrace the change at face value
>
> **participants**—those who accept the change and go through the motions
>
> **observers**—those who watch from the sidelines and withhold judgment of the need for and merit of the change
>
> **skeptics**—those who need to be convinced of the need for and merit of the change
>
> **overt resisters**—those who openly resist change
>
> **covert resisters**—those who resist the change behind the scenes

People can be in one category for one change effort and in a different category for another change effort. If people believe the company is in a "change or die" situation and have a chance to be coarchitects of the change effort, then they may welcome the opportunity to play a leading role. Conversely, people who have been left in the dark or burned by change efforts in the past may resist change with the utmost vigor.

People leading change efforts should be realists. Resistance is a natural part of most change processes. Few people embrace change that will affect them when someone else proposes it. The only person who welcomes change is a baby with a soiled diaper. People leading change efforts should recognize that resistance may have merits. They should try to learn why people are reluctant to accept and implement the proposed change. When people do not understand the need for change or what is involved in the change effort, their resistance may actually be confusion. Their questions should not be seen as resistance. People who propose change should remember that other people have not been thinking about the change as much as they have or for as long. They also need to recognize that other people do not have extrasensory perception. They should look at change through the other people's eyes.

We may be able to learn something from the resisters. Most people do not wake up in the morning and say, "Let's see how I can keep the company from moving ahead today." People who resist change believe that they have a good reason for doing so. They may see something that we don't see. Resisters can serve as a timely reality check by keeping us from having blind faith and becoming overly infatuated with our own ideas.

Resisters need to see the benefits of making the change—and

the consequences for both the company and themselves if the company does not make the change. There will be times, however, when resisters must face a moment of truth. They should be given the opportunity to get on board. However, the invitation to get on board should make it clear that once the decision is made to go ahead, they need to mentally and physically get on board or find a company that shares their perceptions.

Change leaders need to keep an eye on covert resisters. John Kotter, author of *Leading Change*, stresses the need for change leaders not to drop their guard once the change effort is initiated. Covert resisters look for the first sign of a problem to show the change effort was ill conceived. They may even look for the first sign of success to indicate that the problem has been resolved and that the company can return to its old ways.[3]

Breakthrough leaders recognize three other aspects that are associated with people's commitment to change efforts. First, the absence of resistance should not be mistaken for commitment. Going back to the chicken and pig story, there are a lot of chickens out there. Effort needs to be directed to gaining their commitment. Second, while people may resist change, few people resist improvement. Change efforts need to indicate how the change will lead to a better tomorrow. Emphasis should be placed on how things will be better instead of merely different. Third, change efforts need to be led by people at all levels of the company. Top management may foster change by providing air cover, but change efforts should not rely on charismatic style to gain commitment. Charisma has two drawbacks: It is a rare commodity and most people would rather decide for themselves whether to join the change effort rather than relying on someone else's personality to sway them.

Midlevel managers, first-line supervisors, and hourly employees should also be given the opportunity to play leadership roles. Top management needs to ensure that midlevel managers support the change. Midlevel managers can make change happen or kill it in its tracks. They can expedite change by endorsing it or they can derail it by dragging their feet. Midlevel managers play a crucial role in ensuring that two-way communication flows unimpeded.

Top management also needs to be in tune with what is happening on the front lines of change. Front-line personnel will be more committed to the change effort if they have a sense for the overall context of change. First-line supervisors live where the rubber meets the road. Employees usually support change only to the extent their supervisors support them. In many ways, their commitment to the company is tied directly to their commitment to their supervisor. Change has the best chance for success when the whole organization operates as a web of formal and informal change champions.

LEADING CHANGE MEANS SLOUGHING OFF YESTERDAY AND TODAY

Executives need to create an environment where people realize that they cannot prepare for tomorrow unless they are first willing to let go of the past and present. Kurt Lewin, a noted psychologist, developed two models for understanding and managing the change process. Lewin's first model involves a three-step unfreezing-change-refreezing process.[4] The first step involves unfreezing the current approach for getting things done. Before executives try to introduce change, they need to create a situation where the people involved in the change recognize the shortcomings and risks associated with continuing the present into the future.

Kurt Lewin's Three-Step Model for Initiating Change

Step One: Unfreezing → Step Two: Initiating the Change → Step Three: Refreezing

Step One: Unfreezing
Breaking away from the way things have been done
Step Two: Initiating the Change
Identifying and trying new ways to do things or new things to do
Step Three: Refreezing
Reinforcing the new ways or new things to do

Kurt Lewin noted that change efforts are destined to be exercises in futility if people are unwilling to drop what they have been doing. Most people are unwilling to change if they are in their comfort zone. They prefer their comfort zone, even with its drawbacks, to the potential benefits associated with an uncertain future.

Almost everyone has a pair of jeans or khakis that should have been thrown out years ago. Instead, we hang on to them the way a child clings to a security blanket. The jeans may be tattered, but we still wear them. When life at work gets hectic, it is nice to come home and put them on. We know that we should throw them out and break in a new pair, but we still keep them. It usually takes an act of spousal intervention for you to throw them out.

Leaders need to recognize that each person involved in a change process may have work-related habits that resemble time-worn jeans or khakis. Change efforts have the best chance for success when those involved in the change recognize the need to let go and welcome the prospect of doing something new. Unfortunately, some people seem to be unwilling to let go of past and present practices, approaches, and mental models.

Change efforts must start with the deliberate discontinuation of the past. Executives need to be prepared to deal constructively with people who are unwilling to let go. It is said that the Spanish explorer Hernando Cortes burned his ships as soon as he arrived in the New World. Cortes recognized that as long as the ships were anchored offshore, his men could think about returning to their homes. By scuttling the ships, Cortes's men had to deal with the New World. If you want your people to journey into the future, then you may have to provide the spark that burns their comfort zones so that they cannot cling to the present. The most effective spark may be information that shows that we either change or die!

Peter Drucker noted, "Systematic sloughing off of yesterday is a plan by itself. . . . It will force thinking and action. It will make available men and money for new things. It will create a willingness to act. Conversely, the plan that provides only for doing additional and new things without provision for sloughing off old and tired ones is unlikely to have results. It will remain a plan and never become a reality."[5]

Drucker's strategic-planning gap concept helps with the unfreezing process. Drucker stated that executives need to ask: Where is the company at this point in time? Where should the company be at a future point in time? and Where will the company be at that future point in time if it does not change what it is currently doing? The strategic-planning gap is the difference between where the company wants to be and where it will be if it does not change. The larger the gap, the greater the need for change—and the greater the magnitude of the change effort.

Leaders must learn how to transform the anxiety and risks

associated with uncertainty into constructive efforts rather than debilitating behavior. Chris Argyris noted there are two types of anxieties associated with change. Anxiety I is the anxiety associated with doing something new. It includes the risks associated with making a mistake, of looking stupid, and of being punished. Anxiety I is quite natural and should be expected.

Whenever people are put in a situation where they try to do something new, they are temporarily incompetent—they are not in control. This explains why so many people are hesitant to leave their comfort zones. Anxiety I causes *paralysis by analysis* where people are reluctant to pull the trigger of change. They stay in a "ready, aim, aim, aim" mode and never fire. Paralysis by analysis can happen at any level of the company. CEOs can "lock up" when faced with the challenges of embarking on a journey into new markets. It can also happen to lower-level managers when they are expected to adopt new software.

Bob Knowling, a change agent while at US West, captured the nature of Anxiety I when he stated, "Once people have figured out something very different is happening, fear permeates the organization. You can cut it with a knife. I've come to the conclusion that you can unfear an organization. You have to tell people that if they allow fear to paralyze them, it will become a self-fulfilling prophecy; it will be their undoing because they're immobilized; they can't make decisions."[6] A scene from the film *12 O'Clock High* provides an extreme example of how to get people to let go of the past. When the commanding general recognizes the bomber crews are reluctant to fly, he tells them, "Consider yourselves already dead. Once you accept that idea, it won't be so tough."

Emphasizing the benefits of sloughing off the past may be more fruitful than utilizing scare tactics to get people to let go. You can reduce the anxiety associated with trying new things by providing a safety net for the people who are involved in the change process. People are far more willing to experiment if they have the freedom to fail.

People will be more willing to embark on a new journey if they believe that they have the opportunity to make a difference. Steven Jobs had been unsuccessful in his attempts to recruit John Sculley away from his heir apparent position at Pepsi to run Apple Computer. Jobs's stock offers and generous perquisites were not sufficient to entice Sculley to change his career. Sculley tendered his resignation, however, after Jobs challenged him with the question, "Do you want to spend the rest of your life selling sugared water or do you want a chance to change the world?"[7]

Anxiety II is markedly different from Anxiety I. It comes with the recognition of what will result if the change is not initiated.[8] Anxiety II is rooted in the concept of opportunity cost. While Anxiety I focuses on the risks associated with making the change, Anxiety II focuses on the consequences of not making the change. People who are thinking about starting a new venture frequently encounter both types of anxiety. People who are preoccupied with the risks of taking on a second mortgage to finance the venture, as well as quitting a job that offered a stable salary and fringe benefits, rarely become entrepreneurs. Their level of Anxiety I keeps them from leaving their comfort zones and putting their marriages, mortgages, and credit card balances in jeopardy.

Writer Henry David Thoreau captured the essence of Anxiety II when he observed, "The mass of men lead lives of quiet desperation."[9] People are far more willing to initiate change when they recognize that failure to embark on the new will not merely result in lost opportunities but could produce everlasting regret for not doing what could have—and should have—been done. Jeff Bezos attributed his motivation to create Amazon.com to what he refers to as a regret minimization framework. Bezos could not fathom what his life would be like if he didn't catch the e-commerce wave. When he saw projections for business use of the Internet, he quit his job as vice president of an investment firm in New York. Once Bezos realized that the risks of catching the wave were far less than the regret he would have if he continued his career, he started his journey west to the new frontier.

People like Jeff Bezos, who embark on the entrepreneurial journey, or like John Sculley, who jump at the opportunity to be part of a corpreneurial initiative, have either low levels of Anxiety I or high levels of Anxiety II. People who relish the challenge of doing something new are less likely to be constrained by Anxiety I. These people welcome the opportunity to do things that they—and possibly no one else—have never done before. The strength of their Anxiety II can serve as the catalyst for embarking on an entrepreneurial or a corpreneurial journey.

Organizations that are future-oriented and opportunity-driven are less likely to encounter Anxiety I. Leaders can expedite change by creating an environment where the opportunity cost of Anxiety II exceeds the risks associated with Anxiety I. People will jump on the train when they see that the benefits of heading to a new and exciting destination far outweigh the benefits of staying at the station and continuing the status quo. The same reasoning also applies when the consequences of continuing the status quo (staying on a burning platform) outweigh the consequences (fear of the unknown, etc.) of the proposed change effort.

Step two of Kurt Lewin's model—the process for identifying the change initiative—incorporates decision theory and creative problem-solving techniques. This step works best when the people involved in implementing the change, as well as those who will ultimately be affected by the change, are given the opportunity to share their thoughts. The more the people who are going to be involved in implementing the change are given the opportunity to be the coarchitects of the change, the greater the probability they will be committed to making it a success. The more the people to be affected by the change understand its need and benefits, the less likely they will be to resist it.

The need to create an environment that encourages and rewards change efforts is particularly important in step three—refreezing the change—of Kurt Lewin's model. This step increases the likelihood the new way of doing things will become the way of life. One of the guiding principles of psychology is the concept of behavior modification. Behavior modification stresses the need to reward desired behavior whenever it is demonstrated. Positive reinforcement does two things: First, it indicates that the new behavior is valued. Second, it reduces the likelihood that people will continue the former behavior. Behaviors that are rewarded tend to be repeated. Behaviors that are no longer rewarded tend to be discontinued.

The rewards for the new behavior need to be greater than the rewards people find in maintaining the status quo. Step three will also have a greater chance for success if the people involved in the change effort see that they are making progress. Their efforts will be strengthened if they are rewarded, even symbolically, for their efforts. The need for early victories is discussed later in this chapter.

Kurt Lewin's second change model provides a useful framework for expediting the acceptance of change. His force-field model indicates that most situations exist in a state of dynamic equilibrium.[10] Lewin noted that equilibrium exists when the forces supporting change are counterbalanced by the forces restraining change. The force-field model serves as a reality check. Restraining forces will exist in almost every change effort. If they are not identified and addressed, the change effort will be jeopardized.

Kurt Lewin's Force-Field Change Model

Driving Forces → Present Balance Point ← Restraining Forces

The force-field model shows that change occurs when at least one of the following three conditions occurs:

1. Management increases the forces supporting the change. This can be done by increasing training opportunities and by providing rewards for adopting the desired behavior.
2. Management tries to reduce the restraining forces. Knocking down the barriers that hold people back will foster change. Creating an environment where people have a punishment-free opportunity to try the new represents one of the best ways to reduce the risks associated with change.
3. Management tries both approaches.

The red-light–green-light change concept builds on Kurt Lewin's ideas. Certain facets of the proposed change may represent stoplights that stop change efforts in their tracks. If the goal of the change effort is to have employees go from point A level of performance to point B level of performance, managers need to create an environment that makes the improvement in performance possible. Change efforts should begin by asking employees to identify the *red lights* that slow them down and/or impede their journey. The red lights may include poor equipment, lack of training, or insufficient information. These factors impede performance and sap motivation. Employees quickly conclude that management is not committed to them and/or the change effort if these factors exist. Management needs to address these factors before initiating the change effort.

Management should then direct its attention to providing *green light* factors. Green lights enhance commitment. They give people a reason to get out of bed in the morning and improve their performance. Green lights are important because the elimination of red lights—even though it may be appreciated by employees—will not generate high levels of performance. If management wants high levels of commitment and high levels of performance, it needs to provide high levels of rewards. Management needs to ensure that the rewards are relevant to the people involved and that they are large enough to make the effort worthwhile. Management also needs to be sure the rewards are tied directly to—and proportional with—the level of performance.

The two-stage red-light–green-light model provides a good explanation for why employees may not jump at the chance to be part of a change effort. If they don't join the change procession to point B, it is because management has not eliminated the red lights and provided enough green lights to make the journey worthwhile. If employees don't jump on the train, management is at fault, not the employees.

LEADING CHANGE INVOLVES AVOIDING THE "BOILED FROG" SYNDROME

There is a story that if you put a frog in a frying pan and slowly turn up the heat, the frog will boil to death rather than jump out. If you drop a frog in boiling water, however, it will jump out immediately. The strategic-planning gap concept represents a way to reduce the likelihood the company will fall prey to the boiled frog syndrome. If people do not sense a significant gap between where they are and where they need to be, they may not recognize the need to get out of their comfort zone and change what they are doing.

Edgar Shein, as a professor of management at MIT, noted that managers must make nonconforming data highly visible to all members of the organization, and the data must be convincing. Merely saying that the organization is in trouble because profit levels are down, market share is being lost, customers are complaining, costs are too high, or good people are leaving is not good enough. He observed, "Employees often simply do not understand or do not believe it when management says, 'We are in trouble.' "[11]

John Kotter considers creating a sense of urgency to be the first step in leading change. He noted, "Sometimes executives underestimate how hard it can be to drive people out of their comfort zones. . . . When the urgency rate is not pumped up enough, the transformation process cannot succeed and the long-term future of the business is put in jeopardy. . . . The urgency rate is high enough when 75 percent of a company's management is honestly convinced that business as usual is totally unacceptable. Anything less can produce very serious problems later in the change process."[12] More than half of the companies Kotter studied failed to create the sense of urgency needed to enact change.[13]

While innovative leaders may see the need for the company to change what it is doing, executives should recognize that an extra effort may be necessary to jump-start other people's perceptions of the need to discontinue what they are doing. Ignorance, arrogance, and complacency abound in many organizations. Companies that are on the brink of disaster frequently operate in a state of denial.

If the company is not facing a crisis, then management may need to *create* a sense of urgency. Jan Timmer, as CEO of Phillips Electronics, may get the prize for attempting to get his employees' attention. He handed out a hypothetical press release that Phillips was bankrupt to the company's top one hundred executives at a retreat.[14] When managers look for reasons why the company got itself in a bind, such as the loss of accounts or missed deadlines, they should remember the immortal words of Pogo, "We have met the enemy and he is us!"

LEADING CHANGE MUST ESTABLISH RELEVANCE

Management's efforts to create a sense of urgency will not gain a high level of commitment unless there is a sense of relevancy for all involved. Paul Strebel, a professor at the International Institute for Management Development in Lausanne, Switzerland, noted, "Managers must put themselves in their employees' shoes to understand how change looks from that perspective and to examine the terms of the personal compact between the employees and the company.[15] Gerry McQuaid found the ability to create a sense of relevance was critical to gaining a high level of commitment from employees. When he was site manager for Corning's optic fiber plant, he recognized management's earlier efforts to gain a high level of commitment to quality were unsuccessful. Management had emphasized the need to increase Corning's profitability, stock price, and dividends. Workers did not jump on the quality train because they did not consider themselves to be directly in Corning's financial loop.

The workers jumped on the quality train after McQuaid created an environment where they realized foreign competition was trying to put each one of them in the unemployment line. They embraced quality initiatives not because doing so would improve Corning's finances but because it was essential for *their* financial security.

Jack Welch's change efforts at General Electric (GE) also showed the benefits of leveling with workers. He knew there was no way that he could guarantee workers lifetime employment. Instead, he indicated that employees who were willing to learn new skills would be in a position to find work elsewhere if they were not needed at GE. The workers recognized that learning new skills was an investment in their future employability, not just a means for enhancing GE's performance.

LEADING CHANGE MEANS ASKING THE RIGHT QUESTIONS

The three *I*s of strategic management (inquiries, insights, and initiatives) described in Chapter 10 reflect the first and second steps of Kurt Lewin's change process. The first *I* involves making strategic inquiries. By pondering what the future may hold, people are encouraged to mentally break away from the present. Scenarios provide excellent opportunities for people to identify various possible futures.

Assumption analysis, benchmarking, and the analysis of best practices can also stimulate recognition that current procedures can be improved. John Management researchers John Grant and Devi Gnyawali believe assumption analysis provides the opportunity to raise interesting questions about the likelihood of the present being a prologue to the future. Assumption analysis also helps executives determine which drivers of current performance are apt to remain predictable in the near future and which may be jolted by foreign competition, technological advances, and regulatory changes.[16]

When people realize that certain changes are possible, and in some cases, inevitable, they are far more likely to commit themselves to dealing with the new realities. The same is true with best practices and benchmarking. The analysis of companies both in and outside of one's industry can be an eye-opening experience for people at all levels of the company.

Benchmarking analysis and the study of best practices may be particularly beneficial for people who have adopted the State of Missouri's "show me" attitude. Benchmarking helps remove mental blinders that keep people from seeing what is possible. It also enables managers to deal constructively with people who say, "There's no way we can do that!" When people claim that it is not possible to reduce the packaging error rate to less than 1 percent, they see things differently when they learn L.L. Bean ships more than a hundred thousand packages a day at Christmas time, with an error rate of less than one tenth of 1 percent.

LEADING CHANGE MEANS CREATING EARLY VICTORIES

Once the unfreezing process has taken effect, step two—the introduction of change—can begin. This step has multiple dimensions. New ideas can now be developed to address new challenges. Yet, executives need to be selective, recognize the importance that timing plays, and demonstrate finesse.

Breakthrough leaders recognize that they do not have carte blanche nor do they have an unlimited time to introduce the change. They know they need to be selective in what they say, what they do, and how they try to introduce change. Bob Knowling notes that change efforts are similar to triage situations in hospitals. According to Knowling, "You have to think of leading change as like working in an emergency room . . . the change agent has limited resources . . . so you keep coming back to the question. What are our priorities? Some people are going to have to sit in the waiting room."[17] Not every change can be addressed immediately. Some challenges may need to be addressed later, when the company has the momentum and resources needed to succeed.

Executives need to identify those actions that optimize importance and urgency. If they get wrapped up in initiating change efforts that take years before providing any return, people may throw in the towel before embarking on the journey. Conversely, if they spend all their time on urgent but relatively insignificant efforts, people may not believe that tomorrow will be better than today.

While people may be receptive to new ways to do things and new things to do, finesse should be demonstrated when introducing change. Each change effort needs to represent an essential part of an overall game plan for transforming the company. Management needs to make sure the change effort is not seen as another "flavor of the month." Knowling notes, "If you come in and announce, 'Here's the next change program.' You're dead. You just painted a target on your chest."[18]

People need to see that the new way of doing things produces results. Executives need to identify opportunities for early victories when they develop their change efforts. While management may have total faith in the change effort's eventual success, the sooner the rest of the people see they are making progress and there is light at the end of the tunnel, the better. For example, Ford has a systems learning network where middle managers work on projects that have the potential to achieve significant operating results, which they then take to senior management as proof that their ideas work.[19] People at lower levels of the company should have similar opportunities to demonstrate the value of their ideas.

The untapped potential for ideas is particularly evident at the lowest levels of the company. The average Japanese worker submits more than a hundred ideas each year. Toyota has averaged more than two million ideas per year from its workers—and implemented nearly 80 percent of them.[20] American workers rarely submit more than a handful of ideas each year. John Gardner, author of *No Easy Victories*, noted, "There is usually no shortage of new ideas; the problem is to get a hearing for them."[21] He also observed, "The still untapped source of human vitality, the unmined lode of talent, is in those people already recruited and thereafter neglected."[22]

Veteran leaders know the importance of being able to pick "low-hanging fruit." Low-hanging fruit represent events or milestones that are easy to accomplish and produce beneficial results in a short period of time. They are tangible indicators of progress. Low-hanging fruit have three benefits. First, as people see the merit in their efforts, they begin to believe the new way is the better way. Second, low-hanging fruit also keep at bay the naysayers who have been skeptical about the change. Third, capturing low-hanging fruit provides the impetus to reach for higher-hanging fruit. The higher-hanging fruit may include tackling major challenges or seeking innovation.

The pursuit of early victories should not be confused with the pursuit of quick fixes. Quick fixes are superficial efforts that tend to give a false impression that the battle has been won. Quick victories represent situations where there is tangible evidence the company is making progress in its transformation. Early victories help maintain the momentum and energy needed to win the war.

LEADING CHANGE MEANS RECOGNIZING THE PARADOX OF SUCCESS

Executives should exercise caution when they refreeze the new behavior and celebrate success when making progress. Leading change is a never-ending process. Although Frederick Taylor and his followers in the scientific management movement may have stressed the need to find the "best way," it is clear that there may not be any *one* best way.

The moment you believe that you have found the best way, you are dead. Executives need to recognize that although today's change may appear to be the best way, it will be tomorrow's status quo. What is refrozen today in Lewin's step three may need to be unfrozen tomorrow. Today's great ideas may become tomorrow's undoing. Although it is important to have quick victories, celebrations should be put in perspective. John Gardner noted, "Self-congratulation should be taken in small doses. It is habit forming, and most institutions are far gone in addiction."[23]

John Kotter noted that premature victory celebrations kill momentum. He stressed the need for continued movement forward because without momentum, the powerful forces associated with tradition take over. After the celebration is over, the resisters may point to the victory as a sign that the war has been won and the troops should be sent home.[24]

Kurt Lewin may have been perceptive in developing the three-step change model, but he did not anticipate the accelerating rate of change that exists today. As a psychologist, Lewin wanted to help people adopt more constructive behavior, which is why he stressed the need to refreeze the new behavior. Executives must use caution, however, when they reinforce the new behavior. They need to recognize that even though the change initiated today may be quite innovative, it may be obsolete in the near future.

Executives need to stress that all change is subject to change and that no one should get too comfortable with the way things are done. Rosabeth Moss Kanter, author of *The Change Masters*, observed, "Organizations with a formula that works well are doomed to replicate it, handing over their operations to people who control things so that there are no deviations from the formula."[25] In their book *Control Your Destiny or Someone Else Will*, Noel Tichy and Stratford Sherman wrote, "In an environment of unceasing change, few business ideas remain useful for long; after a while, even successful concepts must be abandoned."[26]

LEADING CHANGE INVOLVES BUILDING A LEARNING ORGANIZATION

A few years ago when Peter Senge, the author of *The Fifth Discipline*, introduced the concept that companies need to be learning organizations, most executives dismissed the concept as an academic's theoretical abstraction that had no place in the real world. However, if the concepts associated with learning organizations had been packaged as prerequisites for building core competencies, establishing competitive advantages, and gaining the highest levels of productivity from the company's human resources, then executives may have tuned even more into Senge's ideas.

Competitive advantages were previously based on the extent to which a company had more capital than its competitors. Today, knowledge and ideas are often a company's greatest competitive advantage. Success is now contingent on being able to outthink and outinnovate rather than outspend one's competitors. However, if we want to do things differently, then we need to think differently—and we need to *see* the world differently before we can *think* differently.

Being the market leader does not come from maintaining the status quo or from imitating other companies. Market leadership will not go to incrementalists but to companies that are able to generate breakthrough ideas, have the courage to boldly go where no company has gone before, and have the managerial acumen to operationalize ideas so that they become a reality.

Market leadership comes from busting through the ceiling of commonality. Competitive advantages reflect an organization's ability to do certain things better than other companies. Competitive advantages are the result of experimentation—of learning what works and what doesn't. It occurs when people find new things to do and new ways of doing them.

Companies that want to be at the leading edge need to learn from their various stakeholders. Stakeholders need to be asked—and asked often—what they want and what they expect from the company. The ideas of customers, employees, suppliers, and distributors need to be solicited, and they must be given the opportunity to be coarchitects of the company's change efforts.

Revolutions begin with insights and ideas. To develop revolutionary ideas, you need a revolution in thought patterns, not just knowledge.[27] Ideas are the product of one's thought patterns (mental models) and one's perceptions of how the world works (paradigms). One's mental models and paradigms need to be uninhibited by conventional thinking or a myopic perspective.

Organizations, like individuals, can have learning disabilities and blind spots. Managers and management teams can suffer from selective perception, which keeps them from processing information that is inconsistent with their current managerial mind-sets. When this happens, they either fail to see the new realities or they are unable to modify their behavioral repertoire to meet new challenges.

Learning in its most fundamental form is about listening, asking, reflecting, challenging, experimenting, unlearning, and discontinuing. Learning provides the insights that serve as the cornerstone for the strategies, products, services, and processes that will enhance the company's competitiveness, performance, and vitality.

Learning occurs best in environments where there is contempt for the status quo, where the past and present are not revered, and where there are no sacred cows. Leading change means creating an environment where everyone is free to challenge every assumption and every practice. It also means creating an environment where there are no dumb questions and no dumb ideas because making mistakes is considered part of the learning process. Mistakes should be acceptable as long as people learn from them and do not make the same mistake twice. It also means that complaints from internal and external stakeholders are considered to be learning opportunities rather than an assault on the company. Their criticisms and suggestions should be solicited, welcomed, and rewarded.

Leading change is as much an attitude as it is an overall process. Learning organizations do not refer to negative situations as problems; instead they consider problem situations to be challenges that need to be addressed. People tend to avoid problem situations because they have a negative air about them. However, people tend to be far more motivated when they are faced with the challenge and opportunity to make things better.

LEADING CHANGE MEANS COMPETING AGAINST ONESELF

Market leadership also comes from competing against oneself rather than one's competitors. When companies focus their energy on what competitors are doing, they take their eyes off their customers. They get caught up in market share and competitive response. A competitor orientation also creates the tendency to react to other companies, rather than focusing on what the market values and needs.

Market leadership comes from competing against one's self to delight customers, empower and reward employees, create unparalleled wealth for stockholders, and develop relationships with the company's other stakeholders to the point that they consider the company to be their most valued ally. When you compete against yourself, there is no end to learning, experimenting, and evolving. When you compete against other companies, there is a tendency to celebrate when you are out in front, which can elicit corporate arrogance. Arrogance quickly degenerates into complacency. Rapidly changing markets and escalating customer expectations show little mercy or patience for companies that are complacent and out of sync.

Chunka Mui, coauthor of *Unleashing the Killer App: Digital Strategies for Market Dominance*, noted the need for companies to commit themselves to creative destruction. Mui observed, "Cannibalize your markets, treat your assets as liabilities, ensure continuity for the customer, not yourself. Smart companies are preemptively destroying their own value chains. Recognizing that change is coming that will (render) obsolete their infrastructure, force them into a commodity role, or remove them from the process altogether, many are choosing to hasten the end of the old model."[28]

LEADING CHANGE MEANS BUILDING COALITIONS

Change efforts need to be broad-based rather than the effort of only one or two individuals. While the effort may initially be led by a handful of people, more people need to be brought in to drive the change effort for it to gain momentum. Breakthrough leaders bring people together and help them develop a shared strategy for creating a forward-focused company.

Change efforts are more likely to succeed when they are led by coalitions of individuals or groups that have common interests. Coalitions are particularly beneficial in two areas. First, they provide a broader base of ideas, reducing the likelihood that the change effort will be based on a myopic perspective. Second, coalitions provide a broader base of support for the change. John Kotter noted that a lone executive can be an easy target for those who want to derail a change effort. A change effort that represents a broad-based coalition is much harder to derail.[29]

Leading change must recognize the political side of organizations. Although a few companies may offer the freedom to challenge the status quo, change leaders need to recognize their vulnerability. The precarious nature of change management has not diminished since Niccolo Machiavelli wrote *The Prince*. Bob Knowling stresses the need for change agents to be savvy to organizational politics and organizational turf. He noted, "As a change agent you have to pick which battle you really mean to fight, and never sacrifice the war over a little skirmish . . . a dead change agent doesn't do anybody any good."[30]

Change leaders need to remember that new ideas usually replace existing ideas. The person who came up with the idea for the way things are currently being done probably won't welcome any effort that will modify, reduce, or discontinue his or her idea. When you suggest a new way of doing things, you are in a sense *firing* the current idea. You are declaring the way things are currently being done to be obsolete. You may see the *constructive* side to constructive criticism, but the originator of the current strategy will see the *criticism* part of constructive criticism. The originator of the current strategy will be less likely to be a resister if given the opportunity to be a coarchitect of the change effort.

CONCLUSION: LEADING CHANGE IS ABOUT CHANGING ONESELF

Organizational transformation requires personal transformation. You must be prepared to change yourself before you attempt to influence other people—and you must be prepared to lead by example. It is hypocritical to expect others to be flexible if you are not willing to make similar changes yourself. You must undergo an honest self-appraisal by looking at your own behavior when you are seeking an explanation for why people don't jump on the change bandwagon.

You cast a shadow in everything you do. Every action and every word either reinforces or undermines the change effort. You must be willing to apply the "rule of finger," which suggests that you look at your own hand when you point the finger of blame at others. If you look at your hand, you will see three fingers pointing back at you. You must be the stimulus that fosters the desired response from everyone involved in the change effort. If the results are not there, then it is because you did not create an environment conducive to producing results.

"It is easy to find fault with a new idea. It is easier to say it can't be done, than to try. Thus, it is through the fear of failure, that some men create their own hell."

—E. Jacob Taylor

NOTES

Portions of the material in this chapter originally appeared in the article "Leading Organizational Change" by the author in *Industrial Management,* May–June 1998, pp. 25–31. Reprinted with permission of the Institute of Industrial Engineers, 25 Technology Park, Norcross, Georgia 30092.

1. Thomas J. Watson, Jr., *A Business and Its Beliefs* (New York: McGraw-Hill, 1963), p. 79.
2. Charles Fishman, "Change," *Fast Company,* April–May 1997, p. 66.
3. John P. Kotter, *Leading Change* (Boston: Harvard Business School Press, 1996), p. 133.
4. Kurt Lewin, "Frontiers in Group Dynamics: Concepts, Method, and Reality in Social Science," *Human Relations,* January 1947, pp. 5–41.
5. Ibid.
6. Noel M. Tichy, "Bob Knowling's Change Manual," *Fast Company,* April–May 1997, p. 80.
7. John Sculley, *Odyssey* (New York: Perennial Library, 1987), p. 90.
8. Edgar Schein, "How Can Organizations Learn Faster? The Challenge of Entering the Green Room," *Sloan Management Review,* Winter 1993, p. 87.
9. Henry David Thoreau, *Walden* (New York: New American Library, 1960), p. 10.
10. Kurt Lewin, *Field Theory in Social Science: Selected Theoretical Papers* (New York: Harper & Brothers, 1951).
11. Schein, p. 87.
12. John Kotter, "Leading Change: Why Transformation Efforts Fail," *Harvard Business Review,* March–April 1995, pp. 60–62.
13. Ibid., p. 60.
14. Paul Strebel, "Why Do Employees Resist Change?" *Harvard Business Review,* May–June 1996, p. 89.
15. Ibid., p. 87.
16. John Grant and Devi Gnyawali, "Strategic Process Improvement

through Organizational Learning," *Strategy and Leadership Journal,* May/June 1995, p. 30.

17. Tichy, p. 82.
18. Ibid., p. 80.
19. Arian Ward, "Lessons Learned on the Knowledge Highways and Byways," *Strategy and Leadership Journal,* March–April 1996, p. 20.
20. Daniel Gross, "Power of Suggestion," *Attache,* October 2000, p. 16.
21. John Gardner, *No Easy Victories* (New York: Harper Colophon, 1968), p. 41.
22. Ibid., p. 40.
23. Ibid., p. 42.
24. Kotter, "Leading Change: Why Transformation Efforts Fail," p. 66.
25. Rosabeth Moss Kanter, *The Change Masters* (New York: Simon & Schuster, 1983), p. 70.
26. Noel M. Tichy and Stratford Sherman, *Control Your Destiny or Someone Else Will* (New York: Harper Business, 1994), p. 37.
27. Ward, p. 19.
28. Leigh Buchanan, "Killer Apps," *Inc.,* May 1998, p. 94.
29. Kotter, "Leading Change: Why Transformation Efforts Fail," p. 62.
30. Tichy, p. 82.

2

Visionary Thinking and Breakthrough Leadership

"Leadership will always play a key role during those times when a group faces a new problem and must develop new responses to the situation. One of the functions of leadership is to provide guidance at precisely those times when habitual ways of doing things no longer work, or when dramatic change in the work environment requires new responses."

—Edgar H. Schein, author of
Organizational Culture and Leadership

The process of creating a forward-focused company is light-years away from becoming an exact science. Change is so multifaceted that it is nearly impossible to know all the factors and forces at play. It is even more difficult to determine the dynamic relationships among these factors and forces. Breakthrough leadership calls for perceptiveness, flexibility, and finesse. There will be times when the company needs to move ahead at full speed, while at other times it may be wiser to pull back on the throttle and reassess the appropriateness of the company's course of action. Sometimes, the breakthrough leader will need to be out front leading the charge, while at other times the leader is more effective at making the right things happen by working behind the scenes.

THE STRATEGIC DEPLOYMENT OF SELF

Leaders need to use their talents in a strategic manner by deploying them as skillfully as they deploy the company's resources. Leaders need to allocate their time and attention so that they get the greatest return per unit of time—in a manner similar to the way they allocate the company's capital to get the highest return per dollar invested.

Breakthrough leaders recognize two important points about how they spend their time. First, it is impossible to lead every change effort. There are not enough hours in the day to be involved in every facet of change. Second, it would not be in the company's best interest to be directly involved in every change effort. Breakthrough leadership involves creating an environment where change is initiated at all levels of the company. Change efforts work best when people at all levels of the company are playing a leading role in the change process. Leaders should champion the company's *overall* change rather than be the sole champion for individual change efforts.

Dynamic leaders recognize the need to be selective in their involvement. If they are too removed from change efforts, the troops may wonder whether anybody at the top really cares about the challenges and risks that they are facing. However, if leaders are ever-present, they lose the opportunity to appear at just the right time to break down a barrier or to give the troops a psychological boost. Being ever-present may also indicate a lack of faith in the employees' judgment and ability to make things happen.

Self-awareness plays an integral role in the strategic deployment of the leader's time and talents. Every person has shortcomings. Leaders who are aware of their shortcomings should surround themselves with people who have talents they lack. They should also surround themselves with people who will tell them like it is when the situation calls for objectivity and candor. Leaders need to recognize that as situations change, so must their talents. Paul Wieland, former CEO of Independence Bancorp, observed that at some point your strengths become liabilities. According to Wieland, "Most of us have become successful by developing a set of strengths and working around our weaknesses, but inevitably we push these strengths too far, and they become weaknesses."[1]

Leaders should recognize that every word they speak and every action they take can send ripple effects throughout the company. At no time are the leader's comments off-the-record. At no time is the leader offstage. Times of change are times when even the slightest action or lack of action can make a major difference in whether a change effort moves forward or stalls.

Every person in the company casts a shadow. Leaders should strive to cast the type of shadow that fosters positive change. They must recognize that to lead effectively, they must lead by example. Asking or expecting others to do what you are not willing or able to do is hypocritical. Leaders must be willing to take risks before they can expect anyone else to take risks. They need to understand the dynamics of technological change before they can expect others to embrace new technology. When you lead by example, you gain the respect of those around you. When you expect others to take a journey that you are not willing to take, you are sowing the seeds of distrust, contempt, and resistance.

BREAKTHROUGH LEADERS NEED TO CRAFT THE COMPANY'S VISION OF A BETTER TOMORROW

Crafting the company's vision may be the most important role breakthrough leaders can play in creating a forward-focused company. Breakthrough leadership will only be possible if the company has a clearly articulated vision. The vision serves three purposes. First, it serves as the company's North Star. All decisions, plans, and activities should be directed toward fulfilling the company's vision. Second, the vision must be compelling. It should give each person in the company a reason to jump out of bed in the morning. Third, the vision can serve as the glue that binds all the company's components together. Carlo Brumat, dean of the Duxx Graduate School of Business Leadership in Monterey, Mexico, noted the role visioning plays in fostering a collaborative environment. He stated, "Each of us has a fragmented view of how the world works. The leader's role is to put together and harmonize such views, because only by associating minds in this way can you acquire a full and objective view of the world."[2]

Leaders should use the process of crafting the company's vision to explore possible futures for the company. Journalist Steven Rebello noted, "Truly successful people have the ability to see new paths and the power to persuade others to follow. . . . Vision is the ability to fill in the blanks, to see beyond the blind spots and to move forward while the others are still standing around rubbing their eyes. . . . Visionaries make their mark by breaking rules, taking risks, forging connections. And they alter the landscape with innovations we were hardly aware we couldn't live without. Visionaries share the capacity to see what others can't (or won't) and the courage to bring their vision to life."[3]

Breakthrough leaders recognize that the visioning process is not for dreamers. They know that creating a forward-focused company calls for imagination and realism. Their job is to explore the possibilities and then create the company's future realities. Visionary leaders recognize that revolutions begin with ideas. They also know that imagination is the source of great ideas. Robert Stozier, as executive editor of *Success* magazine, noted, "Perhaps, more important than any other tools, great generals wield with dash that supreme weapon, imagination. The true leader takes risks, springs the unexpected, and dares to dare."[4]

LEADERSHIP CALLS FOR COURAGE AND RESILIENCE

The process for crafting and implementing a company's vision calls for guts and resilience. If a company wants to be on the leading edge, it must take bold initiatives rather than fine-tune the present. The bolder the vision, the greater the risks and the greater the need to let go of the past. Breakthrough leadership requires the courage to boldly lead a company where no company has gone before. It also requires the courage to deal with challenges from those who have a vested interest in maintaining the status quo or some other course of action that meets their needs. While Thomas Watson, Jr., served as chair of IBM, he observed, "Every time IBM moved ahead, it was because someone was willing to take a chance, put his head on the block, and try something new."[5]

Leaders must recognize that there are risks involved with taking the company in a new direction or trying to achieve higher levels of performance. You cannot steal second base if you keep one foot on first base. Performance and morale may drop at the beginning of the journey because it takes time for people to learn. When people try new things they also make mistakes. Change takes people out of their comfort zones. People may feel incompetent when they try to do things they have not done before. Leaders need to build a learning period into the change plan and let people know in advance that mistakes are part of the learning process. Although they may not encourage mistakes, leaders must expect them to occur.

Leaders also need to be the keepers of the faith. They must have the courage to protect the company's basic values when others are tempted to compromise the company's integrity. There will be moments of truth when the company can demonstrate its commitment to doing what it claims to value—or it can take the easy way out. In those instances, leaders must step forward and do the right thing without hesitation.

Leaders need to create an environment where people at all levels know what the company values. They recognize that a strong set of values can provide far better guidance than a one thousand–page company policy manual. Nordstrom demonstrated its commitment to doing the right thing when it developed its "rules" for decision-making: "Rule #1: Use good judgment in all situations. There will be no additional rules."[6]

BREAKTHROUGH LEADERS ARE DECISIVE: THEY DON'T FAIL THE "MATCH TEST"

Breakthrough leaders recognize that change calls for decisiveness. The words *someday* and *maybe* have no place in the process of creating a forward-focused company. Leaders create a sense of urgency so that people resist the temptation to procrastinate. They create a situation where people do not sit on their hands waiting for additional information that may not be available or worth the additional time.

Decisiveness appears to increase with experience. People who have been on the firing line in various situations are more willing to make decisions. They are also more willing to trust their intuitive skills when data are limited. The accelerating rate of change and the consequences of being a day late place a premium on having leaders who don't freeze up when they are confronted with a major decision.

Contributing editor of *Fast Company* Seth Godin noted, "In the old days, risk-averse managers knew they'd never get in trouble for ducking a tough decision. In fact, it might even be the fastest ticket to a promotion: It's one sure way to keep all the dirt off your feet. But these days, if you can't make a decision, you're out of action. Any decision is likely to serve you and your company better than no decision."[7]

Too many people in today's companies would fail the "match test." The match test forces people who have been reluctant to take the risks associated with decision making to make a decision with minimal delay. When they are presented with a decision, they must hold a lighted match in their hand. They have to make a decision while holding a lit match. They learn that you either decide or get burned.

LEADERS MUST DEMONSTRATE "IMPATIENT PATIENCE"

Most people consider the concept of impatient patience to be an oxymoron. Breakthrough leaders know the difference between forcing the issue and giving it time to germinate. Carlo Brumat noted, "Leaders need to transmit a sense of urgency, a feeling life is short and that there's a lot to be accomplished. But if a leader is unreasonable—if he or she expects results overnight—the effect on morale can be devastating. The best leaders balance a sense of urgency with persistence."[8]

Being decisive has its merits, but if the people playing a role in the change effort don't recognize the need for change, decisiveness will have little effect. The purpose of decision making is not merely to make decisions, but to make decisions that will be implemented. Without implementation, the change effort dies quickly.

Leaders need to recognize that decisions are rarely embraced when they are forced down people's throats with a "Just do it!" edict. Decisions that require input and the support of others may need time to germinate. People who develop ideas should not expect their ideas to be embraced immediately by others in the company. They should also recognize that when others ask questions about the idea, it doesn't mean they are opposed to the idea. Questioning should be encouraged so that other people have the opportunity to see the light for themselves.

Mark Maletz, a principal with McKinsey & Company, provided the following observations for effecting real change. First, realize that you probably did not stumble over your brilliant insight or ingenious project idea in one glorious moment. Undoubtedly, you arrived at your idea over time. It was a process. Second, when others (including your boss) don't understand your ideas immediately, don't label them as ignorant bureaucrats—a force to be reckoned with. That attitude will back others against a wall and make it difficult for you to get your point across. Instead, recognize that others may have to go through a similar journey of understanding that you traveled to "get there." Third, self-discovery is much more powerful than preaching from on high—or from below. By helping others to discover for themselves what you are proposing, you won't have to waste time maneuvering or dodging.[9]

LEADERSHIP PROVIDES THE SPARK THAT IGNITES COMMITMENT

In a perfect world, every person in the company would embrace the company's vision and be sufficiently self-motivated to make it a reality. Leadership must recognize that people rarely have blind faith in the company's leaders. Leaders must also recognize that people are committed to the company's vision—and to creating a forward-focused company—only to the extent to which the journey contributes to their own futures.

Leaders need to make every effort to show how fulfillment of the vision will enhance each person's well-being. Warren Bennis, educator and writer, noted how important it is for leaders to be in tune with the human side of change when he stated: "Real leaders have identified and mastered a secret tool: emotional observation. If you can watch people—and, by watching them, figure out what makes them do what they do—you might be able to get them to do something else, something better."[10]

Leaders must create an environment where the people who are motivated to fulfill the company's vision will be empowered and rewarded for their efforts. However, people who are only moderately motivated should also see the merit of contributing at a higher level. Finally, those dragging their feet should realize that they must either get with the program or get out of the company.

If leaders are in tune with what turns each person on, then they may be able to create an environment where good people are transformed into fanatics. When Phillip Diehl was asked how he brought new life to the U.S. Mint, he stated, "We've fundamentally changed people's expectations of our performance. When you change expectations, it's very hard for an organization to relax and slip back into old patterns of behavior."[11] Diehl added, "My goal is to be part of an organization whose members are engaged as whole people. I want them to have a sense of purpose, excitement, and fulfillment. The ultimate performance metric might be to call people on Sunday night and ask them how they feel about going to work the next day. Are they really looking forward to Monday morning? If the answer is yes, then people can do just about anything."[12]

BEWARE OF COVERT RESISTANCE

Leaders must be aware that change efforts may be resisted in many ways. Sometimes resistance is direct, whereas, at other times, it can occur in a more covert manner. Change creates a state of disequilibrium and takes people out of their comfort zones. It also alters positions of power and influence within the company.

Warren Bennis and attorney Anita Hill provide a couple of interesting insights about resistance to change. Warren Bennis observed, "When I was President of the University of Cincinnati, I discovered I spent too much time worrying about those who resisted change. Instead, work with people who want to go forward."[13] Anita Hill noted, "Some of the biggest pitfalls in the process [of initiating change] are taking resistance to change personally and believing that resistance is intractable. Very few people are absolutely opposed to change. Rather, they hesitate because they cannot see immediately how they will benefit from it. You've got to show them. Realize there are many ways to achieve your goal. Learn to use creativity and flexibility to get there."[14]

Mark Maletz offers four observations about resistance:

1. If change has not been very successful in the past, then you need to prepare for the inevitable opposition.
2. Beware of people who say they are supportive of the change effort, but who are not. They will either fail to support/sign off on it or sabotage it.
3. Change agents should not automatically resist resistance—they should learn from it.
4. From the very first day, make the change process transparent. If you are going to make the process transparent, you've got to be willing to admit when you're wrong, or when someone else has a better idea.[15]

Leaders of the change effort should create an environment where people who have reservations about the proposed change are free to voice their concerns and to challenge the assumptions that were part of the decision process. Leaders must be prepared to provide information to support the course of action. The best way to reduce resistance is to give people—especially those skeptical about the need for change—the opportunity to participate in analyzing the company's current situation, crafting the vision, and developing the change effort to make the vision a reality. When it comes time to implement the decision, leaders should do whatever is necessary to gain overt commitment from everyone involved in the change effort. The company will not be able to break away from the pack if people just go along to get along or just go through the motions.

Leaders must be clear that there is a time to discuss, a time to decide, and a time to act. If an employee is not willing to commit to the change effort, then he or she should find another employer that shares his or her perceptions of the future and what it takes to get there. Jim Collins, coauthor of *Built to Last,* provided one view of how to deal with resistance: "How do you get people to share your values? You don't. You find people who share them and eject those who don't."[16] Wayne Calloway, as CEO of PepsiCo., indicated there may be times when drastic action needs to be taken to deal with people who could jeopardize the change effort. He stated, "Occasionally, it's very important to have a public hanging."[17]

The best way to reduce ongoing resistance is to show that it is producing results. The sooner the change effort shows that it is making tangible progress toward its goal, the sooner the resistance will be reduced. Particular attention should be directed to breaking the change effort into periodic milestones. Meeting the milestone targets can be seen as minivictories for the change effort. A change effort's momentum and early victories can help to bulldoze lingering resistance.

BUILDING TRUST CAN GO A LONG WAY TOWARD GAINING COMMITMENT

People are far more willing to embark on a journey if they have faith in their leader's judgment and trust that person to act in their best interests. Trust does not come with one's position. Trust, like respect, arises from an ongoing relationship. Trust is more likely to occur when people are involved in the change process from the earliest possible stage. They are more likely to support and implement ideas and plans they helped to develop than ideas and plans that are dropped on them from above.

Leaders should recognize that listening and asking may be more effective than telling people what to do. John Kotter, educator and writer, noted, "The key is not having all the answers . . . but asking probing questions. If you come in and announce what should be done, then they are less likely to trust you. If you ask for their views, then they tend to believe you value their views. This is important for building trust."[18] Senior editor for *Fast Company* Bill Breen and Cheryl Dahle, senior writer for *Fast Company* observed, "Change kicks in when people start to trust—in the plan and one another. Trust is the glue that invariably holds the change effort together. . . . Getting the buy-in. Overcoming resistance. Building trust. Zeroing in on the objective. These are critical skills that every change team must leverage if it is to have any hope of succeeding."[19]

Brad Cooper, as superintendent of the West Point Mint, sensed a climate of fear about what the future would hold from 220 employees during his effort to transform its operations. He indicated, "I basically walked around. I met with everyone in small groups. I did nothing—because I knew if I started acting before I had built trust, any changes would fail. The more we improved, the more people wanted to keep improving."[20]

CHANGE CANNOT BE DONE BY ONE PERSON . . . GET OTHERS INVOLVED

People at the top of the company often believe they can initiate change by edict. They may get *reluctant* compliance, but they will rarely get the level of commitment needed to leapfrog competition. Change works best when it is a collaborative effort by people who are allied to one another.

The ability to form an alliance is particularly valuable if the person who wants to initiate the change is not at the top of the company. Resistance may come from all sides rather than just from below. This is why it is important to establish a network of relationships based on trust and respect throughout the company. Barbara Reinhold, author of *Toxic Work: How to Overcome Stress, Overload and Burnout, and Revitalize Your Career*, noted, "You have to understand the metabolism rate—the tolerance for change—of your boss or of your organization might be dramatically different from your own. Then look around. Find other people who are willing to take the change journey with you. Never go it alone. Undoubtedly others in your company feel as you do. Your task is to find them."[21]

Warren Bennis observed, "If you're a leader, you've got to give up your omniscient and omnipotent fantasies—that you know and must do everything. Learn to abandon your ego to the talents of others."[22] Bill Breen and Cheryl Dahle also noted the need for enlisting the support of others. They state, "Change starts with finding a backer—someone who can sell your plan to the senior team. Change dies without a fighter—someone smart enough and skilled enough to win over the opposition."[23]

BREAKTHROUGH LEADERS DEVELOP LEADERS

Leadership involves more than merely getting people to follow or even to be allies. Leaders do much more than develop followers; they develop leaders. They know the company cannot rely on one or two leaders to create its future. A company needs leaders at all levels if it is to excel in the marketplace.

Creating the company's future involves a deliberate and continuous effort to create future leaders. Breakthrough leaders create an environment where people are given the opportunity to lead themselves. As people gain experience and confidence, they are given the opportunity to lead others. Every manager's performance review should identify whether the manager is developing people to their potential and developing leadership skills within the group. One Midwestern manufacturer was so serious about the need for leaders to develop leaders that it established the policy, "Any manager who does not have a ready replacement will be terminated!"

Companies that are committed to developing leaders at all levels do not leave the process to chance. They commit considerable time and resources to the development of leaders. Stratford Sherman, coauthor of *Control Your Destiny or Someone Else Will*, indicated, "Perhaps the simplest, hardest, and most telling measure of any company's leadership development program is the allocation of the CEO's time."[24] Roger Enrico, as CEO of PepsiCo, noted, "You must be prepared to commit one-half to one-third of your time to the [leadership] development program."[25] Enrico suggested three additional tips for developing leaders: "You need to put people at risk working on business projects that matter. You should be a learner open to new ideas and feedback, and a coach who can admit mistakes. You must have a personalized, teachable view on (a) leadership, (b) growing the business, and (c) creating change."

There is an interesting story about IBM's strategy for developing leaders when Thomas Watson, Jr., was president. IBM was known for putting young engineers on the firing line by making them project managers very early in their careers. Supposedly, a young engineer was summoned to Watson's office. When Watson asked if the young engineer knew why he was there, the young engineer responded, "Of course, it's Friday and my $10,000,000 project was a total failure. I figure I am about to be fired!" Unlike most executives, Watson exclaimed, "Fire you? We're going to keep you around to see what you learned!" People who hear the story wonder how IBM could afford to keep young managers who made mistakes. The answer is clear: IBM knew it would need to have leaders in the future who had the courage and ability to make $100,000,000 decisions. The $10,000,000 project was an investment in developing insights and experience.

BREAKTHROUGH LEADERS ARE LEARNERS

Breakthrough leadership involves going where no company has gone before. If change does not involve anything that is new, the company will not move ahead. Change and learning go hand in hand. Learning usually involves experimentation and experimentation frequently produces mistakes and/or setbacks.

Leaders should be willing to learn, to experiment, *and* to make mistakes. How leaders handle their own mistakes—as well as the mistakes of others—can have a dramatic impact on people's willingness to experiment. Carlo Brumat noted, "No one knows what the future will bring, how a market will respond, whether a new technology will work. Yet so often, whenever a desired outcome fails to materialize, leaders look for scapegoats. That reaction freezes people's mindsets and destroys imagination. In the sciences, researchers don't look upon a failed experiment as a mistake to be blamed on somebody. Instead, they see it as an opportunity to change their view of how things work. Business leaders need to adopt the same attitude."[26]

CONCLUSION: KEEP MOVING FORWARD

The ever-accelerating, never-ending nature of change resembles a relentless set of waves crashing into the shore. Breakthrough leadership is a relentless process. It involves meeting the challenges of change head on and keeping the organization forward-focused.

Your company must avoid being caught in the paradox of

success. It cannot afford to celebrate its successes for more than a moment. You need to direct your attention to tomorrow and tomorrow's tomorrow. As CEO of PepsiCo., Roger Enrico noted, "As soon as everyone is on the bandwagon with one growth idea, a leader should be working on the next one."[27] Creating your company's future is a never-ending process. You can never let up. The moment you ease up is the moment when the world starts to pass your company by.

"You will never know what is going on unless you can hear the whistles of the bullets."
—George S. Patton, Jr., World War II general

NOTES

1. Pamela Kruger, "A Leader's Journey," *Fast Company*, June 1999, p. 124.
2. Eric Randsell, "School for Leaders," *Fast Company*, April 1999, p. 50.
3. Stephen Rebello, "Visionaries," *Success*, February 1998, p. 39.
4. Robert M. Stozier, "Attack at Dawn," *Success*.
5. Thomas J. Watson, Jr., *A Business and Its Beliefs* (New York: Columbia University, 1963), p. 60.
6. Nordstrom orientation packet.
7. Seth Godin, "Is It Possible to Create a Maybe-proof Company?" *Fast Company*, December 1999, p. 358.
8. Randsell, p. 50.
9. Anna Muoio, "Boss Management," *Fast Company*, April 1999, p. 102.
10. Stevan Alburty, "A Cast of Leaders," *Fast Company*, October 1999, p. 242.
11. Anna Muoio, "Mint Condition: His People Are as Good as Gold," *Fast Company*, December 1999, p. 346.
12. Ibid., p. 348.
13. Muoio, "Boss Management," p. 92.
14. Ibid., p. 100.
15. Muoio, "Mint Condition: His People Are as Good as Gold," p. 396.
16. Stratford Sherman, "How Tomorrow's Best Leaders Are Learning Their Stuff," *Fortune*, November 27, 1995, p. 92
17. Ibid., p. 93.

18. Thomas A. Stewart, "Why Leadership Matters," *Fortune,* March 2, 1998, p. 82.
19. Bill Breen and Cheryl Dahle, "Field Guide for Change," *Fast Company,* December 1999, p. 384.
20. Muoio, "Mint Condition: His People Are as Good as Gold," p. 342.
21. Muoio, "Boss Management," p. 94.
22. Ibid., p. 92.
23. Breen and Dahle, p. 384.
24. Noel Tichy and Christopher DeRose, "Roger Enrico's Master Class," *Fortune,* November 27, 1995, p. 102.
25. Ibid., p. 106.
26. Randsell, p. 50.
27. Tichy and DeRose, p. 106.

3

Developing a Corporate Culture That Embraces Learning and Innovation

"America is in a product war, and the management of innovation is a strategic weapon. . . . Our ability to get better at the innovative process—to drive products from idea to market faster and with fewer mistakes—is the key to winning the war."[1]

—Robert G. Cooper, author of
Product Leadership: Creating and Launching Superior New Products

E ven the savviest executives make mistakes. That is part of learning. The attitude of "If I don't try anything new, then I won't make any mistakes" will speed the company's slide into mediocrity. The greatest mistake a company can make is to not experiment with new products, services, and processes.

A company cannot be at the leading edge if it merely tries to keep up with other companies. For the company to excel, it must be a learning organization that is innovative in its products, services, and processes. Creating a forward-focused company requires more than merely keeping pace with changes that are happening outside the company. The ever-accelerating rate of change places a premium on the company's ability to evolve in a revolutionary manner. Companies that learn quicker and innovate better than other companies are more likely to be out in front. Companies that are slow to learn and merely imitate innovative companies will be relegated to a very precarious existence.

Learning and innovation are closely tied to the company's strategy and culture. If the company wants to be at the leading edge, it must anticipate what its target market will value. It must then be able to develop the products, services, and processes that will be needed to delight its targeted customers. The company will be innovative only to the extent it has a culture where people come up with innovative ideas and are committed to transforming the ideas into reality.

The process of creating a forward-focused company is dependent on the extent to which learning and innovating are a way of life for people at all levels. Perceptive learning enables the company to see the future before its competitors see it. Innovation enables the company to change the future of the marketplace by making current products and services obsolete.

Capital One changed the way the highly competitive credit-card game is played. Capital One combined the power of information technology with a commitment to finding ways to make even its own products and services obsolete. Charles Fishman, contributing editor to *Fast Company*, noted that Capital One's database and high-speed computers enable it to access customer information before the caller hears the first ring. Capital One's computers identify who is calling and predict the reason for the call. Two-dozen pieces of information about the person who is calling are then passed along to a customer service rep. The incoming call, the data review, the analysis, the routing to the appropriate person or division, and the recommending happen in just one-hundred milliseconds.[2] Rich Fairbanks, Capital One's CEO, considers his company to be an innovation machine. He noted, "Fifty percent of what we're marketing now did not exist at this company six months ago . . . fifty percent of what we'll be selling six months from now doesn't exist yet."[3]

THE COMPANY'S CULTURE CAN PLAY A CRITICAL ROLE IN LEARNING AND INNOVATION

Most executives have difficulty articulating the nature of corporate culture and the role it plays in company performance. The relatively intangible nature of corporate culture makes it rather elusive when executives develop the company's strategy and design its organizational processes.

Every company has a distinct culture just as every person has a unique personality. A company's culture is the result of numerous factors and forces. It affects the type of people the company hires as well as how it motivates and rewards people. Corporate culture determines the type of ideas the company will embrace as well as the extent to which people are encouraged to experiment, explore, innovate, and take risks.

Corporate culture plays a crucial role during times of ever-accelerating change. It serves as an invisible guidebook for employees. It indicates what the company values, encourages, and rewards. It provides direction and serves as a compass for making decisions when one's boss is not available for guidance or the company's policy manual does not provide the answer for how a situation should be handled.

The ever-accelerating rate of change and delayered nature of today's companies force people to make judgment calls every day. It is during these "moments of truth" that the company's culture affects whether the company moves forward or falls by the wayside. Corporate culture can be characterized in three dimensions. First, the culture may be strong or weak. Strong cultures have a dramatic effect on employees. Southwest Airlines is known for having a culture that has a pervasive impact on every person at every level. Other companies have cultures that are so weak that they seem to lack any core values or common thread to direct ongoing behavior.

Second, the culture may or may not be in sync with the company's strategy. A company's strategy can be implemented only if the company's culture reflects the attitudes, values, and skills needed to make it happen. If the company's newly crafted strategy calls for the development of innovative products, the company will need a culture that welcomes experimentation and exploration. If the prevailing culture abhors risk taking and punishes mistakes, the company's strategy will never leave the launchpad.

Third, the culture may or may not be adaptive. Some cultures are so rigid that their companies are unable to change with changing times. Cultures that have failed to embrace the power of information technology, women in executive ranks, and a global perspective are out of sync with current realities.

Most executives believe their companies should have strong cultures. The strength of the culture is an attribute in creating a forward-focused company only when it supports the company's strategy, is adaptive, and is in sync with current and emerging realities. Companies that have strong but inflexible or inappropriate cultures will have difficulty staying in the game.

As CEO of Charles Schwab, David Pottruck had to factor in the company's culture when he was faced with the challenge of keeping the company on the leading edge. Pottruck noted, "Build the right culture, and you can grow quickly without losing the qualities that make your company special. Take care of your employees, and they'll take care of your customers. Spend time to explain your vision to everyone in the company, and they'll buy into it."[4] As head of GM's e-GM business-to-consumer unit, Mark Hogan noted the importance of having the culture in sync with current and emerging realities. He stated, "We're using the Net to change the culture in the company because we want to be big and we also want to be fast; in the past, we've been big and slow."[5]

CULTURE IS ABOUT PEOPLE, ALIGNMENT, AND COMMITMENT

A company's culture will have a lot to do with whether people create the company's future or whether the company languishes in the present. All products, services, processes, and profits are the result of people. The company's future is directly related to the quality of ideas that are developed today and the extent to which they are executed by people at all levels in the company. Executives need to recognize that it is a lot easier to change the company's strategy than it is to change its culture. While the strategy may indicate a major shift in the company's product portfolio, in most cases, the products will have to be developed by people within the company. If they are not committed to the company or if they do not relish the opportunity to create products that did not exist before, the company's strategy will be nothing more than words and numbers on a sheet of paper.

When David Pottruck began his efforts to bring Charles Schwab into the new investment marketplace, which included Internet trading, he realized many of Schwab's people did not embrace the changes involved in the transition. A survey of employees indicated that they felt top management was out of touch and that they mistrusted the company's new initiatives.[6] While Pottruck may have had the epiphany that Internet trading was becoming a new reality, he also recognized such a dramatic transition could not be accomplished by a memo or a charismatic speech.

Pottruck and Charles Schwab decided to hold town meetings at various Schwab offices to share their views on why Schwab needed to change as well as their vision for what the company needed to become and what it needed to do. Pottruck and Schwab realized that for the company to make such a dramatic change in its strategy, they would have to share their vision and strategy with employees in a face-to-face environment where people could ask questions about the proposed changes. Their efforts took considerable time and cost more than $1 million. When they completed their tour, Pottruck noted, "Suddenly, everyone in the company was aligned, in terms of mission, values, and priorities. It was a completely energizing experience for the employees."[7]

The change effort initiated at Charles Schwab indicated the need for people at all levels of the company to be aligned. Alignment refers to the extent each person's needs, interests, values, and capabilities are consistent with the company's mission, vision, strategy, and culture. While it may be unrealistic to expect each person's needs to be identical to the company's goals, it is clear that the company will benefit more if they are pointed in the same direction, like the front wheels of a car. If each employee's needs pull the employee in a different direction from what the company needs from the employee to achieve its objectives, the company will have a difficult time moving forward.

The company will have a higher probability of having alignment and a corresponding level of commitment from its people if it makes a deliberate effort to attract people who share the company's values and objectives. This does not mean the company should identify the ideal employee and try to clone a whole workforce from that employee. The concept of "goodness of fit" is tied to the need for alignment. Certain employees thrive in certain corporate cultures. The company will succeed to the extent that it attracts these people and rewards them for their contribution to the company's goals.

The goodness of fit may be detrimental to a company, however, if it is taken to an extreme. If the company is to outthink its competitors, it needs to have a cadre of people at all levels who can think outside the conventional box. Breakthrough ideas rarely come from people who think alike. Breakthroughs usually arise from a diversity of views. Although it may be easier to work with people who are similar to you, executives should make every effort to bring together people with different perspectives, experiences, and skills. Some of the most innovative companies have used cross-functional teams to develop breakthrough products, services, and processes. If companies are to truly capitalize on the talents of their people, their executives should make every effort to create cross-functional companies.

Innovative companies are like salads. They value diversity and create an environment where different people thrive, different perspectives are encouraged, and new ideas are rewarded. Some of the most innovative companies take pride in their unconventional hiring practices. Seth Godin noted, "The next time you review resumes, try ignoring all of the 'perfectly qualified' applicants. In fact, disqualify everyone who is clearly competent to do the job at hand. Do what Southwest Airlines does: Don't hire people with experience at another airline unless you're sure that they can unlearn what they've learned at the other airline. . . . Instead look for folks who are quick enough to master a task and restless enough to try something new."[8]

Andy Esparza, vice president of staffing for Dell Computer Corporation, indicated the need to attract the right talent. He noted, "We specialize in the unreasonable around here. . . . There's a war for talent going on, and we're right in the middle of it. . . . But we realize that our future depends completely on continuing to bring in great people—and more and more of them."[9] Dell Computer also recognizes the need to hire for the future and identified the following five core competencies for hiring executives:

1. The ability to learn fast
2. The ability to thrive in a changing environment
3. The ability to deliver results
4. The ability to solve problems
5. The ability to build teams[10]

Bill Gates noted years ago that his company frequently bought whole companies just to get the talented people who worked there. Gates said that it was easier to buy a company to get talent than to hire talent on a person-to-person basis.

Leaders provide air cover for the troops by keeping an open mind and leading by example. Although they cannot be champions of individual change efforts, they can champion change throughout the company. They knock down barriers, keep two-way communication channels open, and cheer the troops on at strategic moments. Lorraine Monroe, principal of Harlem's Frederick Douglas School, affirms the need for top executives to manage by wandering around. Monroe said, "The farther you get from where the magic happens, the more you lose touch with the day-to-day operations. And instead of dealing with people, you start turning out reports."[11] Chan Suh, CEO of Agency.com, a New York–based advertising agency, noted, "When I don't change things, people say 'Hey, what's going on around here?'"[12]

Leaders need to ensure that ideas are encouraged and rewarded rather than subjected to ridicule, territorialism, parochialism, or bureaucratic barriers. Liz Forrest of Innovation Labs developed a list of ninety-nine idea killers that inhabit most organizations. They include:[13]

- "They'll never buy it!"
- "Are we ready for this?"
- "What will they say upstairs?"
- "You can't argue with success."
- "Obviously you misread the request."
- "Let's be realistic."

The greatest idea killer on Forrester's list may be, "The last guy who came up with that idea isn't here anymore!"

Creating an environment that fosters innovation and creativity involves more than making certain that there are few idea killers; it involves creating an atmosphere full of idea enhancers. Ideas should be solicited on a regular basis and rewarded handsomely. Every effort must be made to promote:

- Looking at things from new perspectives
- The free flow of ideas
- Ongoing experimentation
- Transforming mistakes into learning experiences

Executives should heed the value statement that runs throughout 3M, "Thou shall not kill a new product idea."

TO CREATE A FORWARD-FOCUSED COMPANY, YOU MUST FIRST CREATE A LEARNING ORGANIZATION

Creating a forward-focused company will not be possible unless the company becomes a learning organization. The company will not be at the leading edge unless it masters strategic and adaptive learning. Strategic learning involves developing innovative ways to identify and capitalize on the opportunities that may be on the horizon. It also involves positioning the company to avoid potential threats.

Strategic learning uses innovation to change external conditions. Adaptive learning is designed to help the company keep pace with changing external conditions on an ongoing basis. It is directed toward continuously improving the company's operations. It also involves correcting deviations from planned performance.

Chuck Salter, a contributing editor for *Fast Company*, noted, "Winning companies don't just outhustle or outmuscle the competition. They out-think. Business today is about brains, not brawn. It's about how many ideas you generate, not how many factories you own. . . . Every so often, a company will invent a breakthrough business model that reinvents the rules of competition in an industry."[14] Salter also claims that there is a day-to-day side to competing on ideas. Although breakthrough ideas may make headlines and enable the company to leapfrog its competition, corporate success is contingent on the company's ability to learn on a continuous basis.

Context Integration is a good example of how a company can

turn knowledge into a competitive weapon. Context Integration is a Web solutions company that has turned itself into a learning organization that is committed to gathering and sharing information with its people. Context Integration developed a knowledge management system called IAN (Intellectual Assets Network). IAN stores best practices, tracks new ideas, fields questions, and operates as a kind of group mind. Every day, IAN distributes articles and tips to employees who might find them relevant. When a problem arises, the network tracks down those employees who are the best qualified to solve it. Bruce Strong, vice president of strategic services, noted, "We have positioned ourselves on the frothing part of the knowledge wave. . . . If we're not sharing ideas with one another, with our clients, and with our partners, we're in deep trouble."[15]

Learning organizations do not spend all their time developing new knowledge. They recognize there is no reason to reinvent the wheel if the knowledge they need already exists. Learning organizations develop knowledge networks so they can access critical information. Context Integration's IAN serves as an idea-recycling center. Teams at Context Integration begin each new project by searching IAN for past work that is similar to what they're doing, looking for ideas and practices that they can borrow. The goal is to use anything—models, architecture, source code—that helps them avoid duplicating another team's work.[16]

Thomas Edison indicated that success is the product of 10 percent inspiration and 90 percent perspiration. Bob Young, co-founder of Red Hat, redefined the formula for success. He stated that success is the product of "1 percent inspiration and 99 percent theft."[17] While Young may not have been advocating actual theft, he did recognize that the solutions to some business problems might already exist.

When time is of the essence, the company that can access the best minds, ideas, answers, and practices will be the one out front. Bruce Strong, vice president of Strategic Services at Context Integration, noted, "It's always nice when a project unfolds as planned. It's also rare. The reality at most companies, even smart companies, is that life is filled with unexpected setbacks, problems, and technical glitches. That's why one of the big tests of the power of a knowledge network is whether it helps to solve the latest make-or-break crisis."[18] Strong also said, "One of the best ways to solve an urgent problem is to find the right people to work on it, who have faced it before, or who have so much expertise in a relevant area that they're likely to figure out a solution fast."[19]

Few people will contest the need for companies to study the best practices of companies in and outside their industry. But executives should not become too infatuated with the benchmark companies—especially in their industry. They need to remember that the most radical challenges to established companies usually come from newcomers who don't play by the rules—and who don't have legacy systems to slow them down mentally or physically! They break the rules and become the new breakthrough companies.

It is clear that there are times when utilizing existing answers and business practices may be quite useful. There are at least two situations, however, when borrowing existing solutions may not be appropriate or beneficial. First, companies that want to be at the leading edge must come up with new insights and develop new answers. They need to be able to explore uncharted markets rather than just harvesting existing markets. They also need to develop innovative products, services, and processes rather than just recycling existing knowledge and offering imitative solutions.

Executives need to step back and look at their company and their industry through irreverent glasses. They need to take a fresh look at every situation, every practice, and every assumption. Business process reengineering—when coupled with corpreneurial business strategies—enables companies to look for new opportunities and to develop revolutionary ways to delight individuals or businesses that are not having their needs met well or at all.

The marketplace is changing too rapidly for companies to operate from a reactive stance by responding only to today's needs and relying on today's technology. Robert Reich, Secretary of Labor in the Clinton administration, noted, "The highest earnings in most worldwide industries are to be found in locations where specialized knowledge is brought to bear on problems whose solutions define new horizons of possibility."[20] Reich observed that cutting-edge businesses enjoy higher profit levels because their customers are willing to pay a premium for goods and services that exactly meet their needs. He also observed that knowledge-based companies have a distinct advantage because they cannot easily be duplicated by low-cost competitors elsewhere in the world.[21]

Second, companies must be able to deal with their unique situations or challenges. There may be times when a solution already exists, but numerous problems and/or opportunities faced by companies have unique features or dimensions. In these instances, executives need to avoid the temptation to use generic off-the-shelf solutions. Existing solutions may take less time and money, but they will be effective only to the extent that they match the company's exact situation. Changing times call for new ideas, new approaches, and new solutions.

Learning organizations incorporate processes that resemble tough love. Top management must encourage introspection, multidirectional communication, and constructive criticism throughout the company. When the company is confronted with a problem or performance falls below expectations, people must be free to challenge key assumptions, prevailing perceptions, and the way things are done. For substantive learning to take place, there can be no sacred topics, no sacred practices, and no sacred cows.

The company's overall environment may play an even more important part in creating a learning organization. Numerous conditions must exist before a company can be considered a learning organization. Michael Beer and Russell Eisenstat have done extensive research on what it takes for companies to incorporate learning into their strategies and ongoing processes. They have found that top management impedes learning and change far more often than do people at lower levels of the company. Their research indicates that top management's inability to articulate, share, and justify the company's strategy frequently creates an environment where employees are slow to adopt change. They stated, "Lack of strategic consensus and clarity undermines effective upward communication. Employees [who are] unsure of where the business is supposed to be going cannot help get it there, nor can they warn those at higher levels when the engine is 'skipping the track.' . . . A top-down management style is often the main barrier to honest upward communication and organizational learning."[22] They also noted, "Although it is a normal human tendency to shrink from confronting one's own deficiencies, leaders do so at the peril of their business."[23] Leaders should create opportunities for people at all levels of the company to have an open dialogue with top management.

Few companies demonstrate the internalization and operationalization of a learning organization better than General Electric.

The company's management development institute in Crotonville, New York, is noted for its unprecedented candor. The no-holds barred environment in the institute's "pit" enables new recruits to challenge any idea regardless of who presented it.[24] At Crotonville, people regularly come up with ideas and action plans that foster higher levels of corporate performance. It also provides an environment where managers achieve personal breakthroughs that enable them to change.[25] Crotonville's environment, which challenges current practices, policies, and strategies, has produced several ways to bust bureaucratic practices. One particularly noteworthy technique is GE's CRAP detector. The acronym stands for "Critical Review Appraisal." The CRAP detector takes a look at organizational processes and classifies them according to the degree of difficulty and the extent to which the change will have a favorable impact on the organization.[26] The CRAP detector seeks out processes that will provide breakthrough performance when they are eliminated.

Executives who are serious about having their companies become learning organizations should also incorporate the workout process used by GE. General Electric established the workout process to develop leaders and to improve the company's performance. Workout sessions bring a group of young managers together to identify and address a particular problem or situation. The executive responsible for that area is invited to attend the workout session, but he or she does not run the proceedings. Instead, the executive is drilled about possible dimensions of the problem or situation by the younger managers. Workout sessions bring issues into the open so they can be addressed. They also provide valuable insights for the younger managers into GE's strategies, practices, and operations. The insights play an integral role in developing future leaders for GE.[27]

Alteon Corp. has blended GE's desire for candor with Silicon Valley's beer busts. Dominic Orr, Alteon's CEO, noted, "Alteon managers gather the troops each Friday for a meeting at which 'brutal intellectual honesty' is demanded."[28] Alteon serves beer and wine beforehand, which ensures that people show up and their tongues are loosened. The result is a free-for-all in which staffers grill senior executives.[29]

FOSTERING CREATIVITY AND INNOVATION

There are a number of myths about creativity and innovation. The biggest one is that only a small percentage of the population has the ability to be creative. Gerald Haman, founder of Creative Solutions Network, noted, "People used to believe that creativity was a gift that a lucky few were born with. In fact, all people have a degree of creativity—they just lose it as they grow older. Schools don't foster imagination; stodgy companies discourage people from taking risks."[30]

Creativity can be a self-fulfilling prophecy. Creativity tends to be a product of its environment. If executives believe most people are not creative, then they will design organizational processes that constrain creativity. However, if they believe people have creative ability, they will put processes in place that encourage, enhance, and reward creativity.

Laurie Coots, chief marketing officer at CHIAT/DAY, observed, "You can't force people to be creative. But you can create an environment where creativity is more likely to happen."[31]

Lorraine Monroe, principal of Harlem's Frederick Douglas School, observed, "There's a latent productivity in people; they're just waiting for someone to remind them of their capacity. People are just waiting to be given permission to do amazing things."[32]

Kevin Buzard, manager of business development for Peoples Energy, shares Monroe's views. He stated, "We try to recapture a spirit of childlike innocence. . . . We want our people to see the world with the same sense of wonder and possibility that children see it with."[33]

According to Monroe, "Leaders must convert their organizations from places with pockets of individual creativity into places of community."[34] She added, "A cadre of concerned, creatively crazy people can carry almost any organization."[35]

Breakthrough leaders empower people at lower levels of the company to size up situations and to do whatever is necessary for the company to move ahead. They encourage the formation of cross-functional teams where synergistic results come from cross-pollinating brains, the use of skunkworks where people work behind the scenes to create breakthroughs, and the bootlegging of resources to explore new possibilities. They also do everything within their power to keep the company from being a bureaucratic quagmire where questions that challenge the status quo die of neglect or where innovative ideas die of old age.

Executives who want to create a forward-focused company need to harness the power of technological innovation, which can help the company leapfrog competition. If the technological innovation delights the target market, it may provide the company with a temporary legal monopoly. Leaders need to realize that technological innovation rarely provides a competitive advantage when it is developed in a vacuum; therefore, it must be tied to the marketplace. Avram Miller, as CEO of the Avram Miller Company, noted, "Companies no longer determine the success of products or markets—if they ever did. Customers do."[36] Companies no longer set the agenda of what customers want. Instead, they find out where the agenda is being set and enhance it. The customers decide what is important.[37]

Technological innovation occurs in two different situations. First, there is the traditional field of dreams strategy; that is, "If you build it, consumers will come." Technological innovation begins in the research and development laboratory when the company develops a new product, which it later offers to the market. A number of companies, including 3M, use this strategy. However, companies that use this strategy should make every effort to get their products into the marketplace as soon and as often as possible. Miller observed, "There is no certainty that the market will embrace your innovation . . . so get it in the hands of a group of consumers, find out how they feel, make changes quickly, and get it back in the marketplace."[38]

Breakthrough leaders prefer to use the second strategy, which is making their businesses "customer problem solvers." Their companies seek every opportunity to interact with people and with companies that are not having their needs met. The second strategy can be seen as a market-pull strategy. It begins by listening to the marketplace. It recognizes that existing and potential customers—as well as employees—can be a source of ideas that may be transformed into revolutionary products, services, and processes.

This strategy usually requires considerable air support from top management. James Brian Quinn, author of *Strategies for Change: Logical Incrementalism*, found that air support may not be that common. Quinn observed, "Many senior executives in big companies have little contact with conditions on the factory floor or with customers who might influence their thinking about technological innovation."[39] Quinn's research indicated that continuous innovation occurs when top executives appreciate innovation and manage their company's value system and atmosphere to support it. His research also indicated that companies need a strong market orientation and mechanisms to ensure interactions between technical and marketing people at lower levels.[40]

Leaders need to recognize that while creativity and innovation cannot be forced, they should not be left to chance, luck, or divine intervention. Although creativity and innovation cannot be managed with the same precision as a production line, they do need to be managed to some extent. Creativity and innovation are enhanced when the following conditions occur:

- Objectives are set for creativity and innovation.
- Funds are invested in creativity and innovation.
- Organizational processes are developed to foster creativity and innovation.
- Performance is reviewed in terms of creativity and innovation.
- Rewards are provided for creativity and innovation.

Efforts to manage creativity and innovation can range all the way from being an integral part of the company's strategic plan down to the layout of the company's offices. If management wants creativity and innovation, it must set targets for them. For example, 3M set a goal to have 30 percent of sales after a four-year period come from products that don't exist today. Executives who feel uneasy about setting goals should consider establishing an innovation index to measure whether the company is improving its performance in creativity and innovation.

Rosabeth Moss Kanter used the innovation index in her research to differentiate innovative companies from less innovative companies. The innovation index measures the proportion of effective managers initiating or contributing to new products or market opportunities, new work or production methods, new structures and new policies.[41] Creativity and innovation are often the product of little things as well. Chan Suh, CEO of Agency.com, installed chalkboards on the doors of the offices in his New York–based advertising agency so people can jot down on-the-spot brainstorming.[42]

CONCLUSION: IDEAS CAN BE THE SOURCE OF COMPETITIVE ADVANTAGE

Someone once observed, "If you're going to pay people to come to work, then you might as well tap their brains while they are there . . . it will not cost you any more money!" Executives who want to create a forward-focused company need to recognize that tomorrow's success depends on the ideas their people come up with today. People can be very resourceful if their future depends on it.

If you create an environment that encourages and rewards creativity, people will direct their resourcefulness to efforts that benefit the company. If you create an environment that does not tap their resourcefulness, they may direct their creative talents to activities that do not enhance the company's performance. In some cases, employees who find their creative talents constrained jump ship and share their talents with a competitor. In other cases, they may even create their own companies to compete against your company. When it comes to creative talent, you either use it or lose it!

> *"A new idea is delicate. It can be killed by a sneer or yawn: it can be stabbed to death by a joke or by a worried frown on the right person's brow."*
> —Charles Brower, former president of the
> Batten, Barton, Durstine & Osborne
> advertising agency

NOTES

1. Robert G. Cooper, "Stage-Gate Systems: A New Tool for Managing New Products," *Business Horizons,* May–June 1990, p. 44.
2. Charles Fishman, "This Is a Marketing Revolution," *Fast Company,* May 1999, p. 207.

3. Ibid., p. 218.

4. Joseph Nocera, "A Mug Only 20,000 Employees Could Love," www.company.com, June 2000, p. 161.

5. Dale Buss, "Brighest of the Big Three," *Business 2.0,* June 13, 2000, p. 223.

6. Nocera, p. 164.

7. Ibid., p. 164.

8. Seth Godin, "In the Face of Change, the Competent Are Helpless," *Fast Company,* January/February 2000, p. 234.

9. Chuck Salter and Andy Esparza, "There's a War for Talent Going on, and We're Right in the Middle of It," *Fast Company,* December 1999, pp. 218–222.

10. Ibid., p. 222.

11. Keith Hammonds, "The Monroe Doctrine," *Fast Company,* October 1999, p. 236.

12. Ellen Neuborne, "The Shape of Things to Come," *Business Week,* July 26, 1999, p. 64.

13. Liz Forrest and Innovation Labs could not be located for permission to print the complete list of idea killers. The author would appreciate learning of Ms. Forrest's address.

14. Chuck Salter, "ideas.com.," *Fast Company,* September 1999, p. 294.

15. Ibid., p. 294.

16. Ibid., p. 302.

17. Presentation to the Coastal Entrepreneurial Council, April 18, 2000.

18. Salter, p. 304.

19. Ibid., p. 307.

20. Robert Reich, "The Real Economy," *Atlantic Monthly,* February 1991, p. 36.

21. Ibid.

22. Michael Beer and Russell A. Eisenstat, "The Silent Killers of Strategy Implementation and Learning," *Sloan Management Review,* Summer 2000, p. 32.

23. Ibid., p. 33.

24. Noel M. Tichy and Stratford Sherman, *Control Your Destiny or Someone Else Will* (New York: HarperBusiness, 1993), p. 165.

25. Ibid., p. 159.

26. Ibid., p. 433–434.

27. Ibid., p. 244.

28. Mark Bordon, "When Big Growth Happens to Small Companies," *Fortune,* March 6, 2000, p. 386.

29. Ibid.

30. Curtis Sittenfeld, "What's the Big Idea?" *Fast Company,* April 1999. p. 44.

31. Eric Ransdell, "Work Different," *Fast Company,* June 1999, p. 150.
32. Hammonds, p. 236.
33. Sittenfeld, p. 46.
34. Hammonds, p. 232.
35. Ibid., p. 234.
36. Katharine Mieszkowski, "Who's Fast?" *Fast Company,* December 1999, p. 160.
37. Ibid., p. 152.
38. Ibid., p. 152.
39. James Brian Quinn, "Managing Innovation: Controlled Chaos," *Harvard Business Review,* May/June 1985, p. 73.
40. Ibid., pp. 76–77.
41. Rosabeth Moss Kanter, *The Change Masters* (New York: Simon & Schuster, 1983), p. 26.
42. Neuborne, p. 64.

4

Fostering Speed and Agility

"'Time is money' may have been true in Ben Franklin's time, but 'Speed is profit' is the new business axiom that will make people and companies rich for the foreseeable future."[1]

—Michael LeBoeuf, author of *Fast Forward*

The accelerating rate of change along with its associated discontinuities have forced managers to learn how to drive in the fast lane. The days of placing the company on cruise control and going with the flow of surrounding traffic are gone. If you're not the first-mover or a very fast follower, you're dead. Companies that fail to be at the leading edge look like sloths to consumers. Timing can also make a difference in corporate success. Companies need to have the sense of timing displayed by the cliff divers of Mexico. Executives who hesitate miss the waves of change and crash in the shallows.

Today, being a day late means more than being a dollar short—it means bankruptcy. To operate on an eight-to-five, five-day schedule in a world that has gone to a seven-days-a-week, twenty-four-hour clock is corporate suicide. While sophisticated corporate strategies still play a major role in the success of a company, a world of ever-accelerating change places a premium on perceptiveness, focus, timing, decisiveness, and speed.

The abilities to sense changes early and to make quick adjustments are essential competencies in a world of rapid change. Few people have demonstrated this skill more proficiently than Wayne Gretzky. A sports commentator once asked Gretzky to explain how he had become such a successful hockey player. The commentator wondered how Gretzky could be so good. After all, Gretzky wasn't known for being the fastest, strongest, or best shooter in the league. Gretzky explained that other hockey players tend to play the puck where it is. Gretzky said that he looks at the flow of play and anticipates where the puck will be, then skates to that point on the ice. He said that if you anticipate where the puck will be and put yourself there before anyone else, you usually have a clear shot at the goal. Gretzky noted that when you're in that position and have your stick ready, you don't have to be the world's greatest shooter to score a goal.

While Gretzky's success may be attributed to his keen sense of timing, a closer look reveals that timing is the result of four distinct capabilities: anticipation, speed, agility, and perceptiveness. This chapter profiles the role anticipation, speed, agility, and perceptiveness play in fostering organizational success. Ironically, the four capabilities can go under the acronym ASAP, which stands for "as soon as possible."

ANTICIPATION: GIVING THE COMPANY A HEAD START

Arian Ward, as leader of Learning and Change at Hughes Space and Communications Company, observed, "The key role of leaders is to recognize the winds of change coming and to proactively prepare to integrate it into business strategy."[2] Yet the phrase "I wish I had known . . ." is being heard with increasing frequency today. Rapid change benefits those who are perceptive, nimble, and innovative.

Wayne Gretzky demonstrated the benefits of having a head start over one's competitors. While most executives dream of having 20/20 foresight into what the future holds, the next best thing would be to have 20/20 foresight into what the future *may* hold. Executives who practice anticipatory management by running "What if?" scenarios are in a better position to see what the future may hold. Scenarios are like radar because they extend management's mental horizon. By running scenarios, executives may be able to identify emerging factors and forces. Scenarios can be seen as taking a mental journey into the future by exploring various possibilities. By seeing possible situations and events earlier, management has additional lead time to position the company so that it can capitalize on opportunities or prevent problems. Scenarios help to prevent management from being blindsided by events that could be detrimental to the company. If the leading manufacturers of mainframe computers had run scenarios about the possible use of personal computers, they may have committed resources to the development of PCs instead of being totally out of synch with market demand.

Scenarios may not be able to provide a crystal clear picture of the future with perfect certainty, but they do encourage executives to explore possible futures. Scenarios may provide valuable insights by posing "What if?" questions. If corporate strategy is the product of how management sees the world, then it is likely that the newly found insights will produce more innovative strategies for companies that embrace anticipatory thinking. Insights into the whole range of possible future situations also give management the incentive to develop contingency plans to address these various possible futures.

Executives need to recognize that their plans are based on assumptions about future market conditions. They also need to recognize that no plan is flawless. As soon as the company's real-time information system shows the first sign that the company's game plan is not in tune with new realities, the company may be able to initiate a plan that is in a better position to meet the contingencies. Companies with contingency plans that are in tune with possible futures enjoy a much quicker response than companies that must start from scratch when their plans are derailed.

Anticipatory management gives executives the opportunity to operate from a proactive stance. Companies that anticipate change will be the initiators and beneficiaries of change. Companies that fail to incorporate anticipatory management will be the victims of change. They will be relegated to a red alert type of existence until they are blindsided for the last time.

SPEED: A DECISIVE ADVANTAGE IN THE RACE TO WIN CUSTOMERS

Management researchers John Grant and Devi Gnyawali emphasize the need for companies to have the ability to operate in the
fast lane. Grand and Gnyawali state, "Because of the increasing
speed with which ideas can travel and products can be delivered,
the need for organizations to convert either threats or opportunities into effective new offerings has never been greater."[3] We live
in a time where people are infatuated with speed. We want our
computers and related products to work at the blink of an eye. We
also expect companies to respond immediately to our needs,
wants, and desires. Regis McKenna, author of *Real Time: Preparing for the Age of the Never Satisfied Customer*, observed, "Our
appetite for speed is insatiable. This supercharged world . . . is a
marketplace in which the ticking of real-time technologies is teaching the consumer to expect and demand immediate satisfaction."[4]
McKenna defines real time as the shortest possible lapse between
idea and action, between initiation and result.

Michael LeBoeuf, author of *Fast Forward*, noted, "With massive change comes incredible opportunity . . . those who are aware
of what's happening and prepared to act fast will be those who
will enjoy unprecedented success . . . when change is the problem,
speed is the solution."[5] The marketplace has always been characterized by survival of the fittest. In a world of ever-accelerating
change, the marketplace may now be characterized by survival of
the swiftest. The breakneck pace of competition is particularly evident in the following comment made by Craig Barrett, as president
of Intel: "We are going down the road at 150 miles per hour, and
we know there's a brick wall some place, but the worst thing we
can do is stop too soon and let somebody else pass us."[6]

Anthony Carnevale, author of *America and the New Economy*, noted that in today's economy, companies compete in the
following four races against the clock:[7]

- *The First Race:* Developing innovations in technology, products, or work processes
- *The Second Race:* Getting innovation "off the drawing board" and into the hands of consumers

- *The Third Race:* Increasing efficiency or quality of the innovation or developing new applications
- *The Fourth Race:* Using what has been learned in the previous steps to move to another innovation

The first and second races are receiving considerable attention today from companies that want to operate from a visionary or proactive position. The first race has spawned the "close to customer" movement as well as the formation of alliances between leading producers and leading users. Genentech provides a good example of a company that has embraced the need for speed and innovation when its executives stated that they expect to be the first company to commercialize rDNA technology.[8]

The second race is benefiting from various technological breakthroughs. Prototype development and rapid manufacturing are particularly noteworthy. The abilities to develop a prototype and to test it for consumer response have always been crucial steps in the introduction of new products. John Hennessy, dean of Stanford's School of Engineering, noted, "The gap between research and what's in production has narrowed to almost nothing."[9]

Sony is a master of the quick prototyping process. It is not unusual for a company today to take an entire year to transform a concept into a prototype. Sony is committed to having a prototype ready within five days. This capability gives Sony the opportunity to get a number of versions of a new product into the hands of potential consumers. Sony is then able to quickly turn the prototypes that garner the most favorable responses into actual products.

The desire to accelerate the introduction of new products has accentuated the need for reducing cycle time in the manufacturing process. For example, Teledesic chose Motorola to supply satellites for its system, which will provide high-speed Internet access by satellite. Motorola was selected because it trimmed satellite-manufacturing time down to little more than four days, compared with an industry average of two years.[10]

Flexible manufacturing allows companies to modify production processes between diverse products. This capability allows a company to respond rapidly and efficiently to customer needs. In Japan, automobile companies with flexible manufacturing are trying to develop systems that are capable of making new models in the buyer's choice of color and options in three working days. Concurrent design and manufacturing further accelerates the speed with which a new product can be introduced to the marketplace.

Technological innovations are now challenging the proverbial speed barrier. Recent advances in technology have made rapid prototyping a reality. It is now possible to go directly from the computer-aided design to the manufacture of actual products. Rapid prototyping technology has been combined with rapid manufacturing technology. These two technologies leapfrog the traditional die-and-mold–making steps that can swallow up several years of work.[11] For example, Chrysler uses rapid prototyping machines to design and make intake manifolds. The manifold, which is shaped like an octopus, can be made in transparent plastic in four to eight days. The old way of bending and welding steel tubes took as long as three months.[12] The ability to do desktop manufacturing, where plastic prototypes and actual products can be made using computer-aided design, a laser, and jet-type printers, is not far away.

A few companies are trying to eliminate the need for prototypes altogether. Boeing demonstrated its ability to skip constructing a tangible prototype when it designed the 777 twin-jet airplane entirely by computer. Boeing used a three-dimensional computer model that enabled it to solve virtually every design problem through computer animation.[13] According to Jay Hay, vice president of Ford's Structural Dynamics Research Corp. (SDRC) program, "We're trying to eliminate the prototype stage and do all the testing on the computer. If you can make all your changes to the design when it's a 'virtual' car, then the process is much cheaper and faster."[14] Ford uses software to create virtual prototypes that are so close to the real thing that engineers no longer need physical models to see how parts fit together, which saves time, money, and a lot of headaches. Engineers still make models, but they do so mainly to confirm their computer simulation tests. Hay noted that with the master model, "Everyone is on the same page at the same time. And that's the key to moving faster."[15] With its cad-cam-cae manufacturing technology, Ford has cut the average cycle time from fifty-five months to thirty-two months. Now Ford is pushing to get the time down to twenty-four months.[16]

The need for speed has raised some interesting questions about the role that quality plays in today's marketplace. Speed and quality are essential in most markets. There are instances, however, when speed may be more critical than quality. The competitive advantage associated with being first to market may be dramatic. Writer David Dorsey noted, "Speed-to-market matters. The irony is that you don't need to be the best. You just need to be there fast and to create a dependency on what you offer. You produce a new system that becomes a standard that others must adopt in order to deal with people who are already using your service or product, and that process snowballs until the majority of users are dependent on your system."[17] Dorsey indicated that if the company can achieve "escape velocity from the industry's existing array of products, then nobody will be able to offer a competing product."[18]

Management's efforts to enhance speed should not be restricted to new product development. Management should also review the company's ongoing operations to see if corporate performance can be enhanced by increasing the speed of operations. John Ellis, as contributing editor for *Fast Company*, noted, "As boundaries are erased and time compressed, transactional speed becomes imperative. The oft repeated wisdom, 'The new economy favors speed over size' is only half the truth. The other half is that giant, fast-paced companies will crush quick, smaller ones. But this business of speed and time is, by itself, an overwhelming force. Once you get used to e-mail, snail mail isn't the same."[19] According to Ellis, "These days, if the Internet is not central to your business, the belief among ranking chieftains is that you will soon be out of business."[20] The ordering process appears to be a target-rich environment in the quest for speeding organizational processes. The Internet can provide incredible savings in time and cost. Its ability to provide product information to customers may also provide major savings.

General Electric found that each customer call costs about five dollars to handle by the time the call was fielded. By using the Internet, GE was able to cut the cost to twenty-five cents. GE also found that by using the Internet in its Fleet services, the company was able to go from having telephone inaccuracies of 45 percent to having one tenth of a percent inaccuracies by using its software on the Internet.[21] Jack Welch, as CEO of GE, demonstrated his commitment to making electronic commerce and the use of the Internet an integral part of GE when he decreed, "Every division would be fully operational by the end of 1999 . . . or else!"[22]

Increasing speed may be beneficial in the human resources area as well. Companies that do not have the right number of people in the right place with the right capabilities will be passed by companies that are able to meet their human resource needs in a more timely manner. While a company may lose a customer because it did not have a certain item in stock, not having the right person in a mission-critical position can jeopardize the company altogether.

Mike Maples, cofounder of Motive Communications based in Austin, Texas, observed, "Our really high hiring standards and slow hiring practices got us in trouble . . . we lost our competitive advantage. So we carefully started tracking our hiring process. We coined the term 'perfect hiring,' which meant hiring 'A players on time.' Then we held a contest in which each team (engineering, marketing, etc.) would lose a point for every week a position remained open past the target hiring date. Now we treat our hiring forecast as seriously as our revenue forecast, and there's hell to pay for missing either one. . . . You need to be fully staffed to attack a market."[23]

PROCEED WITH CAUTION: RAW AND UNBRIDLED SPEED CAN SPELL DISASTER

A few words of caution and clarification about speed are warranted at this time. First, although speed may appear to be a virtue, raw and unbridled speed can derail a company. Executives at the helms of rapid-growth companies need to handle the throttle with finesse. The speed associated with new product introduction, rapid growth, and massive corporate change can lead to disaster. William Sheeline, as journalist for *Fortune* magazine, noted, "The fast lane is paved with businesses that failed to spot the hazards in time."[24] Rapid-growth companies frequently crash when their executives drive beyond their headlights. Jim Sinegal, as CEO of Costco Wholesale, noted, "When you are growing very fast, you can't afford to outdistance your management."[25]

Executives should try to extend the company's headlights— or, better yet, equip the car with radar—to see things earlier. If the company cannot extend its headlights, then it needs to enhance its agility by improving its steering and braking systems so it can avoid objects in its path, or stop before hitting them. Sheeline echoed Sinegal's caution when he stated, "Prudence sometimes indicates easing back on the corporate throttle to give employees and internal systems time to adjust."[26]

Speed is like a fast computer processor. Without the right software, a computer cannot do anything productive no matter how fast it is. It is the software that provides focus and agility. This is similar to a question raised at a time-management seminar. A participant asked if he should take a speed-reading class. The instructor responded, "I can teach you to read one million words a minute right now." The instructor then stated that if you know what *not* to read—and don't read it—that is better than reading one thousand words per minute. The instructor noted that the trouble with speed-reading is that by being able to read quickly, people will read almost anything.

The old saying "Please engage your brain before you engage your mouth" seems to apply to the relationship between speed and decision making. Executive time can be divided into numerous categories. In the overall scheme of things, there is a time to think, a time to analyze, a time to reflect, a time to decide, and a time to act. While executives need to guard against paralysis by analysis, they also need to recognize that there are times when reflection may be more important to the company's future than swift action. Although it may be easier and quicker to implement last year's strategy again this year, to do so could spell disaster. Some things take time and should not be rushed. Creativity and the development of people are crucial to the company. They cannot be rushed.

One of the most important talents for a top executive is the ability to put things in perspective—to see the big picture and to be able to separate the important from the urgent. Although the economy might operate twenty-four hours a day, seven days a week, executives need to ensure that they have blocks of time for themselves on a regular basis so that they can maintain a sense of balance and perspective. Without breaks, they can get caught up in the "tyranny of the urgent" or fall prey to pursuing speed merely for the sake of speed.

If speed is all that matters, then all players who return kick-offs and punts in the NFL would be recruited from track teams. When speed is matched with agility, however, truly incredible things can occur. Barry Sanders of the Detroit Lions combined these skills to become one of the greatest running backs in football history. Companies that can develop Sanders's ability to see an opportunity, dodge obstacles, and accelerate past the competition will leave competitors in the dust. For example, National, a Japanese bicycle manufacturer, has gained considerable recognition for its ability to make and deliver a custom-made bicycle in three days. National's agility and speed is particularly impressive when you consider that it offers customers the opportunity to choose from 11 million styles and sizes.[27]

AGILITY: THE ABILITY TO TURN ON A DIME

Agility can give a company a decisive edge over companies that fail to grasp its importance. The need for agility applies to entrepreneurial companies as well as to established companies. Companies that lack perceptiveness and agility are destined to fall prey to the here today, gone tomorrow syndrome. If failed corporations were given funerals, many of their tombstones would read, "Here lies XYZ Corporation, its managers never knew what hit them!" Yet agility should not be viewed as a survival skill. Instead, it should be seen as a means for thriving in the years ahead. Just as companies recognized the need to continuously improve the quality of their operations to remain competitive in the 1990s, companies must recognize the need for agility in the years ahead.

Agility applies to numerous dimensions of a company's operations, such as the ability to develop and introduce new products and services; the ability to enter new markets; the ability to respond to customer concerns; the ability to change from one process to another; and the ability to compress the cycle time associated with receiving an order, all the way through to collecting the funds after the product's delivery.

Jack Welch has been praised for creating an environment where change is implemented quickly. His commitment to get GE up to speed in business-to-business commerce on the Internet was evident when he directed his top 600 executives to develop an e-commerce strategy for every dimension of GE. According to Welch, "One cannot be tentative about this. Excuses like channel conflict or marketing and sales aren't ready cannot be allowed to divert or paralyze the offensive. Delay and you risk being cut out of your own market, perhaps not by traditional competitors but by companies you never heard of twenty-four months ago."[28]

Agility Requires Perceptiveness

Stan Davis and Christopher Meyer acknowledged the impact of the accelerating rate and comprehensive nature of change in their book, *BLUR: The Speed of Change in the Connected Age.* They stated, "The pace is so furious, the meltdown so severe, the erasing of borders so complete that, the whole picture is going out of focus."[29] Companies that see changes coming and possess the ability to move quickly will not only be able to prevent problems that could cause their demise; they will be able to capitalize on the opportunities that come with those changes.

Agility is of little value if the company is continuously blindsided. Although the company may be able to adjust quickly, agility works best when the company has lead time. The company that sees the future first has a head start over companies that are preoccupied with what they are currently doing. Lead time determines whether the company will be a leader or a loser.

The need for perceptiveness and agility has never been greater. It appears that more and more companies are adopting a responsive rather than proactive type of strategy. This shift was evident in the mid-1980s when GE announced that it was reducing its emphasis on formal long-term planning. GE executives concluded that it was becoming too difficult to forecast what the future would bring, so they adopted a strategy that emphasized responding to changes in the marketplace. They recognized that when a plan is developed and implemented, the company's resources are committed. The commitment of resources reduces the company's ability to change to meet future changes. GE then shifted to a quick-response strategy that was designed to sense the changes earlier and to have the ability and resources available to respond to the changes quicker than its competitors. Jack Welch captured the importance of responsiveness when he stated that companies need to be able to "change the tires while the car is still rolling!"

Compressing Cycle Time Can Provide a Competitive Edge

The race to win customers can be viewed as a set of hurdles. Success is contingent on the company's ability to clear each hurdle and to go from start to finish in the least amount of time. The Cycle Time from Market Opportunity Identification to Market Offering chart profiled in Figure 4-1 indicates the series of hurdles that need to be cleared if the company wants to delight its customers and possibly gain a temporary legal monopoly. The process begins with the company's ability to identify emerging customer interests. Companies that can identify a need; develop a product or service concept; design the product or service; then produce, offer, and service that product or service in the least amount of time will win customers.

Figure 4-1. The cycle time from market opportunity identification to market offering.

Identification of Customer Need	Develop Product/ Service	Design Product/ Service	Make Product/ Service	Market Product/ Service	Provide Product/ Service	Satisfaction of Customer Need

◀Identification▶◀ Innovation Time ▶◀ Operational Time ▶◀Service▶
   Time   Time

◀——————Time to Market ——————▶

◀———————————— Total Corporate Cycle Time ————————————▶

◀——————— Opportunity Identification to Satisfaction Cycle Time ———————▶

Companies that outsource key dimensions of the value chain should choose their allies carefully. A company can only be as fast as the slowest link in its overall value chain. A company's ability to sense and seize opportunities will be dependent on the agility of its suppliers and the companies in its distribution network.

Alan Solomon, a Ford SDRC veteran, noted, "If a company really wants to do things differently, then it needs to think about its process for developing products from the moment a new idea gets sketched on a napkin to the day a new product gets shipped to customers. You need to take an end-to-end view."[30] Solomon found that opportunities for accelerating cycle time are immense and said that Ford SDRC is trying to slash development times in half. He also noted, "The faster a company goes, the deeper into its organization it has to reach."[31]

Executives Must Have the Ability to Focus on What Really Matters

Just as it is clear that no company can be all things to all people, it is also clear that no company can pay attention to everything going on around it and within it. For a company to be agile, it needs to be able to focus on what really matters. Focus means knowing what the yes's are and what the no's are. Companies with a clear sense of mission and a clearly articulated vision for where they want to be in the next three to five years are far less likely to be distracted or seduced by short-lived opportunities.

Focus not only enables management to direct its attention to the truly important issues, it also enhances the company's ability to respond quickly when variances occur. Focus is enhanced by management systems that incorporate managing by objectives, time-activity networks, and sensitivity analysis. Managing by objectives forces the company to identify what it is striving to accomplish. Time-activity networks like PERT and CPM help identify the most critical paths. Sensitivity analysis, such as Pareto 80/20 analysis, helps to identify the fewest (20 percent) actions that will make the greatest (80 percent) difference.

These techniques identify in advance the factors that need to be monitored closely. Although these techniques have been around for years, today's online, real-time information technology, like the one used by Cypress Semiconductor profiled in Chapter 12, make it possible for people at all levels of the organization to monitor even the smallest variances. Information technology permits management to focus its attention on exceptional variances. The sooner a variance is recognized, the quicker the company can respond. The need for timely feedback is reflected in the Merrill Lynch advertisement, "It's not what you know that matters, it's when you know it that matters."

If awareness of the need to change is a prerequisite for initiating a change effort, then having an early warning system that facilitates quick response is a necessity. Having crucial information on a real-time basis permits real-time adjustments. Alan Solomon of Ford observed, "When things are already running fast . . . you have to give the right people the right information at the right time."[32] You also need to have an environment where people are not left in the dark or blindsided—especially with bad news. Harold Geneen, as CEO of IT&T (years ago), insisted on operating with a "no surprise" environment. He was known for his policy, "I want to hear bad news . . . and I don't want to hear it late!"

Dominic Orr, CEO of Altheon WebSystems Inc., distinguishes between speed in making decisions and speed in implementing decisions. He noted, "Fast execution and fast delivery—that's easy. Fast decision-making is harder." Orr explained that although today's environment often requires team-based decision making, special effort needs to be made to ensure the team does not take too much time. According to Orr, "Making high-stakes decisions as a team is important. But we don't have time for an endless debate or for office politics."[33]

Orr said:

> Brutal intellectual honesty reduces endless debate and office politics . . . and speeds decision-making. We've distilled that company-wide philosophy into a few simple rules. We focus on collecting as many facts as quickly as we can, and then we decide on the best—but not necessarily the perfect solution. Think Socratic method at the speed of light. There's no silent disagreement, and no getting personal, and definitely no 'Let's take it offline' mentality. Our goal is to make each major decision in a single meeting. People arrive with a proposal or a solution— and with the facts to support it. After an idea is presented, we open the floor to objective, and often withering, critiques. And if the idea collapses under scrutiny, we move on to another idea, no hard feelings. We're judging the idea, not the person. At the same time, we don't really try to regulate emotions. Passionate conflict means that we're getting somewhere, not that the discussion gets out of control. But one person does act as referee—by asking basic questions like 'Is this good for the customer?' or 'Does it keep our time-to-market advantage intact?' By focusing relentlessly on the facts, we're able to see the strengths and weaknesses of an idea clearly and quickly.[34]

The value of focus is evident in two airlines that wanted to tailor their efforts to the challenges in their industry. Jan Carlzon, president of Scandinavian Airlines, noted in his book, *Moments of Truth*, that his airline was floundering until it decided to focus its attention on the business traveler. Once this decision was made, the company was in a better position to adjust its operations to meet the needs of that particular target market. Scandinavian Airlines made every effort to identify the connecting flights and locate them as close as possible to the arrival gates. Herb Kelleher, as president of Southwest Airlines, noted that by not having hub-and-spoke systems or assigning seats, his airline could turn around a plane much quicker than traditional carriers that continued doing business as usual.

PERCEPTIVENESS: THE ABILITY TO TIME CORPORATE INITIATIVES

Lasting success is not the result of being able do a one hundred-meter sprint in less than ten seconds. Lasting success is more like a never-ending relay race of decisions and actions. There are many examples of new ventures once heralded by the media for their meteoric rise that experienced an almost equally swift free fall into oblivion. They went to an early grave once their unique product offering was no longer in sync with the market. Established corporations can also fall prey to the here today, gone tomorrow syndrome. They put themselves in harm's way if they zig and the market zags, or if they fail to respond quickly enough to a shift in the marketplace.

Competition is quick to jump on the bandwagon for markets that show promise. The challenge is amplified when more lead time is needed to develop competencies to meet the needs of a sophisticated market. When this is the case, companies either need to be more perceptive and start sooner or they have to be more agile so they can respond quicker. A study by Ming-Jer Chen and Ian MacMillan indicated, "Competitive actions and responses matter to performance; initiators of actions and early responders gain market share at the expense of late responders."[35] Richard Sherman, senior vice president of Strategic Research at Numetrix Ltd., a Toronto-based software provider, noted, "Those manufacturers that redesign their processes to be more responsive will be able to grow their businesses faster than their less agile competition."[36]

Seth Godin, author of *Permission Marketing*, draws the distinction between speed and velocity. He noted that the newly competent in Silicon Valley, and elsewhere, confuse speed with velocity. The culture of these revolutionary companies is to sprint as fast as possible—all the time. He defines velocity as the company's ability to zig, zag, and zoom—to make significant changes when changes are necessary. He claims that you can have velocity without speed. If you drive around in circles, you may make the speedometer look impressive, but it won't get you across the country very fast.[37] Godin further noted, "Give me five serially incompetent 9-to-5 executives with a focus on velocity, and I can change the world—over and over again."[38]

Sensing "Windows of Opportunity"

The accelerating rate of change in the marketplace has placed a premium on having foresight and the ability to quickly modify the company's capabilities and corresponding market offerings. Although it may be true that there are more opportunities now than at any time in the past, entrepreneurs and executives need to recognize that windows of opportunity may be opening and closing more rapidly than at any other time. The battle to gain customers in some industries is now being fought in real time. Companies that quickly spot emerging opportunities and position themselves to provide what the market values will thrive; companies that lag behind may not survive.

Entrepreneurship is usually associated with identifying and serving an emerging opportunity. Sustained growth for established enterprises is usually contingent on the company's ability to capitalize on additional market opportunities. The need to identify market opportunities, however, tends to overshadow the importance of having a keen sense of timing. Paul Wahl, as CEO of SAP America, observed, "Our remarkable growth in recent years is due in large measure to having a very strong product on the market at precisely the right time."[39]

Yesterday's era of everlasting mass markets has been replaced by an era where market niches and micromarkets appear on the radar screen for only a finite period of time. Companies with perceptive timing are able to sense the window being formed, position themselves to serve the market when the window opens, capitalize on the opportunity, and then exit before the window closes on them.

Although companies might want to be first to market, management needs to ensure that their companies are not so far out in front that they outdistance or lose sight of the marketplace. For example, Corning Glass developed fiber-optic cable ten years before the market was ready. Panasonic's strategy of being "slightly ahead of its time" is less risky than being "way ahead of its time." Companies that are way ahead of the market are also vulnerable if the market changes what it values.

TRIAGE MANAGEMENT: NO ROOM FOR PARALYSIS BY ANALYSIS

Corporate agility is contingent on being able to decide quickly and to act quickly. The accelerating rate of change has placed managers in situations that resemble the triage environment of hospital emergency rooms. Decisiveness is of paramount importance in triage situations. Triage represents an area of health care where the ability to size up the situation, determine what is truly critical and urgent, and take swift action can make the difference between life and death.

Corporate success depends on management's ability to outthink, outdecide, and outimplement its competitors. The ability to decide and implement flourishes in environments where there is a sense of urgency and where people are able to keep their heads under fire. When timing is critical and information is limited or not available, the intuitive insights that come from varied experiences foster split-second decision making and responsiveness.

In an ever-changing world, corporate triage situations are occurring with increasing frequency. Decisiveness enhances the company's ability to seize the moment when it is presented with a challenge. Decisiveness is necessary so personnel can do whatever it takes at that moment to recover a customer who has not been given proper service. Decisiveness is also of paramount importance to get a product delivered on time when the expected carrier fails to come through.

CONCLUSION: TIMING IS A MULTIDIMENSIONAL COMPETENCY

The good old days of stability, linearity, and predictability are gone forever. Turbulence and discontinuity are no longer occasional occurrences. There will be times when the company's agility, speed, anticipation, and perceptiveness will provide the company with the opportunity to seize the moment and gain a formidable advantage.

Your company's future will be contingent on whether it has the ability to sense the need for change, the ability to learn what needs to be done differently, the ability to develop innovative approaches for providing value to the marketplace, and the resources available to initiate changes. Your company will capitalize on emerging opportunities by developing opportunistic strategies and an innovative corporate culture. With increasing discontinuity, however, your company's ability to improvise will also be a valuable attribute. In times of discontinuity, perceptiveness and agility will give your company the ability to respond quickly. Although it may not be possible for you to sense every opportunity and prevent every problem, every effort should be made to create an environment where your company is able to operate from an offensive stance.

"You either make dust or you eat dust!"
—U.S. West advertisement

NOTES

1. Michael LeBoeuf, *Fast Forward* (New York: G.P. Putnam & Sons, 1993), p. 12.
2. Arian Ward, "Lessons Learned on the Knowledge Highways and Byways," *Strategy and Leadership Journal,* March–April 1996, p. 18.
3. John Grant and Devi Gnyawali, "Strategic Process Improvement through Organizational Learning," *Strategy and Leadership Journal,* May–June 1995, p. 30.
4. Regis McKenna, "Real Time," *Inc.,* September 1997, p. 87.
5. LeBoeuf, pp. 207–208.

6. Andy Reinhardt, "Intel," *Business Week,* December 22, 1997, p. 73.
7. Anthony Carnevale, taken from an excerpt from "Putting Quality to Work: Train America's Workforce." Carnevale's thoughts originally appeared in *America and the New Economy* (Washington, D.C.: American Society for Training and Development, 1990).
8. James Brian Quinn, "Managing Innovation: Controlled Chaos," *Harvard Business Review,* May–June 1985, p. 78.
9. Joan O'C. Hamilton, "Stanford: Eggheads and Entrepreneurs," *Business Week,* June 23, 1997, p. 92.
10. Peter Elstrom, "The Internet Space Race," *Business Week,* June 1, 1998, p. 48.
11. Ibid.
12. Gend Bylinski, "Prototypes," *Fortune,* January 12, 1998, pp. 120b–120c.
13. Anna Bernasek, "Pattern for Prosperity," *Fortune,* October 2, 2000, p. 104.
14. Gina Imperato, "SDRC Wants You to Go Faster," *Fast Company,* October 1999, p. 92.
15. Ibid., p. 92.
16. Ibid., p. 90.
17. David Dorsey, "The People behind the People behind E-Commerce," *Fast Company,* June 1999, p. 198.
18. Ibid.
19. John Ellis, "Change Partners," *Fast Company,* October 1999, pp. 351–352.
20. Ibid., p. 351.
21. Howard Rudnitsky, "Changing the Corporate DNA," www.Forbes.com, July 19, 2000, pp. 39–40.
22. Ibid.
23. Rekha Balu, "Hiring Right Means Hiring Fast," *Fast Company,* June 2000, p. 396.
24. William E. Sheeline, "Avoiding Growth's Perils," *Fortune,* August 13, 1990, p. 55.
25. Ibid.
26. Ibid., p. 58.
27. LeBoeuf, p. 121.
28. Rudnitsky, p. 39.
29. Daniel H. Pink, "One Thing's for Sure—the World's a Blur," *Fast Company,* April–May 1998, p. 88.
30. Imperato, p. 90.
31. Ibid., p. 92.
32. Ibid.
33. Cathy Olofson, "So Many Decisions, So Little Time," *Fast Company,* October 1999, p. 62.

34. Ibid.
35. Ming-Jer Chen and Donald Hambrick, "Speed, Stealth, and Selective Attack: How Small Firms Differ from Large Firms in Competitive Behavior," *Academy of Management Journal,* vol. 2, 1995, p. 462.
36. "Building a World-Class Supply Chain," *Fortune,* July 7, 1997, p. 54.
37. Seth Godin, "In the Face of Change, the Competent Are Helpless," *Fast Company,* January–February 2000, p. 234.
38. Ibid.
39. "Building a World-Class Supply Chain," p. 54.

Part II

The Need for Bold Initiatives

New realities require new approaches to leadership. Breakthrough leadership is about creating new realities. New realities call for a whole new way to view the role leaders play in the change process and the approaches they will need to take to enable their companies to thrive in the years ahead. Executives have been quick to blame intense competition, economic uncertainty, and the relatively high cost of capital as reasons that their companies have turned in less than stellar performances in the past few years. The real reason for lackluster corporate performance may actually lie within their companies.

Too many executives operate with a myopic perspective. They are unable to see the myriad opportunities that are mushrooming around them. Their tendency to make decisions by the numbers has made matters even worse. Their shortsightedness and limited imagination have prompted them to be overly cautious in a world that is exploding with opportunities and that beckons innovation. Some executives are so arrogant that they fail to see that what worked well yesterday may not even keep them competitive today. Other executives are so caught up in making certain nothing is falling through the cracks that they have become ignorant to the changes around them. Whether they succumb to arrogance or ignorance, their complacency about the need to create a forward-focused organization will result in corporate mediocrity.

Instead of operating from a reactive stance and trying to cope with change, they should adopt a proactive stance that will permit the company to be innovative and initiate change. Executives who anticipate the future may be in a position to influence probabilities, possibilities, and payoffs. If they are truly corpreneurial, then they may be able to create temporary legal monopolies.

If executives are truly committed to achieving breakthrough performance, they must realize that it cannot be purchased. Breakthrough performance cannot be achieved via merger or a leveraged buyout. In most cases, mergers and acquisitions are merely reactive, stop-gap measures. They are desperate attempts to buy a future for a company that fell asleep at the switch. Executives can no longer afford to be seduced by short-term opportunities or tempted to jump-start their companies with the balance-sheet gymnastics that resemble the popular shell game run by con artists. Executives need to recognize that breakthrough performance must be developed from within, and that it cannot be developed overnight. It takes committed leadership, and it may take at least a decade to develop the qualities needed to achieve and sustain a true competitive advantage.

Lasting success will only come to companies that are visionary and committed to going the distance. Visionary executives identify the company's desired strategic position, develop innovative approaches for making the right things happen, and commit resources to them even though such actions may reduce short-term profitability. They also have the patience to resist being seduced by short-term quick fixes. The following chapters provide insights into how executives can create forward-focused companies in a world of permanent whitewater.

5

Developing New Mental Models for New Challenges

"To every man there comes in his lifetime that special moment when he is figuratively tapped on the shoulder and offered that chance to do a very special thing, unique to him and fitted to his talent; what a tragedy if that moment finds him unprepared or unqualified for the work that could have been his finest hour."[1]

—Winston Churchill, prime minister of England during World War II

C reating a forward-focused company involves making decisions today that will affect the company's future. Today's decisions will influence tomorrow's decisions because today's decisions have a bearing on the company's markets, products, services, and processes in the years ahead. Leadership involves creating an environment where people grow and ideas flourish. It is an environment where people are always scanning the horizon for emerging opportunities and developing innovative products, services, and processes to capitalize on targeted market opportunities.

Most managers, including those who make it to the top, have a tendency to be preoccupied with the present and immediate future. Their perceptual fields are composed primarily of existing markets, existing customers, existing technology, existing competitors, existing capabilities, existing strengths, and existing weaknesses. To make matters worse, most executives rarely break out of their industry's boundaries to experience the dynamics of a world undergoing an incredible transformation or to learn the perceptions and visions of executives in other fields and markets.

Executives who are preoccupied with what is immediately within their reach are prone to develop corporate strategies that merely fine-tune current products and practices. The tendency for executives to direct their attention almost exclusively to existing tangible factors and the present time is called management by braille. Management by braille limits one's depth perception. It prevents executives from scanning the horizon for faint signals of what may lie ahead. Their preoccupation with what can be quantified and measured keeps them seeing emerging trends and considering less tangible factors.

Management by braille is evident in what is called the yellow-banana syndrome. A number of years ago, a top executive's reluctance to support various initiatives was challenged by a major stakeholder. The executive responded by saying, "When I go to the grocery store, I only buy yellow bananas . . . I want to be able to eat the banana now. I don't have the patience to wait for green bananas to turn yellow!"

A FUTURE ORIENTATION IS ESSENTIAL

Breakthrough leadership involves developing a shared and compelling vision for what can be, what should be, and what must be. The ability to develop such a vision is contingent on having the ability to embrace what the future may hold. In their book *Competing for the Future*, Gary Hamel and C. K. Prahalad provided valuable insights about the extent to which top executives actually think about the future. Their research found that, on average, senior management devoted 2.4 percent of its energy to building a collective view of the future.[2]

Hamel and Prahalad's observation raised the question, "If the top executives of some of the economy's top companies aren't focusing on their company's future, then who is?" Their research provides good news as well as bad. The bad news is that most top executives are managing more than leading. Without a strategic perspective, executives are destined to live a perpetual "fire-fighting" existence. The good news is that any company with executives at the helm who commit serious time to preparing for the future will have a significant advantage.

MENTAL MODELS AND PARADIGMS

Peter Drucker observed that before we can prepare for the future, we must be willing to slough off the past.[3] Companies that are successful today may find it difficult to prepare for tomorrow. The paradox of success causes many companies to cling to their current way of doing business. This paradox is reflected in the "If it isn't broke, don't fix it" or "You can't argue with success" mentality that plagues many companies today. The celebration of success can backfire because it makes it more difficult for people to challenge the way things are being done. Success may cause executives to be blind to new realities and deaf to the challenges made by people within the company and to the complaints or suggestions made by customers and other stakeholders outside the company.

The better the company is at something, the more successful it has been, and the greater the market share it enjoys, the greater the likelihood that it will fail to see a major shift in the market. Success tends to put executives in a mental comfort zone and they no longer seek breakthroughs. In times of rapid change, it will not take long for their companies to be dethroned by maverick companies that fail to pay homage to them or their way of doing business.

What causes so many executives to miss the emergence of critical new realities? Every person has mental models that serve as the basis for how he or she sees the world. Mental models either can help a person deal with the changing world or they can be an anchor that keeps him or her from journeying effectively into the future.

Alvin Toffler, as a futurist, coined the term *future shock* to capture the anxiety that occurs when the future invades the present. When people are surprised, they tend to operate from a reactive stance. It is difficult and unusual for a company to thrive under red alert conditions. Companies that are out of touch will not be able to align and synchronize their strategies and operations with new realities. History provides numerous examples of people and companies that were blindsided by new realities. Here are a few of the more noteworthy examples:[4]

> *"Heavier than air flying machines are impossible."*
> —Lord Kelvin, British mathematician, physicist, and president of the British Royal Society, 1895

> *"Who the hell wants to hear actors talk?"*
> —Harry M. Warner, Warner Brothers Pictures, 1927

> *"A severe depression like that of 1920–21 is outside the range of probability."*
> —The Harvard Economic Society, November 16, 1929

> *"We don't like their sound. Groups with guitars are on the way out."*
> —Decca Recording Company executive, turning down the Beatles in 1962

> *"With over fifty foreign cars already on sale here, the Japanese auto industry isn't likely to carve out a big slice of the U.S. market for itself."*
> —*Business Week*, August 2, 1968

> *"I think there is a world market for about five computers."*
> —Thomas Watson, chairman of IBM, 1943

> *"There is no reason for any individual to have a computer in their home."*
> —Ken Olson, President of Digital Equipment Corp., 1977

"They couldn't hit an elephant at this dist——"
—General John B. Sedgwick's last words
in the Battle of Spotsylvania, 1864

Each of these statements reflects the negative impact mental models can have on one's perceptions, decisions, and behavior. In some cases, the people were still able to adjust and survive. General Sedgwick's mental model cost him his life.

Mental models filter information and screen people's perceptions of the world around them. People tend to see things that are consistent with their models. Mental models are like boxes. Their walls keep people from going outside the box—or thinking the unthinkable. Their boundaries keep people from seeing changes the future may hold. Mental models also affect people's ability to see certain things that may be in clear sight, and in some cases, right in front of them.

Sony, IBM, GE, and Microsoft provide recent examples of the role mental models can play in developing corporate strategies. Each of these examples emphasizes the need for companies to bring together people with a variety of backgrounds and to create an environment where people are encouraged to challenge the way things are done.

For years, IBM seemed to be fixated on making mainframe and personal computers. The top brass did not recognize the valuable role that offering business solutions—especially via the Internet—could play in IBM's future. It was only when things deteriorated to a twenty-year low that the board of directors realized the need to bring in a CEO from outside who could bring a fresh perspective. Fortunately for IBM, Louis Gerstner arrived on the scene just in time to ask the tough questions and to encourage the development of new initiatives that were needed to revitalize IBM.

Jack Welch is considered to have been the best corporate executive in the latter part of the twentieth century. Yet Welch did not recognize the importance of the Internet until his wife showed him how it was becoming an integral part of people's lives and corporate life. When she showed him a Web site where people were commenting on GE and Welch's style of management, he realized he was missing out on one of the most important dimensions of modern commerce.

It is said that Bill Gates also failed to recognize the early signs of the role the Internet could play in business strategy and operations. Supposedly, members of his management team had to gang up on Gates to get him to incorporate the Internet into Microsoft's strategy.

Sony provided a good example, however, of the need to approach a situation with a fresh perspective from the very beginning. When Sony decided to enter the music business, top management decided to staff its music venture team with people from outside the music industry. Top management recognized it would be difficult to gain a competitive advantage if it staffed the team with people who had spent their careers in the music business. Sony wanted its music division to be innovative so it put together a team of people from various fields, including its video-game business. Sony believed outsiders would ask probing questions, challenge prevailing wisdom, and offer innovative approaches that would allow the company to separate its music business from the pack.

Beware of Corporate Maginot Lines

People who are infatuated with the past rarely have the ability to prepare for a different future. Executives need to recognize that mental models that may have served them well may be totally inappropriate when conditions change. The Maginot Line provides a good example of how a mental model can make sense at one time and be totally obsolete at a later date. The French built a fortified line of defense following World War I to protect their country from German invasion. The Maginot Line was massive, expensive, and visually impressive, but it was rendered useless in 1940 by the Axis forces in World War II. The French were so focused on a frontal assault along the French border that they did not expect the Germans to invade France through Belgium, nor did they expect Axis planes to drop paratroopers west of the wall in strategic locations.

It is not unusual for people at lower levels of an organization or who operate at an organization's fringes to have mental models that are quite different from the models that are being used by people at the top. General Billy Mitchell provided an excellent example of what can happen when different mental models collide in an organization. Mitchell was known for his innovativeness and willingness to challenge the status quo. Those in command of U.S. military forces did not share his ideas about the role air power would play in future wars. During his court martial in 1925, Mitchell boldly predicted that planes launched from aircraft carriers would one day attack the United States. It is ironic that Frank Knox, secretary of the U.S. Navy, claimed, "No matter what happens, the U.S. Navy is not going to be caught napping," *three days* before the Japanese attack on Pearl Harbor on December 7, 1941.

Executives whose mental models are more in sync than others have the potential to achieve breakthroughs. As the saying goes, "The one-eyed man rules in the kingdom of the blind." This observation raises an interesting question, Which is worse: to have no mental model at all or to use an inappropriate or outdated mental model? It may be better to have no mental model as long as you are committed to analyzing the unique nature of the situation and to developing a mental model that reflects new realities.

The following list profiles a few of the mental Maginot Lines that have been circumvented by companies that saw the new realities of the ever-evolving marketplace:

- While conventional pizza parlors were building new sites and renovating older facilities, Domino's was developing a nationwide franchise network for delivering pizzas.
- While conventional banks were installing ATMs to compensate for Monday-to-Friday banking hours, Intuit was creating software to reduce the need to go to banks altogether.
- While ergonomic keyboards were being designed to reduce carpel tunnel syndrome, a husband-and-wife team at Dragon Software (who had worked at IBM on this technology) were creating a voice-recognition system that would reduce the need for using the keyboard altogether.
- While conventional brokerage houses were trying to figure out how to compete with discount brokers, new companies were being created that would tap the power and speed of the Internet to enable people to nearly bypass brokerage houses and fees altogether.

Each of these changes demonstrates the dramatic effect new mental models can have over models that are not in tune with new realities. It is interesting to note that, in most cases, the new breed of competition came from outside the established boundaries.

TO REDUCE SURPRISES, LENGTHEN AND BROADEN YOUR MENTAL RADAR AND SONAR

Surprise occurs when reality is not what we expected it to be. People and companies are surprised because they have the tendency to be blind, deaf, rigid, and "legacy brained." Executives who want to reduce the likelihood of being surprised need to

- Knock down the walls of their mental boxes so that they can see new realities.
- Extend their mental radar so that they can catch a glimpse of what may be on the horizon.
- Activate their mental sonar so that they can sense what may be lurking just below the surface.
- Open their ears so that they can hear voices that have not been heard.
- Develop perspectives and broaden their education so that they can think new thoughts.
- Stimulate their minds so that they will have the dexterity needed to try new things.
- Exercise their bodies so that they will have the energy needed to leave their comfort zone.
- Let go of their memories of the past and their infatuation with the present so that they can welcome a different tomorrow.

Mental models filter our vision and blind us to what may be going on around us. They block signals of what the future may hold. Companies suffer when their executives either do not see the signals, will not acknowledge the signals, or are unwilling to deal constructively with the signals. While most executives exclaim, "How could we have known?" a closer look reveals that the new realities were visible. Executives are not surprised because the new realities could not be seen; they are surprised because:

- They weren't looking for the signals.
- They wouldn't know how to read the signals if they saw them.
- They failed to incorporate the signals into their decision processes when they did see them.
- They didn't act on them when they had the opportunity to do something about the new realities.

PRESCRIPTION: NO MORE LEGACIES AND A STIFF DOSE OF REALITY!

Two prerequisites must exist before executives can create a forward-focused company. First, they must be willing and able to drop everything that impedes progress. Embarking on a new journey is less difficult when executives are not loaded down with anchors of the past. Second, they must look reality straight in the eyes and not blink. Creating a forward-focused company is about changing reality—and changing reality requires a no-holds-barred environment where people are free to think new thoughts and to challenge everything.

Breakthrough leadership acknowledges that where we have been and where we are now may have little bearing on where we need to go. Leadership rarely involves incrementalism. The automatic linearity associated with continuous improvement rarely provides the ability to blow competitors out of the water.

Breakthrough leadership is far more likely to occur when you operate with a clean slate. You cannot create a forward-focused company by merely adding one more dot each year to a series of older dots. It usually involves starting a whole new vector! Although the company may bring some of its core competencies along on the journey, it shouldn't automatically bring its existing products, processes, and services.

Breakthrough leadership incorporates many of the qualities found in new ventures. Entrepreneurs start a venture because they see a gap in the current marketplace or an emerging opportunity. Entrepreneurs see reality and attempt to change it, or they see a new reality emerging and attempt to capitalize on it. New venture success is usually contingent on the size of the gap and the extent to which the new venture introduces innovative products, services, or processes. Ventures that merely offer continuous improvements may manage to survive. However, ventures that produce discontinuous change—where nothing on the market even comes close—thrive because of their bold innovativeness. The entrepreneur's ability to see what *is* and what *can be* provides the basis for creating a company. When Pierre Omidyar saw the power that the Internet could bring to the auctioning process, he created eBay.com to link millions of buyers and sellers. When David Filo and Jerry Yang saw how difficult it was for people to access information on the Internet, they created Yahoo! Their ability to see gaps in today's reality and the possibilities in tomorrow's opportunities strengthen their resolve to boldly go where no person has gone before.

Executives of established companies can benefit from the irreverence to the status quo and candor demonstrated by most entrepreneurs. Executives need to create an environment where each person is able to challenge every idea, every decision, and every plan. Each business plan—and almost every decision—is based on mental models about what the future holds. Each mental model includes assumptions about what competitors, customers, employees, distributors, suppliers, legislatures, and the public will do. If mental models are partly the product of past experiences and current perceptions, then they are far from being infallible.

Executives need to ensure that plans and decisions are fair game for reality checks. Assumptions and perceptions need to be identified and tested on an ongoing basis. The more rapid and radical the change, the more frequently the reality checks should be conducted. To be effective, mental models must be based on a consistent and realistic set of assumptions. They must also be explicit so they can be monitored. Early warning alarms need to go off when performance indicators show signs that the plan may not be providing the desired results so that the models can be modified or new ones developed that are in tune with the new realities.

It is amazing how long a period of time some companies can be in trouble before their executives wake up and change their mental models. Some companies are able to see the new realities in time to develop new models and change the way they do business. In other companies, new executives need to be brought in to help develop a new model for doing business. Karl Albrecht observed that one of IBM's challenges in the early 1990s was to correct the problem that caused its CEO, John Akers, to be "in [the] saddle of a horse that was going in the wrong direction."[5] Eventually, it became clear that IBM needed a new jockey with a fresh perspective to restore IBM's vitality. Louis Gerstner was brought in to turn the company around.

A company will not be able to see and deal with reality unless it has a culture that encourages people to challenge prevailing mental models. Executives need to ensure that internal and external messengers are not shot! People must be confident that their candor will not place them in jeopardy. Customers, suppliers, and distributors must believe that their feedback and suggestions are welcomed and will not be treated as criticisms. People at all levels of the company must believe that their views are solicited, welcomed, and valued.

FedEx provides an interesting example of how constructive criticism is sought. Laurie Tucker, head of FedEx's virtual order software group, noted, "It's my role to offer challenges to the existing way of doing business. This group is the future of the company."[6] She added, "The challenge that Fred Smith and Dennis Jones and I share has been to get people to think in a bigger way. This new world isn't just about keeping the core business strong. We have to find new businesses and be more in tune with the future. . . . This company has always listened to the customer. Now it's about anticipating the customer. There's no time for incremental improvement."[7]

NEW REALITIES CALL FOR NEW PARADIGMS

Mental models are usually viewed on an individual basis. Although the concept of paradigms appears to be similar to the concept of mental models, paradigms tend to be *shared* frameworks for viewing the world. One's mental models are usually the product of one's experiences and perceptions. Paradigms tend to reflect the way groups of people, companies, industries, and societies view the world and how it works. The collective or shared nature of paradigms means that they are more durable and less pliable than an individual's mental models. The shared nature of paradigms also means that they are less likely to be challenged. History is full of examples of paradigms that lasted generations, centuries, or even longer. There was a time when the masses believed that Earth was the center of the solar system, humans couldn't fly faster than the sound barrier, and the four-minute mile could not be broken.

Executives need to recognize the resilience of most paradigms. When there is an inconsistency between reality and the prevailing paradigm, people may still cling to the paradigm. Some paradigms are so strong that people will deny their reality even if it stares them in the face. While some people may see the light and be willing to adopt a new paradigm that is consistent with new realities, executives need to recognize it will take considerable time, effort, and data for some people to let go.

New paradigms almost always require fundamental changes in the way the company does business. Executives may find that words alone will not persuade people to see the light. Executives need to show people how the new paradigm reflects new realities. Executives also need to note how human nature can cause people to be reluctant to adopt a new business paradigm. It is human nature for anyone who has developed an idea, product, service, or process to be reluctant to let it go in favor of something that reflects a new paradigm. Product managers will be reluctant to phase out a product that they developed. Stockbrokers are not likely to be champions for offering discount brokerage services or electronic trading. Change takes people out of their comfort zones. People who have created their own comfort zones, been in them for some time, and found them to be very rewarding will be reluctant to leave their comfort zones for a new paradigm. Extra effort may be needed to help them see why change is so important and how it will benefit them.

The concept of an epiphany seems to be very timely in today's marketplace. An epiphany is a sudden awakening to the nature of things. When Jeff Bezos, as a successful young Wall Street hedge-fund manager, learned that the Web was growing by 2,200 percent, that knowledge was an epiphany for him. He quit his job and began his search for a business opportunity that would use information technology and the Internet to provide new ways of doing business. Amazon.com was one of the first businesses to catch the e-commerce wave. Although the company experienced a wild roller-coaster ride in the stock market because of concerns about whether it will be able to generate the level of profit necessary to justify its valuation, there is little doubt about Amazon. com's ability to generate customers and its effect on conventional bricks-and-mortar retailing.

Although few executives are card-carrying members of the Flat Earth Society, certain paradigms have lasted well beyond reason. The following generally accepted paradigms have served as the basis for many business practices:

- Managers are the ones who make decisions.
- Price is all that matters.
- Location is everything.
- Ninety-three percent is the optimal level of quality; higher levels are cost-prohibitive.
- Anything over a 15-to-1 price/earnings ratio for a stock is too risky.

These five statements were considered fundamental rules or truths for numerous businesses for so long that few people even challenged their validity.

A considerable part of our quality of life and the strength of our market economy have been the result of people who had the courage to challenge existing paradigms and the innovativeness to develop new ones. They were the ones who boldly challenged the status quo by asking, Why do people have to leave their home or office to do banking, to buy stock, to buy a book, to get an education, or to buy airplane tickets? They were the ones who challenged the need to use a stamp to send mail, the lack of portability of desktop computers, the need for airplanes to have propellers, and the need for most products to be made of wood or metal. Once they realized there must be a better way, they developed products that changed the way people work and live. They were the ones who developed voice recognition software, the mouse, laptops, personal digital assistants, the microwave oven, e-books, and e-mail.

People who challenged prevailing paradigms created their own futures in spite of the choruses of doubters who said: "But that's not the way it's done." "But who would want to do it that way?" "There's no way . . ." "You've got to be kidding." "No one in her right mind would . . ." or "What fool came up with that idea?" It is interesting to note that many of these products were considered frivolous when they were first introduced. Managers, purchasing specialists, and accountants wondered why people would need a Xerox photocopier when carbon paper had done the job just fine.

The next generation of managers, purchasing specialists, and accountants wondered why people wanted Post-it® notes when a piece of paper with a strip of tape could do the job. Microwave ovens were also subjected to considerable skepticism. Skeptics wondered why anyone would spend hundreds of dollars to cook a hot dog, bake a potato, or pop popcorn in a few seconds. Skeptics challenged why anyone really needed to "zap" a cup of coffee. Skeptics also played the health issue card to challenge whether the food was really cooked. They also raised concerns about microwave rays leaking from the ovens. Skeptics also challenged how any serious computer company could expect adults to use a childish mouse. It is ironic that products that were once ridiculed, such as cell phones, are now considered by many to be necessities. Frequent users are often heard asking their elders, "How could you live without them?" It is amazing how attitudes and behavior for millions of people can change in such a short period of time.

PARADIGM CREATORS OR PARADIGM SURFERS?

Joel Barker sheds considerable light on the nature and shifts of paradigms in his book and video, *The Business of Paradigms*. He differentiates between paradigm shifters and paradigm pioneers. He notes that paradigm shifters create the new rules.[8] The rules in turn make it possible to do new things or provide new ways of doing things. When a paradigm shifts, all the companies that were in that field go back to zero. A shift can make everything that existed before obsolete. Companies that had significant competitive advantages may lose everything.

The shift associated with digitalization and e-commerce had a dramatic effect on Encyclopedia Britannica. Supposedly Bill Gates approached Encyclopedia Britannica about doing a deal that would digitize its contents and make it available using Microsoft's distribution clout. When Encyclopedia Britannica scoffed at the idea, Gates turned around and offered Encarta to consumers for fifty dollars or for free as part of a bundled software package.[9] Although Encarta may not have been as comprehensive as the thirty-two-volume Encyclopedia Britannica, it took up far less space and could be updated for a lot less money and time. Encyclopedia Britannica's failure to sense the paradigm shift and to modify its operations had a devastating effect on what had been the industry's premiere product for decades.

Paradigm shifts tend to do two things. They catch many people who have enjoyed the existing paradigm off guard. They also open the door to a whole new set of possibilities. Under Ted Turner's direction, CNN showed that people wanted news when it occurred rather than the one half-hour per weekday evening news offered by the three networks. Fox showed the networks there was room for a fourth network that offered original programming. Polaroid showed there could be a way for people to see their pictures develop before their eyes rather than waiting for days. The introduction of wireless electronic devices showed conventional companies that people would jump at the chance not to be tethered to their office or home. Michael Dell, with his "Dell Direct" paradigm, proved companies did not have to make their own components to be market leaders.

Joel Barker believes companies do not need to be paradigm shifters. He noted that companies can be successful if they are paradigm pioneers. While paradigm pioneers may not cause the shift, they are quick to capitalize on it. Paradigm shifters usually come from outside an industry or operate at its fringe. The difference between shifters and pioneers is similar to the difference between inventors and entrepreneurs. While inventors may develop a revolutionary product, they rarely have the managerial ability or resources to bring it to market on a large scale. Paradigm pioneers are similar to entrepreneurs. Entrepreneurs frequently take an idea that was developed somewhere else (via acquisition, licensing, or joint venture) and make it available to consumers who are not having their needs met sufficiently or at all.

Lasting corporate success is contingent on two things: ideas and execution. It may turn out that somewhere between a 50/50 and a 30/70 split may be the best formula for the optimal balance of shifting and pioneering. No company can be out in front all the time. Conversely, few companies will survive if they are followers. A company that is too far out in front of the marketplace may have its revolutionary product die on the vine before the market values the product's qualities. A company that is slow to adopt the processes associated with a new business model will suffocate in the dust of companies that have embraced the new paradigm.

The history of combat is full of examples of how people broke or changed the rules. During America's Revolutionary War, it became clear to the patriots that they could not win if they tried to match the open battlefield strategy employed by the British, in which row after row of soldiers faced front. The lack of comparable weapons and soldiers forced the patriots to explore less conventional tactics. Before long, they adopted the hit-and-run guerrilla tactics used by some Indian tribes. While the British officers claimed the tactics were not gentlemanly, the patriots were busy winning their independence.

American generals scratched their heads in Vietnam when they couldn't figure out how the North Vietnamese Army was able to continue supplying its troops even though all the roads were made impassable by U.S. bombers. Years after the war was over, a U.S. general had the opportunity to ask a North Vietnamese general how they supplied their troops without using the roads. The North Vietnamese general said that they turned the riverbeds into roads. They built roads, much like bridges, just below the water's surface. The North Vietnamese merely saw the rivers to be the "aquatic roads" that they had always been for centuries in most countries. While U.S. high-altitude surveillance planes were looking for conventional roads, the North Vietnamese were using underwater roads that incorporated underwater bridges!

It would be interesting to take a trip back in time to see the reaction of others when someone suggested, "We should build a large wooden horse on wheels, fill it with soldiers, and leave it outside the gate!" to the military leader who was trying to invade the ancient city of Troy.

A keen sense of timing may make the difference between people accepting a revolutionary idea and them considering its developer to be a complete fool. Fred Smith had his timing right when he created Federal Express. He launched his overnight delivery service at a time when the world was speeding up and people were willing to pay a premium to have it delivered the next day. He saw a gap in the market and had the courage to go ahead even though most people said it couldn't be done or few people actually needed overnight service.

Jack Welch may not have been at the leading edge of the shift to the e-commerce/Internet paradigm. He was, however, quick to commit GE to the new paradigm once it became clear that the company could not continue doing business as usual. Early in 1999, he challenged GE's largest business units to reinvent their business before some upstart destroyed them. Within the year, GE's cost for online transactions was down to $5, compared with its conventional cost of $50. Its auction transactions went from $200 million in 1999 to $5 billion in 2000.[10]

PREPARING YOURSELF AND YOUR COMPANY FOR A DIFFERENT FUTURE

Most executives feel more comfortable dealing with profit-and-loss components than with discussing mental models and business paradigms. Yet, companies will be able to generate profits and build wealth only to the extent to which executives use mental models and business paradigms that are in tune with market realities. The following observations and recommendations may help executives to ensure that their mental models are in sync with the ever-evolving marketplace, sense change earlier, and ensure their companies are in sync with new realities:

Observations

- People who say it can't be done will be trampled by those who make the impossible possible.
- Those who hesitate lose to those who seize the moment.
- If you cannot anticipate or create trends, then participate in trends.
- Market niche or segment waves of opportunity are forming quicker, cresting earlier, and closing out quicker!
- Change usually hits us when and where we least expect it.
- Bad things can and will happen . . . and they will happen twice as soon as you expect.
- Your observations, insights, and ideas will probably not be

embraced by others . . . especially those who have the most to lose by change.

- If it is your idea, then it will take twice as long for others to implement it than if it was their idea.
- Just because an idea is not the same as what is being done doesn't mean that it is a bad idea.
- Remember what Alvin Toffler said, "The future invades the present at different speeds."[11]
- *Maybe* will probably become *certainly*.
- There will come a time when the impossible will be possible.

Recommendations

- Recognize that your mental models are the product of a lifetime of experiences and education. You will gain new insights and develop new mental models only when you perceive the world in a different manner. To gain new insights you will need to have new experiences.
- Get out of your comfort zone.
- Have out-of-mind, out-of-body, out-of-specialty, out-of-company, out-of-industry, out-of-the-present experiences often!
- Escape the conventional-thinking mental box.
- Get on your tiptoes so that you extend your mental horizon.
- Spend at least two hours a week contemplating two to five years from now.
- Periodically do a 360-degree rotation so that you see the whole world around you and reduce the likelihood that someone else is sneaking up on you or that you'll be blindsided.
- Have at least one meeting per month with people who have different vantage points to discuss the future of business.
- Read what the people at the fringe are writing and don't be so quick to discount radical ideas or trends.
- Interact with people from different walks of life . . . the more different the better.
- Take newcomers in your company to lunch . . . and listen to what they have to say.

- Get to the fringe; interact with people who are different from you . . . the weirder the better.
- Go to conferences about remotely related technology.
- Identify at least three things from three very different industries that may have applications to your business.
- Challenge every assumption.
- Realize that *someday* could be *tomorrow.*
- Never say never.
- Expect the obvious, but prepare for the unexpected.
- Hope for the best but prepare for the worst.
- Constantly run "What if?" scenarios.
- Think the unthinkable.
- Run worst-case scenarios.
- Go from whether or not . . . to when?
- It is rarely an issue of whether or not something will occur. It will occur so get ready! Deal with it. Make change your ally rather than your adversary.
- Determine which strategy could help your company become the first mover or a fast follower.
- Identify what could be the forward pass in your industry that makes the conventional running game look about as graceful as elephants trying to mate.
- Ask, ask, ask, and then listen, listen, listen to your customers, competitors, employees, and suppliers.
- Learn, learn, and learn. Step back and learn from every situation. A line from the film *The Natural* noted, "I believe we have two lives . . . the life we learn with and the life we live with after that." Live the second life.

CONCLUSION: DON'T EXPECT CHALLENGING THE STATUS QUO TO BE AN EASY JOURNEY

You need to recognize three important points when you commit to creating a forward-focused organization. First, there will always be surprises, but you can reduce the likelihood of being blindsided by extending your mental radar and checking the reality of your mental models. Second, there will be problems and setbacks; know the difference between problems that come with trying to make progress and the problems that come with clinging to the past or present. Third, you will have to challenge prevailing wisdom and break the rules to position your company for a better tomorrow.

> *"The people who get on in this world are the people who get up and look for what they want, and if they can't find them, make them."*
>
> —George Bernard Shaw, poet

NOTES

1. Craig R. Hickman and Michael A. Silva, *Creating Excellence* (New York: New American Library, 1984), p. 35.
2. Gary Hamel and C. K. Prahalad, *Competing for the Future* (Boston: Harvard Business School Press, 1994), p. 4.
3. Peter F. Drucker, *Managing in Turbulent Times* (New York: Harper & Row, 1980), p. 43.
4. Christopher Cerf and Victor Navasky, *The Experts Speak* (New York: Pantheon Books, 1984).
5. Karl Albrecht, *The Northbound Train* (New York: AMACOM, 1994), p. 2.
6. Scott Krisner, "Laurie F. Tucker," *Fast Company,* December 1999, p. 168.
7. Ibid., p. 172.
8. Joel A. Barker, *The Business of Paradigms* (video produced by Charthouse Learning Corp., 1989).
9. Jerry Useem, "Withering Britannica Bets It All on the Web," *Fortune,* November 22, 1999, p. 344.
10. Elizabeth Corcoran, "The E Gang," *Forbes,* July 24, 2000, p. 146.
11. Alvin Toffler, *Future Shock* (New York: Bantam, 1970), p. 21.

6

Embracing the Concept of "Futuring"

"Only the day dawns to which we are awake."
—Henry David Thoreau, American
naturalist and author

E xecutives who realize the need to extend their time horizons frequently jump on the long-range planning bandwagon. Most long-range planning efforts are exercises in futility because executives fail to recognize the context within which long-range planning must exist to be successful. Too many executives approach long-range planning the same way they mistakenly approached the process of managing by objectives years ago. They saw it as something that could be plugged into the organization immediately without regard for whether prerequisite or concurrent conditions were in place.

Karl Albrecht, author of *The Northbound Train*, cautions against the tendency for companies to get too wrapped up in the planning process. He notes that many organizations are so engrossed in planning that it impairs their ability to respond to changes, threats, and opportunities. Albrecht stated that, in some instances, developing a plan is "such an exhausting process that thereafter nobody wants to change it, even if some major environmental event occurs."[1]

Whether it is referred to as long-range or strategic planning, one thing is clear; most people approach it in a too mechanistic and deterministic manner. If the marketplace were stable and the future fairly predictable, the development of detailed long-range plans would be relatively simple. The marketplace, however, is anything but stable. The accelerating rate of change, technological breakthroughs, new competitors, and the emergence of new markets have produced discontinuities. Conventional planning techniques that were developed in a linear and incremental world do not have the flexibility needed to address multifaceted and rapidly paced change. Conventional planning techniques also fail to incorporate entrepreneurial forces that change what it takes for businesses to succeed.

Entrepreneurial and visionary companies change the competitive landscape by injecting new ways of doing things and new things to gain a competitive advantage. Entrepreneurial and visionary companies are different from reactive companies in how they view the marketplace. The difference may be seen in the following example. Two sculptors approach two blocks of marble. Each sculptor surveys the block and studies the grain. The first sculptor steps back and contemplates what she will do with the block. The second sculptor starts slowly chipping away at the block. The first sculptor asks the second sculptor what he is doing. He responds, "The ultimate object is already determined within the block. I need to find it in the grain and let it out." The second sculptor then asks the first sculptor about her approach. She responds, "While the grain may be set and the size of the block may be given, the ultimate object is what I choose to make it!"

Most planning efforts are doomed before they even begin because they are too rigid or too incremental. Although plans still need to be developed, targets identified, and deadlines set, the overall planning process needs to become more organic and flexible. The overall planning process needs to reflect the first sculptor's attitude and approach. When planning incorporates future possibilities and the impact of innovation, it resembles "futuring" more than planning.

FUTURING IS NOT FORECASTING NOR IS IT INCREMENTAL

Futuring is different from long-range planning in at least three distinct areas. First, it recognizes that the future will not be an extension of the past. Futuring expects events that cause discontinuities to occur. Second, there may be numerous possible futures. The future will be a function of various factors as well as various possible relationships among those factors. Third, innovation will play an even greater role in the future. Innovation has the potential to accelerate the rate of change and to cause fundamental shifts in the nature of business and life.

Traditional forecasting techniques have drawbacks because they tend to be extrapolations from the past. Unexpected events, however, cause discontinuation from the past. A forecast is like a mental model that does not change with changing times. Executives are frequently blindsided because forecasts miss early indicators of discontinuities. These discontinuities can be the result of environmental factors, such as the unusual weather patterns caused by El Niño, major economic shifts caused by war in the Middle East, or the emergence of new markets or industries created by a technological breakthrough.

Few companies in the 1970s foresaw OPEC's oil embargo and how it would affect their operations. Nearly twenty years later, few companies foresaw the exponential use of the Internet. Most retailers believed it would be business as usual where established companies competed against each other for market share. Few companies foresaw how quickly wireless communication would be developed or the breadth of impact it would have in various industries.

Discontinuities destroy linearity and predictability, causing turbulence for those who expected stability. Yet discontinuities are what creating a forward-focused company is all about. Creation is defined as the act of bringing something new into the world. It involves starting a new vector rather than adding another dot to a linear series of dots.

Creation involves exploring, experimenting, and testing the limits. It means doing what others say cannot be done that way, for that little cost, that well, that soon, or at all. Creating a forward-focused organization involves creating discontinuities that give the company temporary legal monopolies.

FUTURING OPENS THE COMPANY TO UNLIMITED OPPORTUNITIES

Executives should direct their attention to exploring future possibilities and identifying the position the company should occupy in the years ahead. Instead of trying to develop detailed formal plans, executives need to adopt the proactive philosophy of anticipating—if not creating—change. "Proactivity" is based on two premises. First, your job is to influence the world around you as much as possible. Second, if you are to be subject to change, then be the initiator of the change.

Reactive executives view the world from a problematic perspective. Proactive executives view the world in an entirely different light. Jack MacAllister, as CEO of U.S. West stated, "I'm not comfortable with the status quo, because the status quo leaves you a step or two behind the time line. You should take the past in its own context, project what the world might be, and then proactively position yourself so you can preempt the future, instead of just reacting to it."[2] Proactive executives view the world from an opportunistic perspective.

Executives can spend their time in three different ways. First, they can spend their time solving problems and putting out fires, which is a fairly reactive type of existence. Second, they can try to anticipate potential problems and invest their time in preventing them or positioning their companies to minimize the consequences. This is more proactive and productive than the fire-fighting existence associated with solving problems. It is amazing how many problems can be prevented with a little foresight and resourcefulness. Third, executives need to elevate themselves above problem solving, and even problem prevention, so that they can direct their attention and the company's resources to creating, cultivating, and capitalizing on emerging opportunities.

When executives operate from a reactive stance, they have less time to think things through or to explore the possibilities.

When timing is critical, most executives tend to approach situations as they did in the past or by trial and error. This approach can be costly for two reasons. First, what worked well yesterday may be totally inappropriate tomorrow. It takes time to develop innovative approaches. Second, even though the trial-and-error process associated with winging it can produce an occasional success, it places considerable stress on the company's human resources.

There is an interesting irony associated with managing in today's marketplace. The question has been raised, "Does there have to be a crisis for a leader to emerge?" Executives who are particularly good at preventing problems, via foresight and resourcefulness, don't get a lot of fanfare. By preventing fires instead of fighting them, they don't make the news, nor do they need to be involved in high-profile actions or speeches. Their foresight and resourcefulness puts their company on a path that allows it to evolve without radical reorganizations, crash programs, or a desperate search for a charismatic leader.

Futuring is built on the concept of anticipatory management. In times of rapid change, it is easy for companies, especially growing ones, to drive beyond their headlights. The ever-accelerating rate of change puts companies in a situation where they may not be able to see what is in front of them until it is too late to do anything constructive about it. Anticipatory management encourages executives to do two things: First, executives need to consider various possibilities for what may be ahead of them. By asking "What if . . . ?" questions, executives may be able to identify potential threats in time to either prevent them or minimize their consequences. Second, executives are encouraged to extend their mental headlights. By extending their time horizons, executives not only see things earlier; they have the lead time needed to deal with them in a constructive and evolutionary manner. Anticipatory management reduces the need for the company to swerve or to hit the brakes.

With foresight, executives can put their companies in a position not only to prevent or minimize problems but also to turn potential threats into lucrative opportunities. Peter Drucker noted that within every problem there is at least one disguised business opportunity. Visionary executives not only prevent problems; they *identify* opportunities. Companies that are entrepreneurial may even *create* opportunities. Visionary executives separate their companies from the pack by anticipating key events and by positioning their companies to seize the moment when possibilities become a reality.

FUTURING HELPS EXECUTIVES DEVELOP TIMELY ANSWERS

Anticipatory management recognizes executives can operate from three different levels. Most executives spend their time coming up with answers to questions. Better executives spend their time identifying the questions that need to be answered. These executives provide the lead time needed for their staffs to come up with the answers. The best executives, however, go one significant step further. They come up with the answers *before* anyone outside the company—customers or competitors—even knows the questions.

When most executives are asked, "What business are you in?" they usually respond by identifying the products or services their companies offer the marketplace. Futuring encourages executives to view their world with a longer time horizon and from a broader perspective. Executives should view their companies as customer problem solvers rather than as producers of certain products or as providers of certain services. Customers don't really want to buy a product or service. Products and services are merely a means to an end. Customers want to have their problems solved. Customers will be delighted only to the extent to which the products and services meet their specific needs.

It is easy for executives to get caught up in their company's existing markets, products, and services. It is also easy for executives whose companies are in highly competitive markets to get caught up in ensuring that their companies retain their current customers and maintain their market share. Gary Hamel and C. K. Prahalad, authors of *Competing for the Future*, noted, "However well a company meets the articulated needs of current customers, it runs a great risk if it doesn't have a view of the needs customers can't yet articulate, but would love to have satisfied. . . . Any company that can do no more than respond to articulated needs of existing customers will quickly become a laggard."[3]

Executives need to recognize that the company may need to

change its target markets as well as its products, services, locations, and infrastructure. Hamel and Prahalad developed the Beyond Customer-Led Matrix[4] profiled in Figure 6-1 to encourage executives to explore gaps in the current market. The matrix encourages executives to identify and investigate unexploited opportunities. The unexploited opportunities noted in the three shaded quadrants include the unarticulated needs of customers already being served, the articulated needs of customers not being served, and the unarticulated needs of customers not being served. Each quadrant may provide numerous growth opportunities.

Figure 6-1. Beyond customer-led matrix.

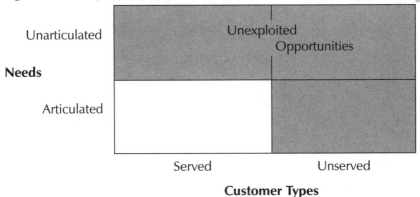

Executives need to invest more time in market exploration. Market exploration, however, is not the same as market research. Most market research techniques are too narrow and too superficial to identify true opportunities. Hamel and Prahalad observed, "Too often the questions asked of customers by market researchers—'Do you prefer a widget with a green strip to one with a red strip?'—provide little scope for fundamentally challenging traditional product concepts or creating real competitive differentiation. Although market research can be helpful in fine-tuning well-known product concepts to meet the demands of a particular class of customers, it is seldom the spur for fundamentally new product concepts."[5]

Akio Morita, cofounder of Sony, also had reservations about the value of conventional market-research techniques. He believed that if you ask people how they would like a product to be improved, they tend to limit their suggestions to minor modifications.

Morita believed most consumers are not able to identify major innovations or breakthroughs because they do not have the mental dexterity to think about them. Morita encouraged the people at Sony to anticipate what consumers would truly value even if the consumers did not know it yet.

The difference between whether a company will experience moderate growth or significant growth may be contingent on the extent to which it explores uncharted areas. Hamel and Prahalad noted that there are three kinds of companies: "Companies that try to lead customers where they don't want to go; companies that listen to their customers and then respond to their articulated needs; and companies that lead customers where they want to go but don't know it yet. Companies that create the future fall into the third category. They do more than satisfy customers, they constantly amaze them."[6]

Futuring enhances an executive's perceptiveness and sense of timing. It encourages executives to look beyond the present. Futuring reflects the Wayne Gretzky approach to managing profiled in Chapter 4 by anticipating where the market will be rather than focusing exclusively on market conditions in the present. Executives should try to identify what their current customers will need in the future. They also need to identify who their customers should be in the future. The Future-Positioning Matrix profiled in Figure 6-2 indicates three types of opportunities that should also be explored by the company.

In addition to knowing their present customers' immediate

Figure 6-2. Future-positioning matrix.

Future Product/Service Needs	Future Product/Service Development Opportunities	Wide-Open Future Opportunities
Products and Services		
Present Product/Service Needs	Present Product/Service Offering	Gaps in Present Product/Service Offering
	Present	Future

Customers

needs, executives should identify what these customers will need in the future. Executives should also identify who their future customers should be. By identifying their present needs, executives may be able to identify their future customers' future needs. This lead time may help the company to develop products and services for markets that are not being served. Executives who want to create their company's future should identify the wide-open opportunities that may emerge in the future.

Sony's development of the Walkman™ provides a good example of having the product before the customer even recognized the need. The development and phenomenal growth of the Walkman can be attributed to Sony's perceptiveness and innovativeness. Akio Morita sensed the opportunity for a small, high-quality portable tape player when he saw a teenager carrying a boom box at the beach. The massiveness and blaring sound prompted Morita to encourage Sony's research and development team to create a small tape player with a jack for earplug speakers.

When the Sony team realized that jogging was not merely a fad, it explored ways for Sony to get a piece of the action. The team thought that if people were going to spend a lot of time jogging, then sooner or later they would want to find a way for it to be more pleasurable. It also noted that a large number of the people who jogged also liked listening to music on high-quality sound systems. The team then set out to capitalize on Sony's core competence of miniaturization to create a high-quality, compact, and affordable tape player for joggers. The Walkman has been an outstanding success because it made the time spent jogging more pleasurable by making the minutes or hours seem to pass more quickly.

The ability to sense what the market wants before the market overtly indicates the need is what drove Fred Smith to create Federal Express. As noted in Chapter 5, Smith recognized that companies and individuals would soon cherish the opportunity to have items delivered overnight. The ability to sense what the market wants before the market overtly indicates the need also drove Steven Jobs and Steven Wozniak to create Apple Computer. They knew the time would come when the masses would want personal computers that were easy to use. While most people considered such efforts to be a folly and very risky, Smith, Jobs, and Wozniak did not consider their ventures to be risky. They believed the market for their services and products was inevitable. Smith, Jobs, and Wozniak changed the way people work and live.

DEVELOPING A TEMPORARY LEGAL MONOPOLY

The Future-Positioning Matrix reinforces the Gretzky concept of anticipatory management. If executives can identify what customers will need or want *before* the customers even know it, the company may gain the lead time needed to develop the products, services, or processes by the time customers start their search. This is having the answer before anyone else knows the question in its purest form. Executives who are able to identify an emerging opportunity and develop products or services to meet the market gap when it occurs may be able to position their companies so they have the distinction of being first to market or first movers.

Someone once asked, "What is the ideal business situation?" Two responses to the question are particularly noteworthy. The first response was, "A post-office box where people send cash!" While this idea may be appealing, few companies are likely to succeed unless they also offer the market valuable products or services in exchange for the cash. The second response, "A legal monopoly," reflects the essence of the Future-Positioning Matrix.

Companies that are able to develop competencies to serve emerging market gaps will thrive in the years ahead. This is particularly true for companies that position themselves to be first to market. If they offer what the market wants and their timing is right, then they will be in the enviable position of having 100 percent market share. First-to-market companies have the market to themselves. This is quite different from most companies that spend considerable resources just trying to maintain their market share in saturated markets.

The dynamics of today's ever-changing marketplace make it nearly impossible for any company to maintain a monopolistic position. Customers' needs, interests, and desires may change from one day to the next. Technological breakthroughs can provide a company with the ability to leapfrog even an established market leader. Executives who want to create a forward-focused company must seek opportunities where they may be able to create temporary legal monopolies.

CREATING A FORWARD-FOCUSED COMPANY BY RIDING THE WAVES OF CHANGE

Futuring has some striking similarities to surfing. Surfers know that the quality of their ride will be contingent on their ability to be in the right place at the right time with the right skills. They also know that the quality of their ride is contingent on the size, speed, shape, and duration of the wave. A company's success is contingent on its ability to offer the market the right product or service, at the right price, in the right place, and at the right time. Its success will also be linked to the size, shape, and duration of the market opportunity. Success will also be affected by the nature and extent of competition. Just as surfers dream of the day they will have great waves to themselves, executives should position their companies to have a number of temporary legal monopolies.

The accelerating rate of change in the global marketplace can be seen as a never-ending set of ever-changing waves. While executives wish they could call a time-out to catch their breath, they need to recognize that the days of occasional change followed by a few years of consolidation are gone. Companies have entered an era when change-change-change is becoming the prevailing cycle. Changing consumer expectations and technological breakthroughs have caused the cycle of one new model every three years to be replaced by the cycle of a one-day shelf life. The dramatic rate and nature of change is evident in numerous markets. It is particularly evident in software and buyer-seller relationships. Not that long ago, people would go to a retail store to buy their software in a shrink-wrapped box. Now, they can either have it downloaded almost instantly over the Internet or subscribe to an applications service provider. The introduction of new versions and upgrades of software is happening with such speed and frequency that we often get daily upgrades.

Executives who are committed to creating a forward-focused company must position their companies to catch the right waves and avoid the ones that could jeopardize their very existence. Although it may not be possible to foresee every wave, companies that do not sense the changes early will drown. Futuring helps executives develop strategies that enable their companies to capitalize on the waves of change and to create a corporate culture that welcomes change. Companies that truly embrace futuring will enjoy a great ride. Companies that fail to embrace futuring will be tossed about like the book and music retailers that failed to see how the ability to access and download music, magazines, and books would change the marketplace.

HELP WANTED: ONLY EXECUTIVES WITH VISION NEED APPLY

Futuring is not limited to sensing what the future may hold. Sensing what the future may hold is a prerequisite to being able to position the company to capitalize on the changes that could affect it. Companies need to be driven by a corporate vision about what the company should become in the future. Companies that lack a vision are destined to either drift, and thereby drain their limited resources, or be seduced by short-term opportunities or flavor-of-the-week management fads that offer little lasting value.

For a company to be truly successful, it must develop executives at all levels who have the following characteristics:

- The vision to see tomorrow today
- The perceptual dexterity to identify emerging opportunities
- The ability to develop innovative strategies for positioning their companies to occupy propitious niches
- The leadership skills to transform myopic perspectives and sedentary complacency into entrepreneurial dynamism

Visionary leadership can transform the company's strategy and culture from where it has been to where it will need to be to capitalize on the changes that lie ahead.

The importance of having a vision for what the company should become was illustrated in the movie, *The Carpetbaggers*. The film profiled the life of a Howard Hughes type entrepreneur and adventurer. In one scene, the entrepreneur and his partner secure a government contract to deliver the mail between two cities.

When the partner who is a pilot asks the entrepreneur what they should name their new business, the entrepreneur responds, "International Airways." The partner exclaims, "International . . . we are only going from L.A. to Frisco!" The visionary entrepreneur then states, "This year." He was naming it for what it will be, not what it is.

Jack Welch provided a vision for what he wanted GE to be in the future soon after he took the helm. He stated, "A decade from now I would like General Electric to be perceived as a unique high-spirited, entrepreneurial enterprise . . . a company known around the world for its unmatched level of excellence. I want General Electric to be the most profitable highly diversified company on Earth with quality leadership in every one of its product lines."

Most executives at the helm of today's companies spent their careers ascending the corporate hierarchy in one industry. Their background may actually jeopardize their company's future. Executives with a single industry heritage tend to develop a myopic and narrow perspective. Their tasks, training, and travel have been industry specific. In a sense, they are operating within a mental box, with high walls that keep them from seeing the dramatic changes taking place around them.

The ascent of most executives up the corporate hierarchy was spent in two areas. First, they were implementing plans they did not develop. Second, they were responding to unexpected threats rather than capitalizing on emerging opportunities. When these managers finally make it to the executive suite, they are unprepared for the complexities and intangibles associated with leading the company in an ever-evolving global marketplace. The skills and perspectives that produced prior success are usually not the ones needed to create their company's future.

LEADING REQUIRES BIFOCAL MANAGEMENT

Someone once noted, "The company that does not prepare for the future will have no future!" It would be easy for executives to say, "Wait a minute, if we don't take care of business today, we won't be in business tomorrow!" Operational matters must be addressed, and they need to be done well. Companies that fail to control costs, provide on-time deliveries, and monitor accounts receivable quickly lose efficiency, customers, and money.

Lasting success will be achieved only by companies that have executives who practice bifocal management. That is, their executives are able to focus their attention on strategic issues *and* operational matters. There is a sports metaphor that aptly illustrates bifocal management. Golfers frequently stand at the tee of a par-three hole dreaming what it would be like to get a hole-in-one. The best golfers take the wind, exact distance, and the slope of the green into consideration when they select a club. As they position their feet, they envision the flight of the ball and where it needs to land to roll into the cup. The best golfers do one other thing with the same precision . . . they keep their heads down so they don't "whiff!"

The best golfers demonstrate bifocal vision when they mentally aim for the pin while keeping their heads down and their eyes focused on the ball. They know the importance of distance and direction. They also know the importance of execution. Some golfers hit the long ball, but their games suffer either because they can't play the short game, they are penalized for going out of bounds, or they add unnecessary yards to the hole by spraying the ball in a zigzag fashion all over the course. Other golfers are very deliberate in their approach to the game. They practice constantly so that they will make few mistakes. Unfortunately, their preoccupation with not making mistakes keeps them from wanting to play truly challenging golf courses. To them, the prospect of losing a ball in the water beside an island green or getting a double bogey keeps them from accepting the challenge of a championship course.

The debate over whether to focus more on the short term versus the long term is similar to the debate over the importance of having good ideas versus the effective implementation of ideas. The futuring part of bifocal management encourages the company to focus on innovation, while the part of bifocal management that prevents things from falling through the cracks enables the company to focus on the continuous improvement of execution.

While the company's position, market, industry, and culture may affect its time horizon, each executive has a tendency to view the world with his or her own particular time horizon. Some executives are preoccupied with the tangible nature of the present. Others seem to feel comfortable with the intangible and uncertain nature of the future.

In their book *Built to Last*, James Collins and Jerry Porras wrote, "A visionary company doesn't seek balance between short-term and long-term. It seeks to do well in the short-term and the long-term."[7] Their study of visionary companies indicated that these companies seek to do very well in both time frames. Jack Welch stated, "You can't grow long-term if you can't eat short-term. Anybody can manage short. Anyone can manage long. Balancing those two things is what management is."[8]

The higher the position in the organization, the more the job involves conceptual rather than technical matters, a long-term rather than a short-term time horizon, and issues about the type of business the company should *be* rather than how the company should *do* business. Executives need to extend their vision beyond today. For that matter, they need to extend their mental horizon beyond tomorrow. They need to be concerned with tomorrow's tomorrow.

FUTURING FOCUSES ON TOP-LINE MANAGEMENT

Most companies judge their managers according to what they have done to enhance the company's profit recently rather than what they are doing today to enhance the company's performance five years from now. Executives have developed considerable prowess when it comes to enhancing the bottom line. When their company's growth slows, they enhance profitability by cutting expenses. Training and development, research and development, preventative maintenance, capital investment, as well as the development and adoption of new technology are cut to the bone when their company's profit wanes.

When executives run out of expenses to cut in their desperate quest to show a profit, they dust off their finance textbooks to enhance their company's return-on-investment (ROI) formula by reducing the company's assets. Their logic is that if they can't improve the net profit part of the ROI equation, then they can improve ROI by reducing the amount of their assets. The shift from improving the company's income statement by radical surgery is followed by balance sheet gymnastics that reduce the company's assets. While their efforts to reduce expenses and then assets may temporarily spike their company's profit and ROI figures, executives need to recognize they are taking large—and possibly irreversible—steps in liquidating their companies.

BOTTOM-LINE MANAGEMENT WON'T CUT IT

Some executives have fine-tuned their ability to make their companies look good in the short term so proficiently that they have become celebrities. Unfortunately, most executives' preoccupation with enhancing the present has not been matched with a corresponding level of commitment to the future. Futuring begins with a commitment to growing the company's long-term top line. Top-line management focuses on creating new streams of revenue, identifying and capitalizing on emerging opportunities, and building organizations that will stand the test of time.

Top-line management has two major advantages over bottom-line management. First, you can only go so far in cost cutting and financial restructuring before you get diminishing returns. There are no limits, however, to the number of emerging opportunities in the ever-evolving marketplace. Second, people are far more willing to make a lasting commitment to a company that is growing than to one that is cutting every corner and compromising fundamental business issues and values. People are far more committed to an enterprise that is exploring emerging markets and developing innovative products, services, processes, and systems than they are to a company that is selling its assets and pruning its payroll. Being involved in building a company that has a promising future is far more motivating than biding one's time while waiting for the inevitable pink slip.

Top-line management is more of an art than a science. It involves perceptions rather than spreadsheet gymnastics. It involves judgment rather than software. Most executives prefer to deal with the more tangible and deterministic here and now. Yet, it will be the executives who recognize the need to focus on the messy and uncertain future who will be valued in the years to come. There is an abundant supply of the cutters and the slashers in today's companies. In the years ahead, companies will need visionaries rather than bean counters. They will need people who know how to build rather than how to downsize and how to capture the human spirit rather than play shell games with financial statements. In the years ahead, companies will need executives who can unleash the innovative talents of people throughout the enterprise rather than the type of managers profiled in Dilbert cartoon panels. Timid and cautious managers must be replaced with executives who have the vision to see new possibilities and the courage to do the right things.

This may be a good time to clarify a major point about top-line management. The goal of top-line management is not to increase revenue but to make the company even stronger in the years ahead. Collins and Porras stress the need for executives to have core values that foster a commitment to being an outstanding enterprise. They emphasize the need for management to focus more on building core competencies to foster long-term competitive advantages rather than being engrossed in individual products. To build an outstanding company, top management must make a commitment beyond one product or even one product life cycle.[9]

Collins and Porras believe leaders should direct their attention to being clock builders rather than time tellers. They see executives who focus their attention on a fixed point in time as time tellers. They believe executives should be clock builders who direct their attention to building the type of organization that does well consistently in various environments. According to Collins and Porras, an organization that knows what it values and what it wants to be is in a far better position than one that relies exclusively on its chief executive to stand at the summit and pronounce his or her vision. They believe the company's core values and core competencies are more important for the future of the business than the person who is at the helm at any point in time. They believe the chief executive's role is to ensure that the core values are appropriate, that every facet and action in the company reflects those values, and that the values contribute to the company's core competencies that give the company the ability to maintain its competitive edge.[10]

Even Al Dunlap, who used what the media referred to as a chainsaw turnaround strategy in his efforts to revitalize Sunbeam and Scott Paper, acknowledged the need for top-line management. *Fortune* magazine noted that Dunlap developed a reputation for being a CEO who "storms into ailing companies, hacks at costs, fires thousands, and walks away really rich."[11] Dunlap noted, however, that rebuilding a company is a two-phase process. The first phase usually involves restructuring operations to stop the bleeding and to get the company pointed in the right direction. The second phase focuses on growth. Dunlap noted, "Mickey Mouse could do the cost-cutting. It's much harder to know where to add and where to build."[12]

There is no question that every company has room for some belt-tightening. Changes in the marketplace will continue to force the streamlining of certain operations and the elimination of others. These efforts are essential for the company to stay competitive. These efforts, however, will not be enough to move a company to the head of the pack.

The strategy and culture needed to cut costs are quite different from the strategy and culture needed to grow the company. If the company is to thrive in the years ahead, it must be positioned to capitalize on emerging opportunities rather than continue to squeeze the last bit of revenue from saturated and declining markets. The company must also be committed to developing innovative products and services that will delight customers rather than making superficial changes in aging products. Finally, the company must have the type of environment where people would quit their jobs with other companies in a heartbeat to become part of the company rather than one where they don't want to get out of bed in the morning.

NO MONDAY MORNING QUARTERBACKS!

Many people believe that having all the answers or solutions to problems is all that it takes to succeed. This is not always the case. Timing is also important. Anticipatory management encourages executives to ask questions like, "What if we lose our major customer?" or "What would happen if our primary source of supply for an essential product or service was bought by one of our competitors?" Knowing which questions to ask—and having the foresight to ask them when there is still time to proactively come up with the best answers—is essential for the company to thrive in the years ahead.

Futuring should not be seen as an effort to make executives see the world through rose-colored glasses. Futuring must be reality-based. It encourages executives to identify possible future realities. Hamel and Prahalad stress the ability to anticipate changing customer needs and to invest in new competencies. They stated, "If senior executives don't have reasonably detailed answers to future questions, and if they are not significantly different from the 'today' answers, there is little chance their companies will remain market leaders."[13] Futuring also encourages executives to identify and acknowledge current realities. Bill Breen and Cheryl Dahle noted that executives need to be brutally honest about their company's current situation. They assert that a company will never figure out where it is going if it doesn't take a cold, hard look at where it is coming from.[14]

Futuring will not provide executives with a crystal-clear picture of the future. It should, however, provide insights into possible futures. By asking perceptive "What if?" questions and running "If . . . , then . . ." scenarios, executives may be able to develop strategies that will position their companies to capitalize on emerging opportunities. The process of asking questions and running scenarios may also provide insights into factors and forces that could derail their companies.

Executives also need to realize they cannot build fail-safe systems. The lack of certainty about what tomorrow will bring makes the development of contingency plans a necessity. For every area of opportunity or vulnerability, executives should develop at least one contingency plan. By developing contingency plans in advance, the company may be able to respond quickly when it becomes apparent that its original plan will not produce the desired results.

All strategies, tactics, and budgets are based on assumptions about what the economy, customers, competition, and technology, etc. will do as the company's plan is being implemented. As situations unfold, executives need to monitor performance and conditions to determine whether the plan needs to be modified or replaced by another plan. The appropriateness of the contingency plan, and how quickly it is implemented, will determine whether the company will be able to maintain its forward progress. No company has the luxury of having the time needed to develop contingency plans for every possible threat or vulnerability. Contingency plans should be developed, however, when the probability of error is high or the consequences of error are too high—or when both conditions exist.

Conclusion: Foresight and Commitment Go Hand in Hand

If you want to create a forward-focused company, you must be committed to looking toward the horizon, championing break-through innovation, developing high-performance incentive systems, empowering people to do extraordinary things, supporting continuous improvement, and fostering symbiotic relationships. You must also make a commitment to not compromise quality, be seduced by short-term opportunities, or succumb to quick fixes.

You may not be able to predict the future, but you do have the ability to gain insights into future possibilities. Anticipatory management will not enable you to foresee every possible event. There will still be surprises, Murphy's Law will still show itself, and the best laid plans are still destined to have flaws. Efforts to sense trends, clues, and cues for what the future may hold will still give your company an edge over companies that focus only on the present.

Anticipatory management will help you minimize the likeli-hood your company will be a day late and a dollar short. You may not know exactly what the future will bring, but you should recognize situations will occur that have the potential to slow your company down or derail it altogether. Your company will be more likely to thrive in the years ahead if you have the foresight to start its journeys into the future early, build buffers into plans, monitor ongoing performance, sense exceptional deviations early, have contingency plans ready to implement at the first sign of variance, and have resources in reserve to make the changes possible.

"You must have the freedom to look beyond what has been done before . . . I couldn't find quite the car I dreamed of: so I decided to build it myself."

—Professor Dr. Ing. h.c. Porsche

NOTES

1. Karl Albrecht, *The Northbound Train* (New York: AMACOM, 1994), p. 62.
2. "Maverick," *Financial World,* September 4, 1994, pp. 32–33.
3. Gary Hamel and C. K. Prahalad, *Competing for the Future* (Boston: Harvard Business School Press, 1994), p. 102.
4. Reprinted with permission of Harvard Business School Press. From the book *Competing for the Future* by Gary Hamel and C. K. Prahalad, Boston, p. 103. Copyright © 1994 by Gary Hamel and C. K. Prahalad.
5. Hamel and Prahalad, p. 101.
6. Ibid., p. 100.
7. James C. Collins and Jerry I. Porrus, *Built to Last* (New York: HarperCollins, 1994), p. 44.
8. John A. Byrne, "How Jack Welch Runs GE," *Business Week,* June 8, 1998, p. 82.
9. Collins and Porrus, p. 31.
10. Ibid., pp. 7–8.
11. Patricia Sellers, "Can Chainsaw Al Really Be a Builder?" *Fortune,* January 12, 1998, p. 118.
12. Ibid., p. 119.
13. Gary Hamel and C. K. Prahalad, "Competing for the Future," *Harvard Business Review,* July–August 1994, p. 127.
14. Bill Breen and Cheryl Dahle, "20/20 Change Agent," *Fast Company,* December 1999, p. 402.

7

Toward a "Corpreneurial" Approach to Creating a Forward-Focused Company

"The game is no longer won or lost by who has the deepest pockets or access to the most capital. It is more and more being played on the basis of who can deploy resources to create customer value and competitive advantage."[1]

—Karl Albrecht, author of *The Northbound Train*

We are in an era of fascinating contrasts marked by the dawn of new ventures and new industries. In this era of emerging markets and technological breakthroughs, growth opportunities have never been so plentiful. However, this era is also marked by the sunset of a number of companies and industries. If companies are to grow and remain vibrant, they must be able to identify, cultivate, and capitalize on the multitude of opportunities that lie ahead. The traditional incremental approach of making minor modifications in current products, services, processes, and markets will not guarantee growth. Incrementalism may not even ensure survival. Companies that are committed to growth need to be more innovative, more venturesome, and more entrepreneurial.

GROWING YOUR COMPANY USING THE THREE *U*s

A company can increase its top line by using any of the three *U*s of growth. First, the company may grow by increasing the number of *u*sers. With this strategy, the company simply tries to find more customers who may be similar to those already being served by the company. The company may also try to attract different types of customers. McDonald's used this strategy when its television advertisements appealed to consumers in their so-called golden years. McDonald's marketing research indicated that a disproportionately low percentage of elderly people frequented fast-food restaurants. More recently, a company that makes disposable diapers launched an advertising campaign that encouraged parents to let their kids take their time in being toilet-trained. The company's growth strategy attempted to keep toddlers as consumers beyond the typical period of time. The strategy is similar to the efforts by cosmetic companies to encourage preteens to wear makeup.

The second *U* involves trying to increase the *u*sage by existing customers. Orange growers use this approach. They promote orange juice as a beverage that can be consumed at any time of the day, instead of only with breakfast. The third strategy involves finding additional *u*ses for the company's products and services. A disposable diaper company introduced a disposable diaper that served as a bathing suit. The company recognized that most disposable diapers are not durable enough to hold up to the challenges of water, so the company introduced a more durable diaper that could be used as a bathing suit. Arm & Hammer should get an award for this type of strategy. Arm & Hammer's advertisements claim that its baking soda can also be used to reduce odor when it is poured down the sink. It also promotes using baking soda as an air freshener for the refrigerator and freezer and for dusting it on carpets to cover pet odors.

CHOOSING THE APPROPRIATE TOP-LINE GROWTH STRATEGY

Executives should consider strategies that go beyond making minor modifications to existing products. They should consider offering different products or services, appealing to different market segments, and entering different geographic areas. These strategies range from the traditional avenues of geographic expansion and vertical integration all the way to bold initiatives that involve entering emerging markets with revolutionary products that incorporate first-generation technology. Some strategies can be implemented with less risk, fewer resources, and in a shorter period of time. Other strategies require a considerable commitment of time, innovation, and capital.

In his book *Corporate Strategies*, H. Igor Ansoff identified four particular growth strategies. The strategies are profiled in his Growth Vector Components Matrix in Figure 7-1.[2] The four conventional growth strategies are market penetration, market development, product development, and diversification.

Figure 7-1. H. Igor Ansoff's growth vector components matrix.

Product / Mission	Present	New
Present	Market Penetration	Product Development
New	Market Development	Diversification

Market Penetration Is the Most Conventional Growth Strategy

The market penetration strategy involves doing more of the same but on a larger scale. For this reason, it is frequently called the concentration strategy. The company continues to concentrate all of its efforts on what it has been doing. It simply attempts to increase sales by getting its present type of customers to buy more of its product or service offerings.

The company may increase its advertising, lower prices, or provide additional brands of the same product. It may also make its product or service offering more accessible to existing and potential customers in its present geographic market. The company may consider entering additional geographic territories by opening additional stores or distribution channels to appeal to potential customers beyond its present reach. It may also establish e-commerce links to capture sales beyond its bricks-and-mortar capabilities.

Market penetration strategy appeals to many companies because it does not appear to have much risk. It is a linear and incremental growth strategy. The company merely fine-tunes its operations, which may reduce the likelihood that things will fall through the cracks as well as the company's vulnerability to competition. Market penetration strategy may enable the company to operate more efficiently, which will give it a price advantage in the marketplace. Starbucks Coffee Company demonstrates the market penetration strategy. It had established more than two thousand units in 2000.

Companies adopting the market penetration growth strategy should be aware of at least four types of risk associated with it. First, the company is likely to encounter intense competition as the market matures unless it has a strong proprietary position. Second, the management team tends to get caught up in operational matters rather than searching for emerging opportunities and dealing with strategic issues. Third, a major shift in consumer interests could cause the market to dry up. Fourth, a major technological breakthrough could render the company's product or service offering obsolete almost overnight.

Market Development Targets New Segments of Customers

The market development strategy is more venturesome. Even though the company may not be making any major changes in its original product or service offering, management is making a deliberate effort to grow by appealing to a whole new target market. Companies using this growth strategy rarely turn their backs on the markets they have been serving all along. Instead, they broaden their reach to include a different set of potential customers. The company's product or service offering may not be modified much, but other aspects of its marketing mix will probably be tailored to meet the targeted segment's needs.

Market development frequently involves finding new types of users or new uses for the company's existing product or service offering. Nancy Abt came to the conclusion that there must be a better way to help people cool off in the heat of summer. Her company developed and received a patent on The Cool Advantage. Her product holds blocks of foam that are soaked in saltwater. When the blocks, which are in polyurethane insulating bags, are frozen, they become colder than regular ice. Her product is sold with a cloth cover that is seamed with Velcro strips, which allows people to wear it while playing tennis or any other sport. By using the market development growth strategy, her company explored other target markets, particularly people who may need heat or muscle relief. Chefs or people who suffer from multiple sclerosis represented potential target markets.[3]

Market development encourages management to adopt a much broader perspective of what the company's product or service offering can do. It encourages management to view the company as a customer problem solver rather than as a business that sells products or services. By looking for different uses and different users, the company reduces the likelihood that it will be caught in the quicksand associated with being a one-product, one-market business. In many cases, the supplementary markets become more lucrative and lasting than the company's original market. In certain markets, perceptiveness and flexibility may be more important than inventiveness.

Product Development Broadens the Company's Offering

The product development strategy is a one-dimensional growth strategy, similar to the market development strategy. Instead of trying to find a new set of customers for its existing product or service offering, the company directs its attention toward broadening its product or service offering. This strategy is based on the premise that since the company already understands its present customers, it should be able to develop additional products to meet one or more of their other needs.

Numerous companies have adopted the product development strategy. Retail stores that began offering one particular product to the market and then slowly added different products are classic examples. Some stores took this strategy to the extreme and became department stores. Stores that began selling clothes now offer their customers computers, lawnmowers, cut flowers, and almost everything else that their segment of customers would buy from other stores. Bill Gates's Microsoft may be the best example of the product development strategy. He has become one of the wealthiest people in the world by focusing on providing the most continuous stream of software for personal and business use.

Product development is based on two premises. First, if management believes that it will be more difficult in terms of risk, time, and resources to attract more customers, then the company should focus its attention on broadening its product or service offering for its present target market. Management has to find ways for the company's present customers to spend more money with each visit. The second premise sounds a bit greedy. The company operates with the attitude that since each customer has a specific amount of money available to spend for various products and services, the company should broaden its product or service offering so that it gets a larger portion of each customer's budget. Most companies try to grow by gaining a larger share of the market. Companies using the product development strategy attempt to grow by gaining a larger share of each customer, which is also known as "wallet share."

In most cases, companies using the product development strategy have a distinct advantage over other companies because they already have a relationship with their target market when they attempt to sell additional products and services. Product development is based on the premise that it is easier to sell an existing customer a second item than it is to create a new customer.

Gerber demonstrates this approach very well. Gerber's slogan is, "Babies are our only business." Gerber recognizes that a family will spend a certain amount of money on a child in its first few years. If Gerber can't increase the birth rate, then all it can do is try to increase its share of what families spend on baby-related items.

Part of Disney's spectacular growth can be attributed to its use of the product development strategy. Disney's recent use of the product development strategy is evident in its combination "Disney World—Disney Cruise Line" package. Disney recognized the growing interest in cruises and the desire by parents to take their kids with them. Most cruise lines target retirees or young singles. Disney applied its talents and resources to appeal to families when it established its own cruise line. Disney's strategy capitalized on the experience and goodwill it had established at its amusement parks. The construction of Disney's resort in Sabastian, Florida, also demonstrates Disney's effort to gain wallet share by providing oceanfront lodging.

Product development has merit because it reduces the risk of technological obsolescence. It also encourages the company to experiment. This strategy may also bring new people into the company who have different perceptions of what the future may hold and where the company should be headed.

Product development is not without its drawbacks. The company still has limited its perceptual field. The company's potential will always be limited by the opportunities that can be found in one set of customers. The possibility the market may wane represents the most significant drawback associated with this strategy. If the number of potential customers declines or if their disposable income drops, the company's revenue will almost certainly decline. Changing consumer interests may also affect the company's growth.

The company must also guard against spreading itself too thin. This is what happened to many department stores. They added products they did not understand and they did not monitor their inventories well. By spending too much time on a diverse product or service line, they lost sight of their customers' needs. These companies became product-and-inventory-driven businesses rather than customer-driven businesses.

Diversification Is a Two-Dimensional Growth Strategy

With diversification, the company tries to increase sales by appealing to different markets with different products or services. Diversification involves going where the company has not gone before. It is like a general attacking on two fronts. Diversification usually places considerable strain on the company's cash flow and profitability. The company is also more likely to make mistakes. Diversification requires learning about different markets and developing different products or services. This strategy works best when the company ventures into related markets and deals with a related technology, product, or service.

Safety-Kleen Corporation is a good example of diversification. Safety-Kleen originally delivered a device to service stations for degreasing parts. The company was losing money on that product. Management, however, found there was an opportunity to recycle substances like antifreeze and transmission fluid that could not be dumped anymore. It also found an opportunity in supplying cleaning agents. The company broadened its cleaning agent offering to include 60 percent of the dry cleaners in its territory. Safety-Kleen's mission statement was changed to reflect the change in its products, services, and customers. The company's new mission became, "To become the world's biggest processor of hazardous waste fluids." Safety-Kleen is making progress in fulfilling its mission. Before it diversified, the company was losing money on $1,000,000 in sales.[4] Safety-Kleen's sales exceeded $1.6 billion in 1999.

THE COMPANY'S GROWTH STRATEGY CAN ALSO INCLUDE VERTICAL INTEGRATION

Vertical integration can take two forms. Reverse vertical integration occurs when the company gets involved in doing what its suppliers have done for it. Forward vertical integration occurs when the company gets involved in the manufacturing or distribution stage phase that follows what the company has been doing. Vertical integration is usually undertaken to give the company additional economies, better control over quality, or an exclusive source of supply or distribution. Some companies have undertaken both forms of integration.

Three Buoys provides an interesting example of vertical integration. Three young men who were fresh out of college started this business. They found there was growing interest in houseboat rentals on one of Canada's lakes. Soon after they started renting houseboats, they realized that the existing brands of houseboats were not user friendly. They also found that they were difficult to clean. Three Buoys approached a boat builder to build a house-boat that would meet their needs.

Three Buoys then put together an investment syndicate to buy all the boats they needed. Three Buoys next vertically integrated into the houseboat-building business. Before long, Three Buoys had developed the second largest fleet of boats in Canada. Only the Canadian government has more boats. Three Buoys then verti-cally integrated in the other direction. They bought resorts where they could dock their boats. The resorts also provided bases for selling grocery items and other products and services. After estab-lishing itself in Canada, Three Buoys started exploring locations that offered even larger population bases and a longer rental season.

Ansoff's Updated Three-Dimensional Matrix Identifies Additional Strategic Options

H. Igor Ansoff updated his original 2×2 matrix to incorporate three growth vectors: market geography, market need, and prod-uct/service technologies. The Dimensions of the Geographic Growth Vector Cube depicted in Figure 7-2 profiles a variety of combinations and directions that management can use to modify the company's strategic portfolio.[5] Ansoff's three-dimensional ma-trix indicates that management should consider whether the com-pany should maintain its present position in each of the three dimensions or consider new market geography (regions or na-tions), a new market need, or new product or service technologies. Ansoff noted the extreme choices are to continue serving its tradi-tional market need and geographic market with its technology on one hand (the shaded cube labeled A) or to move vigorously to a new position on all three dimensions (the shaded cube labeled B).[6] The choice of strategy should be based on numerous factors, in-cluding the company's ability to gain and sustain a competitive advantage.

"Corpreneurial" Growth Strategies Incorporate Innovation and Perceptiveness

Ansoff's four growth strategies profiled in his original 2×2 matrix have been supplemented by this author to highlight five "corpre-

Figure 7-2. Dimensions of the geographic growth vector cube.

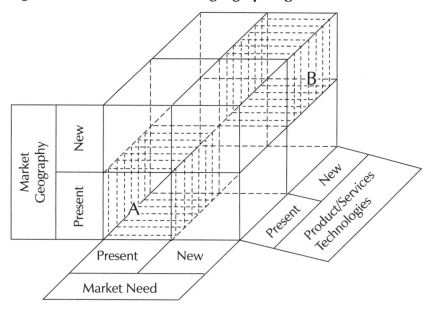

neurial" growth strategies. Corpreneurial strategies may be particularly useful in creating a forward-focused company. The term *corpreneurial* is used because it reflects more venturesome growth strategies. Corpreneurial implies an entrepreneurial approach to transforming an existing venture. Corpreneurial strategies are different from conventional growth strategies because they may involve going wherever the opportunities may be without regard for where the company is in the present.

Corpreneurship is not the same as the concept of intrapreneurship. Intrapreneurship tends to be viewed as an effort to improve corporate performance by unleashing the innovative talents of the company's human resources. In many cases, intrapreneurship represents management's efforts to improve the company's internal operations and processes rather than capitalize on external opportunities or develop technological breakthroughs. Intrapreneurship also tends to have an incremental theme to it. Attention is directed toward finding better ways to do the things that the company is already doing.

Corpreneurship is more entrepreneurial than intrapreneurial. In corpreneurship, management is prepared to slough off today in its efforts to capitalize on a different tomorrow. It involves creating corporate teams to capitalize on emerging market opportunities and to develop new technologies. While the intrapreneurial company does things it may not have done before, the corpreneurial company does things no company has done before. Corpreneurial companies, through their perceptiveness and innovative capabilities, change the way the game will be played.

Timothy Tuff, as president of Alcan Aluminum Corporation, demonstrated many of the qualities that must be infused into more traditional corporations if they are to capitalize on the opportunities that lie ahead. Tuff developed a team to foster an entrepreneurial culture, promote new ideas, and make product development as simple as casting an ingot. *Business Month* reported that Tuff's team was responsible for finding the technology, funding the project, and designing products that did not yet exist. Alcan set a goal that 25 percent of total corporate revenue must come from its new ventures within a specific time frame. Tuff's team spurred the development of dozens of new ventures.[7]

Adding Corpreneurial Strategies to Ansoff's Original 2 × 2 Matrix

The dynamics of today's marketplace place a premium on having the ability to capitalize on new and different opportunities. Ansoff's original matrix has been modified to incorporate the dynamics of emerging markets, changing consumer needs, and the accelerating rate of technological change. Figure 7-3 depicts Ansoff's original 2 × 2 Matrix Modified to Reflect Corpreneurial Growth Strategies. The 2 × 2 matrix has been expanded by this

Figure 7-3. Ansoff's original 2 × 2 matrix modified to reflect corpreneurial growth strategies.

Products ⟍ Markets	Present Products	Different Products	New Products
Present Markets	Market Penetration	Product Development	Product Innovation
Different Markets	Market Development	Diversification	Product Invention
New Markets	Market Transfer	Market Creation	Pure Corpreneurship

author to a 3×3 matrix to incorporate five corpreneurial growth strategies.

The headings for the rows and columns have also been modified. Ansoff's original 2×2 matrix had headings of *present* and *new*. The 3×3 matrix continues to use the *present* heading, but it replaces Ansoff's *new* with the word *different*. In Ansoff's matrix, any time the company did something that it had not done before, the matrix classified that behavior as new. The 3×3 matrix distinguishes new from different. If the company is to embark in a direction that already exists in the marketplace, then the company is merely doing something different from what it had done before. If, however, the company is embarking in a direction where no company has gone before, then this is something that can be considered to be new. The distinction is significant. Because a company does something different from what it has done before, it does not guarantee that the marketplace will reward it.

When McDonald's decided to offer drive-in services and prepackaged salads, the marketplace did not herald McDonald's as the most innovative fast-food franchise. Some fast-food franchises already provided these products and services. Although it may have been different for McDonald's, these changes were not new to the marketplace. The *new* heading in the 3×3 matrix indicates that a service, product, or a process is provided for the first time altogether and the company is at the leading edge.

PRODUCT INNOVATION STRATEGY ADDS CONSIDERABLE VALUE TO THE MARKET

The product innovation growth strategy goes beyond the traditional product development strategy. The company continues to direct its attention to the needs of the people or organizations in its present target market; however, it attempts to introduce a markedly superior product or service by developing new technology. The basic product or service may have been around for years, but the corpreneurial company uses state-of-the-art technology to create a new generation of the product.

Yamaha provides an excellent example of product innovation. Yamaha had 40 percent of worldwide piano sales years ago, yet overall demand was declining by 10 percent per year. Instead of settling for a stagnating or declining market, Yamaha's executives sought ways to foster growth through technology. They knew growth would need to come from offering the market a piano that could do things no other piano could do. Yamaha combined digital and optical technology to develop the means to retrofit a conventional piano to play great works for $2,500. Yamaha took the original player piano concept and matched it with state-of-the-art technology. A compact disk programs the piano to play particular tunes.

Yamaha was already committed to the production and marketing of pianos and other musical instruments. Management chose product innovation as its primary strategy for revitalizing the market. Yamaha did not pursue the typical avenues for turning its situation around. Kenichi Ohmae, as head of McKinsey and Company's Tokyo office, said, "It didn't buckle down to prune costs, proliferate models, slice overhead or all the other typical approaches. It looked with fresh eyes for chances to create value for customers."[8] Yamaha was perceptive enough to recognize that people's interest in and appreciation for the piano continued to grow over the years. The decline in piano sales had come from some people's reluctance to spend years learning how to play it. Yamaha therefore looked to technology as a way to speed the learning process and highlight the true beauty of the piano. Yamaha demonstrated that product innovation relies more on perceptiveness than extensive research and development. The piano already existed, as did the technology. Yamaha was merely the first company in the piano field to combine them to offer the market something new.

Putting technology into a new package is what makes product innovation an effective strategy. Robert Allio, author of *The Practical Strategist*, observed that in the competitive arena, "Losers hang on to old technology in the mistaken belief that incremental improvements can forestall the effect of a technological breakthrough."[9]

PRODUCT INVENTION INTRODUCES A FIRST-GENERATION PRODUCT OR SERVICE

The product invention growth strategy is more corpreneurial than the product innovation growth strategy. The company is introducing a first-generation product or service. The company is also entering a market it has never served. This strategy exemplifies the risk/return nature of entrepreneurship. The company is taking the risk associated with whether the new product or service is in tune with the needs of prospective customers. It is also taking the risk associated with entering a market with limited first-hand experience.

If the product is markedly better from a technological, convenience, speed, or price perspective and the market is searching for something that is clearly better or less expensive, then the strategy may enable the company to harvest the market. This strategy is particularly advantageous when the company is able to secure a proprietary position.

A number of companies have become leaders by providing products or services that are radically different from what has been offered by other companies. Merck and 3M have been heralded for their ability to introduce new products. Merck's development of Proscar provided a completely different way to deal with prostate cancer. Proscar shrinks enlarged prostate glands and minimizes the need for surgery. Some four hundred thousand men who face surgery each year to remove an enlarged prostate can take a pill instead of undergoing surgery. This $1-per-day drug represents a better alternative to the traditional operation that costs more than $10,000.

3M demonstrated a similar propensity to utilize the product invention growth strategy. The company has consistently ventured into different markets and developed new technologies. The development of the bioelectronic ear to help restore hearing for people with inner ear damage reflects 3M's willingness to go where it has not gone before and to develop products that no company has developed before. The company's ability to bring varying levels of technology to market to meet established needs is the hallmark of the inventive organization.

Limmion Corporation and Bio-Energy International are two smaller companies that illustrate how inventive approaches can address existing problems. Both companies capitalized on the inescapable need to deal with the monumental pollution problems in the United States. Limmion Corp. invented a way to use plants to cleanse ponds of industrial waste, and later to collect the usable waste for recycling. Instead of using more chemicals to clean a pond, Limmion Corp. deploys plants as underwater gardens. The plants' pods are regularly harvested to reclaim contaminants they have gathered. Bio-Energy International obtained the rights to use a new microbe developed through gene-splicing to turn garbage into alcohol. Both companies demonstrate the entrepreneur's creed, "Within every problem there lies at least one disguised business opportunity."

MARKET TRANSFER MEANS BEING FIRST TO MARKET

The market transfer growth strategy is designed to take the company's existing product/service/technology mix into markets that are not being served by any company. This strategy is particularly appropriate for entering markets in third-world or emerging countries.

This strategy may involve considerable risk. The company must have the ability to tailor its marketing mix(es) to the uniqueness of the emerging market(s). The risk associated with market transfer tends to be higher than the risk found in the market development strategy. The newness of an emerging market means few data may be available and that the infrastructure for introducing and supporting the product or service offering may be limited or nonexistent.

Companies using this strategy look for markets that are newly emerging. Emerging countries may represent lucrative opportunities for companies that are willing to be the first to serve them. Emerging countries may provide high levels of profit in the years to come for companies that are willing to take their product or services where no company has gone before. As third-world and emerging countries improve their domestic productivity and increase their export activity, their disposable income and pursuit of a higher standard of living will also increase.

Timing may be the key to success for companies using the market transfer growth strategy. As emerging countries develop infrastructures that facilitate importing and currency exchange, companies operating in established and mature markets will attempt to transfer their marketing efforts to the emerging economies. If companies wait until the infrastructure is established before they initiate this strategy, they may be too late to harvest the opportunity.

Success in market transfer may be contingent on being positioned to enter the window of opportunity the moment it starts to open. If the company waits until the window is fully open before it initiates the market transfer strategy, it is likely to encounter stiff competition from outside—and possibly within—that market. Bill Schroeder of Conner Peripherals captured the importance of speed to market when he stated, "The first guy into a market cleans up, the second guy does OK, the third guy barely breaks even. The fourth guy loses money."[10] Conner Peripherals had the distinction of being the first company to go from start-up to $1 billion in sales in four years![11] Conner Peripherals demonstrated the benefits of being in the right place at the right time with the right capability.

The market transfer strategy may be appealing because it may require only a minimal initial capital outlay. The company may test an emerging market by exporting its existing product or service with minor modification. If the emerging market responds with sufficient vigor, the company may consider additional modifications to tailor its marketing mix to meet the emerging market's particular needs. Again, the issue of timing comes up. If the company is first to market and there is pent-up demand, prospective customers may be flexible in their expectations. When you are the first company to deliver pizza, the pizza doesn't have to be great . . . it just needs to be warm, reasonably priced, and not stuck to the carton.

An aquaculture company based in the United States provides a good example of the market transfer strategy. Management explored the merit of exporting its frozen fish filets to an emerging country and entering into a joint venture with that country's government to build fish farms and processing facilities if their product is accepted and demonstrates economic viability. Management sees this opportunity as almost too good to be true. It had been trying to find a way to generate revenue from the filets that did not meet the company's high standards for U.S. restaurants and supermarkets. Exporting appears to have considerable merit because emerging foreign markets may not place the same standards on the color and size of the filets. Ironically, many emerging markets prefer frozen fish to fresh fish filets because they will not spoil as quickly.

Market transfer strategy illustrates the saying that one person's bitter lemon can be the ingredient for another person's lemonade. One caution needs to be noted at this stage. Companies that attempt to use this strategy to merely dump their excess inventory are destined to see market transfer fail. Market transfer strategy is not the same as throwing a handful of spaghetti at the wall to see if any of it sticks. Market transfer will work only to the extent the company is committed to researching the emerging market and prepared to tailor its marketing mix to that market's unique needs and features. Remember, a company invites competition to the extent that it fails to meet the unique needs of its target market.

William Golden incorporated market transfer when he took his company's cleanup savvy to Indonesia and Malaysia. His company, International Environmental Associates, represented small U.S. environmental companies in Jakarta. Businesses in Jakarta were under pressure to stop polluting. Golden's company won contracts because it extensively researched Indonesian environmental laws—information not readily available in the United States. William Golden also showed his interest in the market by sending his son to live for a time in Indonesia.

MARKET CREATION IS A TWO-DIMENSIONAL GROWTH STRATEGY

The market creation growth strategy involves a two-dimensional risk. The company is entering a virgin market and getting involved in products or services with which it has little or no experience. Market creation involves identifying an emerging market and developing products or services that are already offered by other companies.

Perceptiveness and timing are key ingredients to market creation. Companies that already have the experience could enter the emerging market using the market transfer strategy. Yet, many companies practice management by braille, thereby failing to see opportunities outside their immediate sphere of activity. Their preoccupation with current products and markets keeps them from seeing existing and emerging opportunities.

Companies that use the market creation strategy are market-driven rather than product-driven. They spend their time looking for emerging markets. They figure that if they have sufficient lead time, they can either develop the capability to serve the market or purchase via license or outright acquisition the ability from a company that did not see the opportunity.

A major hotel chain provides an example of the market creation growth strategy. Management investigated the merit of establishing teleconferencing facilities in numerous emerging countries when it recognized that companies in emerging countries lacked sophisticated means for linking themselves with companies in other countries. The hotel chain had already established its prowess in the hospitality field so it only needed to secure telecommunications technology and licenses to provide facilities where people could have a hospitable environment for communicating with others all over the world.

Management of this company recognized that businesses will substitute teleconferencing for airline travel in the years ahead due to rising airfares, the threat of terrorism, the relative inaccessibility of some locations, as well as the uncertainty of airline travel due to mechanical problems, weather, and labor strikes. This company's consideration of a market creation growth strategy was based on the same concept as electronic mail. Businesses are now more accustomed to using e-mail to transport data and documents than air-express. A similar situation may be the case with business travel.

PURE CORPRENEURSHIP MAY BE THE ULTIMATE CHALLENGE

The pure corpreneurship growth strategy combines market creation and product invention. It represents a bold strategy for positioning the company to capitalize on the almost inevitable changes that will occur in the years ahead. With this strategy, management is committed to having the company be the first to enter an emerging market with products, services, or technology that did not previously exist for that or any other company.

The question may be raised, which comes first, technological development or market surveillance? Some companies are *technology-driven* while other companies are *market-driven*. Corpreneurship is neither a technology-driven nor an exclusively market-driven growth strategy. Corpreneurship, in its purest form, is an *opportunity-driven* growth strategy that fosters a synergistic effect by anticipating emerging needs with sufficient lead time to develop innovative solutions to serve them.

As the rate of change accelerates, it will be more difficult for companies to keep up with the pace. Pure corpreneurship forces managers to think beyond present products, processes, services, and markets. If a company wants to be at the leading edge, it should position itself to be the first to enter the market and to have such a superior product or service that potential competitors look elsewhere.

Breakthrough leadership means being more than one step ahead of competition; it means being so far ahead that potential competitors choose not to enter the arena. Ironically, the desire to be ahead of the competition needs to be tempered with the realization that a company could hit the market before the market is ready. This is a common problem for companies that are so technology-driven that they fail to recognize whether the market is ready to be harvested. Conversely, companies that are market-driven often ignore the importance of having a technological advantage. In their zeal to get something to meet unmet or emerging needs in the marketplace, many companies may fail to develop and offer superior products or services.

Some companies have experimented with the pure corpreneurship growth strategy as part of their overall strategy to position themselves to capitalize on the future changes. Airxchange Inc. illustrated pure corpreneurship in action when its cofounder Donald Steele recognized that when people insulated their homes to lower their fuel costs, they unknowingly created a new problem. Indoor pollution was almost inevitable when people tightened up their homes by adding insulation.

Steele had anticipated the market for quite some time. He knew that when a problem gets bad enough and is widespread, Congress would almost certainly respond by enacting legislation. When Congress passed the Air Quality Act, Airxchange Inc.'s top line was catapulted to a new level. He noted, "There's a market when the health and safety codes define one for you."[12] Airxchange has sold tens of thousands of units that are designed to transport harmful gasses and particles out of the home.

Noise Cancellation Technologies Inc. also illustrates pure corpreneurship. Its management recognized the growing interest in noise abatement and that few, if any, techniques were available for eliminating noise. It also recognized that the elimination of noise would be an integral component in the quality of work life movement that was destined to blossom. Noise Cancellation Technologies Inc. developed a system that electronically analyzes the sound waves of noise and then produces precisely matched antinoise to eliminate the noise. Conventional approaches had merely tried to buffer the noise, but Noise Cancellation Technologies offers noise elimination.

The irony of the success of Airxchange and Noise Cancellation Technologies is that both companies were dealing with what can be considered obvious rather than obscure opportunities. Moreover, management considered the opportunities and success to be almost inevitable. In their minds, they were not embarking on high-risk ventures.

CONCLUSION: CREATING A FORWARD-FOCUSED COMPANY MAY REQUIRE A HYBRID STRATEGY

Changes in the marketplace will require changes in a company's strategy. Companies that merely make minor changes in the present will not flourish during periods of rapid change. The traditional incremental approach to doing business will not be sufficient for surfing the waves associated with high-growth opportunities. If your company's strategy is nothing more than an incremental and linear extension of what it has been doing in the past, the strategy will be predictable and easy to leapfrog by competitors that have the courage to boldly go where no company has gone before.

The future will not be better than the past for companies that are fixated on cost-cutting and fine-tuning operations. They will miss out on the myriad opportunities that lie ahead. Hopefully, your company will see the opportunities early enough to adopt one or more of the corpreneurial growth strategies that will enable it to capitalize on opportunities that are forming on the not-too-distant horizon.

"A capitalist economy grows by a process called creative destruction—whereby entrepreneurial innovation combines with technological investment to create new growth industries which inevitably inflict pain and distress on older, less dynamic businesses they displace."

—Joseph Schumpeter, economist

NOTES

Portions of this chapter originally appeared in the article "Developing a Corpreneurial Strategy for Fostering Business Growth and Revitalization" by the author in *Industrial Management,* July–August 1992, pp. 19–25. Used with permission of the Institute of Industrial Engineers, 25 Technology Park, Norcross, Georgia 30092.

1. Karl Albrecht, *The Northbound Train* (New York: AMACOM, 1994), p. 5.
2. This model originally appeared in H. Igor Ansoff's book *Corporate Strategy* (New York: McGraw-Hill, 1965), p. 109. Used with permission of the author.
3. "100 Ideas for New Businesses," *Venture,* November 1988, p. 67.
4. Donald W. Brinkman, "On the Path to Opportunity," *Success,* June 1992, p. 16.
5. Model used with permission of the author.
6. H. I. Ansoff, *The New Corporate Strategy* (New York: John Wiley, 1988), p. 84.
7. Richard Poe, "Their Uncanny Think Tank," *Business Month,* November 1989, p. 62.
8. Kenichi Ohmae, "Getting Back to Strategy," *Harvard Business Review,* November–December 1988, p. 152.
9. Robert J. Allio, *The Practical Strategist* (New York: Harper & Row, 1988), p. 134.
10. William H. Davidow and Michael S. Malone, "Instant Profits," *Success,* January/February 1993, p. 80.
11. H. Skip Weitzen, "Billion Dollar Success," *Success,* April 1993, p. 14.
12. Mark Roman, "New Niches for the 90s," *Success,* April 1989, p. 51.

8

Playing "Two Markets" Ahead

"I owe my success in life to having always been a quarter of an hour beforehand."

—Admiral Horatio Nelson, eighteenth-century
British admiral

Someone once stated, "Only two types of people dance with elephants . . . the quick and the dead!" There is little doubt that this century will bring unheralded change. The rate, magnitude, and comprehensiveness of change will trample companies that are not prepared for it. Corporate success will be contingent on the ability to synchronize actions to the dynamics of an ever-changing marketplace. There used to be room in the marketplace for good companies, good managers, and good products. As long as companies offered something within reason at a price that was acceptable, they could make a profit. It used to be, "Lead, follow, or get out of the way." Today, lagging behind the market will not cut it. If you are not taking the lead and markedly better than others in meeting the market's needs, then you're dead!

Luck has been defined as what happens when preparation meets opportunity. Corporate success is contingent on being able to offer what the market wants when it wants it. Companies have always needed to offer the right products and services at the right time in the right place at the right price. The ability to provide products and services that are in sync with market expectations, however, will be put to the test with the ever-accelerating rate of change in all markets.

Management's concern with the present—no matter how successful the company is—must be complemented with a vision of what the company should be in five to ten years. The future offers a multitude of opportunities. Companies will grow and prosper only if they are led by executives who have the vision to see emerging opportunities and the ability to strategically position their companies to harvest them in a timely manner.

Most executives spend their time in three areas. First, some of their attention is directed to their company's current customers, territories, technology, products, services, and people. Second, some of their time is spent reacting to unexpected circumstances, situations, and threats. Third, some of their time is directed toward overseeing operational matters. Executives rarely spend enough time on strategic issues. Many executives exclaim, "I don't have time to think about the future" or "Things are changing so quickly . . . there is no point in planning any more . . . all I can do is see what is happening and try to respond to it."

Life would be fairly predictable if times were stable and conditions certain. There would be little need for planning, risk taking, or innovation. But as Alvin Toffler indicated in his book *Future Shock*, while change has always been with us, the rate of change is accelerating. In their book *Creating Excellence*, Craig Hickman and Michael Silva noted, "Technical innovations, global communications, and fierce competition can bring change overnight that once took decades or even centuries to manifest themselves."[1]

Most managers use the product life-cycle concept in the planning process. The product life cycle is a misnomer because it really refers to the industry life cycle for that generic product or service. Managers tend to think of the industry as a whole, rather than as particular markets or segments within the overall industry. Numerous markets emerge, grow, mature, decline, and die within the industry's life cycle. Managers who use the product life cycle as the basis for making decisions tend to believe that the industry will last forever, causing them to take the market for granted. Theodore Levitt, business writer and educator, observed years ago, "Industries that assume themselves to be riding some automatic growth escalator invariably descend into stagnation."[2] Levitt argues that there is no such thing as growth industries; there are only industries that are experiencing the growth stage.

Executives serve their companies better when they adopt the *market* life-cycle concept for specific segments or niches rather than the *product* life-cycle concept for the whole industry. The market life-cycle concept stresses the need to identify durable opportunities within one or more industries. Executives should direct their attention and their company's resources toward identifying windows of opportunity within existing markets as well as capitalizing on emerging markets.

AVOIDING THE HERE TODAY, GONE TOMORROW SYNDROME

It may be more difficult to maintain excellence than it is to achieve it. Success needs to be viewed more as a marathon than as a 100-meter sprint. The annals of sports are full of Heisman trophy winners who never made it to the pro bowl and of rookie batters who hit .300 and then vanished from the majors within a few seasons. The same appears to be the case for most companies. It is not unusual for a business to go from being celebrated by the media for its meteoric rise to filing Chapter Eleven within a year.

A closer look at companies that are here today and gone tomorrow reveals that their initial success can be attributed to their entrepreneurs being in the right place at the right time with the right product or service. All the conditions were right. As conditions changed, however, their companies were no longer in a position to capitalize on market opportunities. As their markets evolved, their companies were out of sync with new realities. In their dance with elephants, they made too many wrong steps.

When the here today, gone tomorrow ventures were created, market demand may have been so strong that consumers would have bought almost anything that would meet their needs. As their markets grew and matured, competitors entered the scene who were more in tune with changes in the marketplace. Entrepreneurs of first-to-market companies may have been perceptive and recognized what the market wanted initially, but many lacked the resources or managerial skills to support their company's rapid growth. Hence, many emerging ventures implode.

Postmortems of "here today, gone tomorrow" companies reveal that lasting success requires numerous factors. Companies that are driven by a single market may be destined to fail. Peter Drucker noted that if you stay in one business long enough, you *will* go out of business. Lasting success is contingent on being able to keep up with changes in the marketplace as well as being able to calibrate the company's infrastructure to support sustained growth. Perceptiveness, agility, resourcefulness, and stamina are valuable talents in the dance with elephants. When the rate of change is accelerating and uncertainty is the rule, the ability to turn on a dime may keep the company from being trampled to death.

A KEEN SENSE OF TIMING IS ESSENTIAL FOR SUSTAINED GROWTH

Numerous companies fail not because they do not have good ideas but because their executives do not have a good sense of timing. The timing of initiatives continues to play an integral role in the evolution of an enterprise. The following five types of offensive-timing initiatives need to be addressed during the life of a venture:

1. When to start the venture
2. When to introduce a new product or service
3. When to introduce a new process
4. When to enter a new territory
5. When to initiate major expansion

Timing corporate initiatives also has defensive dimensions. Country singer Kenny Rogers's song *The Gambler*, which is about playing poker, highlights the importance of defensive timing. To paraphrase Rogers, success comes from knowing "when to hold and when to fold." The following is a list of four defensive-timing initiatives that entail reducing or phasing out certain corporate activities:

1. When to drop a product or service
2. When to exit existing markets
3. When to consolidate operations
4. When to sell part or all of the venture

When Nolan Bushnell reflected on his life as an entrepreneur, he indicated that while his ideas were good, his timing was off. Bushnell said that he got out of Atari too soon and out of Pizza Time Theatres too late.

Entrepreneurship is usually associated with creating a company to capitalize on an emerging opportunity. Lasting success, however, only occurs if management is able to develop a strategy and culture that foster sustained growth. The need to identify market opportunities tends to overshadow the importance of having a keen sense of timing.

The accelerating rate of change in the marketplace has placed a premium on having foresight and the ability to quickly modify the company's capabilities. While it may be true that there are more opportunities than at any time in the past, executives need to recognize that windows of opportunity are opening and closing more rapidly than at any other time. Competition is quick to jump on the bandwagon for markets that show promise. The challenge is amplified by the fact that it may take more lead time to develop competencies to meet the needs of a more sophisticated and demanding market.

The word *entrepreneur* is derived from the French term *entreprendre,* which means to initiate something. Success may be tied just as closely to knowing when to exit a market. If the venture is to continue growing, management must explore new opportunities. For this to happen, management must be willing to venture away from its current position, regardless of how comfortable it may be. For the company to enjoy sustained growth and success, it must possess chameleon-like capabilities so that it can be transformed into what it needs to be rather than what it has been.

Jack Welch recognized the need for timing when he became CEO of General Electric. He justified the sale of many of GE's products, facilities, and companies for three reasons. First, Welch recognized that certain markets and products were waning and that if he didn't get out while they had some value, GE would have little left to salvage. Second, GE did not have an unlimited amount of capital. Welch recognized that for GE to be able to invest in its future, it had to free up capital employed in some of its existing operations. Third, Welch recognized that GE would be in a position to create its future and generate considerable wealth for its stockholders if it committed resources to leading-edge technologies and emerging markets.

SUCCESS MAY BE TEMPORARY

Many companies focus their attention only on their current markets. This practice is not only myopic; it may jeopardize the company's survival. Executives frequently use their company's current market(s) as a security blanket. Although the current markets, products, and customers may be comfortable, they can easily suffocate the company's ability to adjust to a rapidly changing marketplace. Too often, executives wait until their companies are in serious trouble before they begin to look for ways to keep their companies afloat. One of the things that separates leading-edge companies from the others is that management does not wait for major problems to arise before it starts looking for ways to strengthen the company.

Successful companies have longer-term time horizons. This gives them two strategic advantages over other companies. The longer-term time horizon enables management to have a more objective view of where the company is and what its future may hold. Managers who live only in the present frequently assume that today's markets and the company's competitive advantage(s) will last forever. Managers of successful companies recognize no market, customer, location, product, process, or service lasts forever.

A longer-term time horizon also permits management to look beyond the company's current market(s). Successful executives believe almost anything is possible. They live by Ferrari's motto, "If you can dream it, we can make it." If the company has sufficient lead time, it can develop new products, new processes, new competencies, and expand into new territories. The longer-term time horizon may also provide the impetus needed for the company to move into an entirely different industry. In its truest sense, a longer-term horizon may even permit management to combine a visionary perspective and with corpreneurial strategies to boldly go where no company has gone before!

Nicholas Murray Butler, Nobel laureate and educator has observed, "People, it has been said, can be placed in three classes: the few who make things happen, the many who watch things happen, and the overwhelming majority who have no idea what has happened." His distinction between people may also apply to companies. Companies can be classified according to when management realizes the need to change and how aggressively it attempts to reposition the company. In this case, there can be visionary companies, proactive companies, reactive companies, and laggard companies.

THE LAGGARD COMPANY IS DESTINED TO FAIL

One of the most important dimensions of a company's evolution is when management recognizes the need to change the company's strategy and operations. Figure 8-1 depicts how the executives at a laggard company may make minor modifications but fail to recognize that the company is no longer in sync with market realities. After two years—or in some markets, just two quarters—of declining sales, the company's executives finally acknowledge that the company has no future in its current market. Executives then undertake crisis-type efforts by entering a state of red alert. Because they waited until their company was clearly declining to start searching for some way to stay alive, their actions tended to be futile.

The X in Figure 8-1 indicates when management realizes the need to take a closer look at the company's operations and the appropriateness of the company's market offering. Managers in laggard companies miss or ignore the first signs of a declining situation. They may even rationalize away the signals and attribute their company's declining sales to a soft economy. It usually takes a major crisis before managers of laggard companies acknowledge the need for major change.

The crisis may be the result of the paradox of success where the company celebrates its success for too long and fails to invest in its future. This is particularly common with companies that believe their patent protection or current competitive advantage guarantees continuing success. These companies celebrate their patent protection too long, and thereby neglect the need to invest

Figure 8-1. The laggard company.

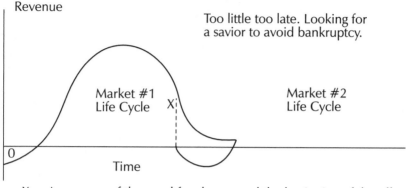

X = Awareness of the need for change and the beginning of the effort
   to reposition the company. This usually occurs after the second
   consecutive period of declining revenue.

in their future, or they believe their products are so superior that
the competition cannot appeal to their customers. In either case,
management is delinquent in fulfilling its responsibility to create
the company's future. More perceptive and innovative competitors
rudely interrupt the laggard company's celebration or awaken
them from their coma-like sleep of arrogance.

Even if management's last-minute crash efforts stop the bleeding, they merely postpone the company's demise. These companies
resemble the gamblers who place and keep their bets on the color
red for each spin of the roulette wheel. The ball may stop on red
once or twice, but sooner—rather than later—the ball will stop on
black.

The marketplace shows little mercy to companies that fail to
keep pace. Strategic repositioning requires substantial lead time,
managerial prowess, and the availability of resources in reserve.
Most laggard companies lack these qualities. In an act of desperation, these companies often seek a savior to bail them out. Unfortunately, most of these companies cannot be revived.

REACTIVE COMPANIES MAY STAY IN THE GAME BUT THEY DO NOT PROSPER

Management teams of reactive companies, as depicted in Figure 8-2,
start looking for avenues for repositioning their companies at the

Figure 8-2. The reactive company.

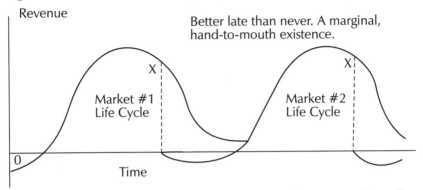

X = Awareness of the need for change and the beginning of the effort to reposition the company. This usually occurs when the revenue begins decreasing at an increasing rate.

first signs of a declining market. The Xs in Figure 8-2 indicate executives realize their market may have peaked after sales fail to reach new heights. Their sense of timing is better than that of executives in laggard companies because they do not wait for the second consecutive period of declining sales to assess the appropriateness of the company's market offering.

Management looks for early signs of declining margins and the lack of repeat purchases as an indication that the company's competitive position or the overall market may be deteriorating. Management may also recognize that the company is having to increase its advertising and sales efforts to maintain its current level of sales. Earlier awareness gives the reactive company more time than the laggard company to modify the company's strategy. Reactive companies recognize price competition can be intense in saturated markets. Although sales may continue increasing for the overall market, profit margins are already deteriorating. Executives need to recognize that cash flow is not a leading indicator of financial problems. By the time cash-flow problems occur, it may be too late to turn the situation around. Cash-flow problems are seldom the real *cause* of the company's financial problems but the *result* of more fundamental problems.

While laggard companies don't know what has happened until it has already happened, at least reactive companies are monitoring key performance indicators. Earlier awareness may give management sufficient time to develop a strategy to keep the company's head above water before it runs out of capital.

Managers of reactive companies, unlike their laggard counterparts, recognize the need for a two-pronged revitalization strategy. The first prong is directed toward harvesting their current market position in the short term. The other prong is directed toward redeploying some of the company's resources to reposition the company to a more propitious market or industry.

These executives realize that it may take an extended period of time to prepare the company to enter new markets, to develop new technology, to train people, and to redesign facilities. They also recognize that their company may experience lean times as it undergoes the transition. Although a number of reactive companies may successfully reposition themselves so that they have a future, the financial crisis and psychological trauma that come with the valley that precedes the repositioning can cause considerable scar tissue.

PROACTIVE COMPANIES DEVELOP SUCCESSOR MARKET OFFERINGS

One of the major differences between proactive and reactive companies is management's sense of timing. Thomas Venable, as CEO of World Technology Group, Inc., noted, "Don't wait to start digging the well until you are thirsty. . . . The CEO cannot wait until a downward trend in revenues and profits is occurring before initiating the product development cycle."[3] Venable also cautioned executives not to wait for declining market share prior to releasing your new products and to not withhold products from the market that will obsolete your existing products . . . if you don't do it . . . your competition will.[4]

Executives in the proactive company depicted in Figure 8-3 recognize the need to start thinking about repositioning their companies earlier in the market life cycle. Proactive managers carefully monitor the rate of growth while their company is growing because they know success can be fleeting. They may not have earned *A*s in calculus or economics class, but they know that the point

Figure 8-3. The proactive company.

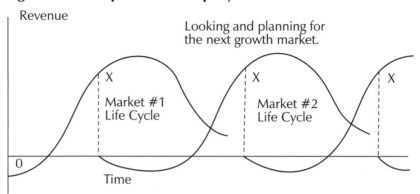

X = Awareness of the need for change and the beginning of the effort
to reposition the company. This usually occurs when revenue is
increasing at a decreasing rate.

of inflection (noted by the Xs) in the revenue curve, represents a
significant change in the company's position. The point of inflection highlighted in Figure 8-3 indicates that even though revenue
may still be growing, it is growing at a slower rate.

By starting the search earlier, proactive executives have additional time to identify emerging opportunities and reposition their
companies to capitalize on their next market life cycle. This lead
time gives them time to develop strategic and operational plans for
introducing a successor product or service to move the company
ahead while its current product or service offering starts to slow.

Proactive companies succeed because they rarely get caught
trying to salvage dying products the way laggard companies do.
They also stand out from reactive companies because they spend
more time creating their futures while reactive companies tend to
operate in saturated markets. While proactive companies are capitalizing on their current growth and success, they are also investing
in tomorrow's breadwinners.

Even though the proactive company may embark on a major
repositioning effort, change should be more evolutionary than revolutionary in nature. The proactive company may be able to sustain its growth because it is a jump ahead of reactive companies,
which are trying to get a piece of the action in their attempt to
make up for declining revenues in their original market.

THE VISIONARY COMPANY PLANS "TWO RACKS" AHEAD

Executives in the visionary company depicted in Figure 8-4 have a jump on the competition. They don't wait for signs of market maturity to initiate change. Management teams of visionary companies are constantly scanning the horizon for emerging opportunities. They look for trends, cues, and clues as to what may be just over the horizon. They recognize that first-to-market companies usually reap the greatest reward. As someone once said, "The first bite of the apple is usually the best." Visionary companies spend considerable time and resources scanning the horizon for fresh opportunities. They not only look for ripe apples but for fertile fields so that they can plant apple orchards to be harvested in the future. This way, they are almost assured of having a bountiful supply of fresh and juicy apples for the decade to come.

Visionary companies operate with a time horizon that is at least twice as long as the time horizon of proactive companies. While proactive companies are preparing for the next market life cycle, visionary companies are directing some of their attention and resources beyond the next market life cycle. While proactive companies look for emerging markets, visionary companies look for markets or industries to create.

Many executives have difficulty conceiving how visionary executives can think that far ahead. Interestingly enough, there may be a close parallel between the managers of visionary companies and the top pool players. Years ago, the champion pool player was interviewed about how he plays the game. He said that when he takes his first shot to break the rack of fifteen balls on the table, he is already planning where he wants the cue ball to be positioned when he breaks the next rack, so that when he finishes that rack he will be in the best position to start the third rack. He attributed his success to playing "two racks" ahead!

Visionary companies operate with a perspective that is similar to the one exhibited by the champion pool player. Both have a clear vision of the type of game they want to play and where they want to be at a certain point in time. Visionary companies plan "two markets" ahead. They recognize that everything they are currently doing may need to be changed to create, cultivate, and capitalize on future opportunities.

One of the reasons 3M has been such a successful company for the last few decades is that it has continued finding new business opportunities. One of 3M's goals is to have 30 percent of the company's sales four years from now come from products that don't exist today. Looking for and capitalizing on opportunities is more than a dream or a slogan at 3M; it has operationalized the development of new products to the point that it is now a way of corporate life.

Visionary executives recognize that playing two markets ahead is not a luxury that few companies can afford. They realize that continuous corpreneurial efforts may be the fuel that feeds the fire of sustained growth and success. Figure 8-4 shows how a visionary company operates in three time planes. While the visionary company may be milking its current markets, it is already preparing its entry into the next market(s) and putting together a team of people to explore opportunities that will be two markets ahead.

The visionary strategy helps to foster a corporate culture that places a premium on the company's human resources. Visionary companies attract, motivate, and retain people who are innovative and who want to be part of a company that is positioned to explore new markets and develop new products or services that meet emerging needs. They also ensure that the company's best and brightest are involved in exploring future opportunities rather than trying to save products that should be put out to pasture.

Figure 8-4. The visionary company.

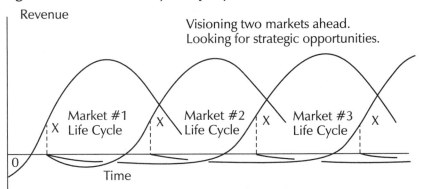

X = Awareness of the need for change and the beginning of the effort to reposition the company. This usually occurs when revenue is increasing at an increasing rate.

The visionary company must have a keen sense for when the window of opportunity is about to open. To jump through the window before it is open could be as disastrous as jumping through it after it has closed. Success may be contingent on anticipating when the window will open. Akio Morita, founder of Sony, captured the essence of visionary leadership when he said, "We should always be the pioneers with our products—out front leading the market. We believe in leading the public with new products rather than asking them what kind of products they want."[5]

Visionary leadership is like skeet shooting. If you aim where the clay pigeon actually is, the shot will be behind it. If you lead too much, your shot will pass in front of the clay pigeon. Management needs to ensure that in its zeal to bring the company's innovations to market, it doesn't introduce its product or service offering before the market is ready. The old saying "If you build a better mousetrap the world will beat a path to your door" applies only if mice are present, if they bother people, and if potential customers know about your product. Morris Siegel, as president of Celestial Seasonings, recognized that his company had developed its line of flavored teas before the health boom had taken hold with the general public. Therefore, Siegel sought distribution through health food stores until grocery stores and supermarkets would carry his company's products.

Most companies commit all their resources to current markets. However, visionary executives carefully calibrate their company's investment of human and tangible resources in current markets. Peter Drucker observed that companies need to have a clear idea of what are yesterday's breadwinners, today's breadwinners, and tomorrow's breadwinners. Drucker also noted that management needs to discipline itself so that its attention and the company's resources are allocated accordingly. The visionary company makes a deliberate effort to re-deploy some of the revenues from the early growth stage of relatively new efforts to fund initiatives that will be tomorrow's breadwinners—and the breadwinners when tomorrow's breadwinners start to wane.

The Allocation of Management's Attention and Company's Resources depicted in Table 8-1 indicates the differences among the four types of companies. Laggard companies commit nearly all their resources to yesterday's breadwinners. Reactive companies divide their resources between the breadwinners of yesterday and

Table 8-1. The allocation of management's attention and company resources.

Type of Company / Breadwinners	Percentage of Management's Attention and Resources			
	Yesterday's	Today's	Tomorrow's	Tomorrow's Tomorrow
Laggard	100%	0%	0%	0%
Reactive	80%	20%	0%	0%
Proactive	0%	80%	20%	0%
Visionary	0%	70%	25%	5%

today. While proactive companies may commit some resources to exploring new opportunities, almost all their resources are allocated to today's breadwinners. Visionary companies may even go so far as to have guidelines that no more than 70 percent of their resources will be committed to current markets. Nearly 25 percent of the visionary company's resources may be committed to tomorrow's breadwinners. The final 5 percent of their resources may be invested in tomorrow's tomorrow!

VISIONARY COMPANIES UTILIZE THE INNOVATION PORTAL

The Celestial Seasons example brings up an interesting point. Visionary companies should seek out visionary customers. If the company wants to be the leading-edge provider of products or services, it should try to develop symbiotic relationships with leading-edge users. The Innovation-Adoption Interface Model in Figure 8-5 highlights that type of relationship. The innovation portal reflects the fertile situation that arises when a leading-edge provider interacts with a leading-edge user. The center of the model represents the ideal situation for executives who want to create their company's future.

Visionary companies succeed because they see themselves as customer problem solvers. By working closely with potential customers, visionary companies may be able to generate early sales. A number of visionary companies have formed alliances or joint ventures with other companies to capitalize on emerging opportunities and corresponding needs. By working closely with leading-edge users, visionary companies have the opportunity to experi-

Figure 8-5. The innovation-adoption interface model.

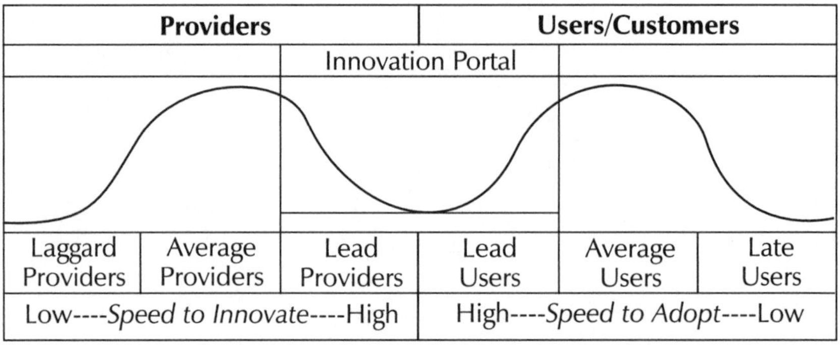

Providers			Users/Customers		
		Innovation Portal			
Laggard Providers	Average Providers	Lead Providers	Lead Users	Average Users	Late Users
Low----*Speed to Innovate*----High			High----*Speed to Adopt*----Low		

ment with real customers in real settings. This situation is superior to conventional marketing research techniques that merely ask potential customers about their intentions. Leading-edge users serve as a beta site for visionary companies. These users may also be in position to supply key resources, including funding for leading-edge providers.

CONCLUSION: TIMING MAKES A DIFFERENCE IN THE DANCE WITH ELEPHANTS

In the years ahead, growth and success will be contingent on whether your company is able to keep pace with rapidly changing markets. Your management team must refine its ability to anticipate emerging markets. It will also need to be more agile in the dance with elephants because the elephants are destined to be leaner and meaner. Few companies will be able to take the lead on every occasion. Things are changing so quickly that it is impossible to anticipate everything that may happen. In those instances, being a fast follower or having the ability to respond quickly may be the difference between thriving and merely surviving.

Companies that spend their time celebrating their current successes will not notice the signs that their markets are starting to erode. To create a forward-focused company, you need to start looking for growth opportunities earlier than other companies do. Your company must adopt corpreneurial strategies by scanning the environment, monitoring market trends, anticipating emerging opportunities, and reallocating resources from current product or service offerings to develop future product or service offerings.

> *"Don't attempt to ride a dead horse in hopes that it will come to life again."*[6]
>
> —Jon Vincent, president of JTV Business and Management Consultants

NOTES

Portions of the material in this chapter originally appeared in the article "Preventing the Here Today, Gone Tomorrow New Venture Syndrome" by the author in *Business Forum*, Summer 1991, pp. 18–22. Used with permission of California State University–Los Angeles.

1. Craig R. Hickman and Michael A. Silva, *Creating Excellence* (New York: New American Library, 1984), p. 176.
2. Theodore Levitt, "Marketing Myopia," *Harvard Business Review*, July–August 1960, p. 26.
3. Stephen C. Harper, *The McGraw-Hill Guide to Managing Growth in Your Emerging Business* (New York: McGraw-Hill, 1994) p. 71.
4. Ibid.
5. James Collins and Jerry Porras, "Organizational Vision and Visionary Organizations," *California Management Reveiw*, Fall 1991, p. 38.
6. Harper, p. 70.

Part III

Strategic Management: The Long-Term Backwards Path to the Future

Strategic management encourages executives to adopt a long-term "backwards" perspective. This approach is quite different from the short-term forward incremental approach. When visionary executives are asked the question, "How do you climb a mountain?" They respond, "From the top down." They know that by mentally envisioning what it would be like to stand on the summit, they can see the best path for climbing the mountain. If they were to climb the mountain from where they currently stand, it would limit them to the path immediately in front of them.

Visionary executives realize that there may be many paths to the summit, and that the best path may not be the easiest, shortest, or even the one they are currently on. With the long-term backwards approach, executives identify where they want the company to be in five to seven years. Then, they work backwards from that date by asking, "If we want to be there in the year 20XY, where will we need to be in the year prior to 20XY?" The process of identifying each preceding year's prerequisite position is calculated until it is brought back to the present time.

The long-term backwards approach has four distinct advantages. First, it recognizes that five to seven years following an incremental approach may lead to a completely different, and probably less advantageous, position. It takes time to identify, cultivate, and capitalize on emerging opportunities. The short-term forward incremental approach can miss emerging opportunities altogether. Second, when executives use the long-term backwards approach, they often realize they are already at least two years behind schedule. Their timetable may indicate a seven-year critical path to achieve the desired five-year strategic position. This fosters a sense of urgency and a bias for action to initiate plans that might otherwise be postponed or never implemented. Third, this perspective unleashes the minds of people throughout the company to find innovative ways to compress the critical path to meet the desired date of arrival. Fourth, it encourages executives to consider entering new markets and emerging industries instead of treading water in mature markets and declining industries.

Fred DeLuca started Subway in 1965 at the age of seventeen to finance his college education. His business plan projected thirty-two stores within ten years. When he and his partner realized that they would not be able to finance their expansion, they redirected their efforts to franchising their business. In 1988, Fred DeLuca's vision for Subway was to have five thousand franchise outlets by 1994, which meant developing between two and three locations per day! This ambitious vision became a driving force for Subway. It had established more than five thousand units by 1990, and by 2000 Subway had more than fourteen thousand units in seventy-five countries. Fred DeLuca's vision and the wherewithal to make it a reality have put Subway in a position to be the largest fast-food franchise in the world.

Strategic management has the following five important steps: thinking, learning, positioning, planning, and monitoring and controlling. The first three steps are the crux of the strategic management process. They emphasize the need for executives to extend their time horizons and to recognize the contextual nature of planning. Step four represents the generally accepted long-range planning process. Step five looks like the traditional approach to controlling; however, strategic controlling is more future-oriented than the traditional rearview mirror approach used by most organizations.

THE STRATEGIC MANAGEMENT PROCESS

Thinking → Learning → Positioning → Planning → Monitoring and Controlling

Step One—Strategic Thinking

- Accepting the need for strategic thinking
- Undertaking strategic inquiries
- Developing contingency scenarios

Step Two—Strategic Learning

- Gaining strategic insights
- Clarifying strategic opportunities and threats
- Identifying possible strategic positions

Step Three—Strategic Positioning

- Creating a unified corporate vision
- Selecting the target strategic position
- Identifying strategic initiatives

Step Four—Strategic Planning

- Formulating the corporate strategy, including comprehensive long-term plans and specific performance goals
- Ensuring that the corporate strategy and all management systems support the corporate vision and long-range plan
- Managing the implementation of the plan

Step Five—Strategic Monitoring and Controlling

- Checking the assumptions that served as the basis for the plan
- Monitoring the effectiveness of the plan and making appropriate changes
- Reviewing the effectiveness of the plan and the planning process

The strategic management process indicates that formulating the long-range plan must be preceded by strategic thinking, creating a corporate vision, and selecting the company's desired future position. It is important to note that strategic management does not attempt to replace long-range planning but to improve it. Strategic management is a broader and more encompassing umbrella. The first three steps indicate numerous areas where strategic planning may encounter problems. Delineating the first three steps also indicates the need for different time horizons, perspectives, mental and technical skills, types of information, and reporting requirements.

The first three steps have not received much attention from top executives. They are a bit fuzzy to most executives because they cannot be placed in mathematical models to produce the single best answer. Most executives feel comfortable around the last two steps because they are more tangible and can be handled in a very logical manner. The last two steps represent the nuts and bolts or the "engineering" side of managing a company, while the first three steps of the strategic management process represent the "imagineering" side of leading a company.

The following chapters profile the first, second, third, and fifth steps of the strategic management process. Strategic planning is not covered because it is fairly mechanical and has received considerable attention in other books. This book has adopted a value-added approach and directs its attention toward the areas of change leadership, which are more timely and have not received as much attention as long-range planning.

9
Strategic Thinking

"A danger foreseen is half avoided."
—Thomas Fuller, M.D.,
eighteenth-century English physician
and writer

It has been said that companies that fail to prepare for the future will have no future. Chapter 8 profiled laggard, reactive, proactive, and visionary companies. In a sense, companies can be categorized as:

- Those that live in the past and reminisce about the good old days
- Those that live in the present and make the most of it
- Those that prepare for the future and position themselves for different times
- Those that create their future by changing the possibilities, probabilities, payoffs, and states of nature

The last type of company has a vision for what it wants to be and develops a corresponding strategy and culture to make that vision a reality.

The classic question, "Quo vadis? Where do we go from here?" challenges even the best executives. There was a time when companies could merely do more of the same. Companies that continue a linear-incremental strategy today need to recognize they may have chosen a self-destruct strategy.

Creating a forward-focused company involves more than developing a long-term plan. Planning for most companies resembles the process of loading data into an electronic spreadsheet. When all the software template's questions are answered, you merely push the print key and the printer pumps out a slick long-term plan. Executives need to be more than planners; they need to be deeply involved in *thinking* about what the future may hold and what they can do to create their company's future.

STEP ONE: ACCEPTING THE NEED FOR STRATEGIC THINKING

Strategic thinking is perhaps the most crucial step in the strategic management process. It can be characterized as the process whereby executives are encouraged to extend their time horizons beyond the typical three- to five-year planning cycle. Through strategic thinking, executives contemplate the world at least twice as far into the future as their long-range plan could reach.

Most executives are quick to exclaim, "Things are changing so quickly that you cannot think that far ahead." Executives need to spend more time thinking about and preparing for the future because the rate and magnitude of change are increasing each day. Executives who fail to embrace strategic thinking are destined to operate from a reactive fire-fighting stance. Their reactivity will impede their ability to identify, cultivate, and capitalize on emerging opportunities.

If times were stable and conditions certain, then life would be fairly predictable. Under these circumstances, there would be little need for strategic thinking, long-term planning, risk taking, or fostering innovation.

Extending One's Mental Time Horizon

The higher the position in the organization, the more the job involves conceptual rather than technical matters, a long-term rather than a short-term time horizon, and issues about what type of business the company should be rather than how the company should do business. Breakthrough leaders see the forest without getting lost in the trees.

Companies that are run by people who practice ostrich management—that is, burying their heads in the sand in response to the accelerating rate of change—are destined to falter because they will be left behind in the marketplace. For example, Montgomery Ward and other retail chains went out of business because they were not in sync with the marketplace. Strategic thinking usually produces anxiety for people who are accustomed to living in the present and reminiscing about the so-called good old days. James Adams, author of *The Care and Feeding of Ideas*, noted, "Strategic thinking is not automatic. It is a divergence from business as usual and is not easy, since it causes us to confront the large uncertainties associated with the future."[1] Strategic thinking means dealing more with intangible rather than tangible factors, as well as dealing with qualitative rather than quantitative variables. Adams observed that it requires a broad, fresh database.[2] Craig Hickman and Michael Silva, authors of *Creating Excellence*, noted that vision can be viewed as "a mental journey from the known to the unknown, creating the future from a montage of current facts, hopes, dreams, and opportunities."[3]

Strategic thinking encourages executives to ponder what the world may be like in ten to twenty years. Most executives express pride in how professional, systematic, and rational they are when conducting corporate affairs. Executives must recognize management will be an art as long as there are situational factors that cannot be quantified. In a world moving toward quantification, most business decisions include qualitative and relatively intangible factors that continue to elude even the most sophisticated mathematical models.

How Long Is Long Term?

The whole issue of strategic thinking raises the question, What is the difference between short term and long term? Short term in one industry may be long term in another. For example, in the software industry, three years may be a long-term time horizon. Software packages may become out-of-date in only a few months. In the biotechnology field, long term may be a five- to seven-year time horizon because of the time it takes to get FDA approval.

Short term means basically dealing with the here and now, where few things can be changed. In the short term, executives usually try to make the most out of the products, processes, personnel, customers, suppliers, technology, capital, and equipment they currently have at their disposal.

Operational matters tend to dominate the short-term time horizon for most executives. Although executives may have good intentions about thinking strategically, they often fall prey to the tyranny of the urgent. Instead of investing their time in thinking about the future, daily emergencies, events, and deadlines divert their attention away from creating a forward-focused company. Thinking about the future is frequently put off until a vague "someday."

Medium term means that certain resources can be substituted, such as machines for labor, products modified, new skills developed, and new ways of doing things initiated. Long term opens the door to all sorts of possibilities. In the long term, everything can be changed. The company can change its products, locations, and processes. It can find new things to do, including moving into emerging industries.

A long-term perspective encourages executives to run various future scenarios, focus on emerging opportunities, and identify possible strategic positions. When executives recognize that there is no future in the status quo and are willing to slough off yesterday, they can direct their attention toward envisioning what the company should become.

Strategic thinking fosters a whole new mentality. If you were to ask your staff to develop a completely new product or a revolutionary way to provide a service and to have it ready within the next thirty days, they would say that it can't be done. However, if you encourage them to find a way to meet the needs of an emerging market that the company may enter three years from now, their response may be far more enthusiastic. They may even say that they can have it ready before then!

When people recognize there is limited value in continuing the status quo or utilizing an incremental approach for the next three to five years, they are more willing to direct their attention toward envisioning what the company should become rather than what it is. The long-term backwards approach, which starts with the projection of where the company wants to be at a future date, facilitates an open-mindedness that is rarely found in companies that have a short- or medium-term horizon. Executives who have a long-term perspective recognize that almost anything is possible. Emerging opportunities can be harvested and formidable obstacles can be overcome if they have sufficient lead time.

Developing a "Kaleidoscopic" Perspective

Executives need to adopt a "kaleidoscopic" perspective. A kaleidoscope is a fascinating apparatus because its image changes every time you turn its cylinder. Executives with a kaleidoscopic perspective make a deliberate effort to look at situations from numerous vantage points. Each vantage point provides new images and insights. Executives who have adopted a kaleidoscopic perspective do mental pirouettes on an ongoing basis. They try to see the ever-changing world from a 360-degree perspective. Most people direct their attention to the world directly in front of them. When they look straight at a situation, their perceptual field is limited to about 150 degrees of the full 360-degree field.

Strategic thinking encourages executives to rip off the mental blinders that have limited their perceptual fields to their company, industry, country, training, and experiences. Strategic thinking also encourages executives to surround themselves with people who have different backgrounds and perspectives. The more diverse the executive team, the broader the perceptual field.

The liberally educated and broadly experienced executive is best suited for strategic thinking and developing a kaleidoscopic perspective. Technical training and in-depth operational knowledge of one industry may have helped managers move up the corporate hierarchy, but the narrowness of their functional perspective and industry background undermine their propensity to think strategically and their mental dexterity. Rosabeth Moss Kanter observed, "Purely technical experts are often unable to put all the pieces together to manage a business in a demanding, rapidly changing environment; Renaissance people are required."[4] Even the much-sought-after engineer with an MBA will need to undergo an extensive mental-broadening process to lead a company in the years ahead.

The ability to distill tangible and intangible factors as well as to see the forest without getting lost in the trees are marks of the visionary leader. Strategic thinking is enhanced when executives interact with people from various walks of life, read mentally enriching and thought-provoking literature, travel to new and different places, study different cultures, and interact with the young people who will be at the cutting edge as consumers and leaders in the decades to come.

Kaleidoscopic thinking reduces the likelihood of the company being blindsided. Yet it is not possible to see everything around us. Executives may need to adopt one of the techniques used by the Secret Service. Its field agents use what they call splatter vision when they scan a crowd. They try to avoid looking for specific objects and specific spots. Instead, they look at the whole field for things that don't fit in, for exceptions, for breaks in patterns, and for anomalies. This technique may have had its roots in World War II. Botanists taught soldiers to look for inappropriate formations in the branches of trees as a way to detect enemy snipers.

By scanning the world around them, executives may be able to identify factors or forces that could blindside them. If the factor or force can be transformed into an opportunity, then seeing it early may enable the company to capitalize on it. If the factor or force has the potential to have a detrimental effect on the company, then the lead time provided by having a kaleidoscopic perspective may enable the company to brace itself for the impact in order to minimize its adverse effects, or to avoid it altogether.

STEP TWO: UNDERTAKING STRATEGIC INQUIRIES

Extending one's time horizon and broadening one's perceptual field are essential components of strategic thinking. Even though strategic thinking may not provide a clear picture of what the future may hold, it provides a foundation for making strategic inquiries. While strategic thinking is intended to encourage executives to recognize the importance of having a long-term horizon and a broader perceptual field, undertaking strategic inquiries encourages executives to investigate what the future may hold.

During periods of rapid change, extending one's time horizon encourages executives to contemplate what may be beyond the horizon. There are no crystal balls available for predicting the future, but extending one's time horizon enables executives to pierce the fog that frustrates them when they attempt to develop long-range plans during turbulent times. Harold Fearon, Bill Ruch, Bill Reif, and Bill Werther, while professors of management at Arizona State University, noted, "While no one can foresee the future with complete accuracy, the seeds of future change already have been planted and broad estimates of the direction and extent of change—and recommendations for the future—can be made."[5]

Step two of the strategic management process recognizes that you cannot have the right answers unless you ask the right questions. Undertaking strategic inquiries plays an integral role in coming up with the right answers. Step two begins with key factor analysis. Executives need to step back and identify the factors and forces that could have a dramatic effect on the company's future. Pareto's 80/20 rule may need to be applied here. It would be nearly impossible for the company to monitor every factor of force. Executives need to identify the few factors and forces that could make the biggest difference.

Environmental scanning is then done to determine whether any of these factors or forces appear on the company's radar screen. Executives then run scenarios to identify how the future may unfold for the key factors. Scenarios should be run for various possible situations. If the company's future will be affected by housing starts, then a number of scenarios may need to be run for various levels of new house construction. If the company's future will be affected by the price of a raw material, then a number of scenarios may need to be run for various levels of availability for that raw material. Scenarios frequently provide insights about opportunities. They also provide insights about potential threats and where the company might be vulnerable.

Strategic insights serve as the basis for developing strategic initiatives to position the company to capitalize on opportunities and eliminate vulnerabilities. Contingency plans should be developed at this time to address beneficial or detrimental situations that may arise. Preparation of contingency plans at this stage will enable the company to make quick adjustments. Companies that sense performance deviations early on and are able to make adjustments in real time will gain valuable ground over companies that are still trying to figure out what went wrong. Monitoring ongoing performance is critical because awareness precedes change.

ENVIRONMENTAL SCANNING GIVES THE COMPANY ESSENTIAL LEAD TIME

Strategic thinking encourages executives to ponder what the future may hold and to see changes at the earliest possible moment. Karl Albrecht has observed, however, that many organizations are out of touch with the wider world. He noted, "Their executives may be so preoccupied with near-term problems . . . these organizations tend to be the sitting ducks that take the worst punishment when a shock wave hits."[6] Ron Zemke, coauthor of *Delivering Knock Your Socks Off Service*, noted that the leaders of the future need to be shock-wave riders. They must be able to see the long waves coming and position their figurative surfboards above those waves. He believes that the more skillful executives will benefit from the rising waves by capitalizing on their movement, while those who fail to see the waves coming, or fail to react appropriately or quickly enough, may suffer serious losses in competitive position and, in some cases, may not even survive.[7]

Karl Albrecht's latest book, *Corporate Radar,* described how the Pony Express declared bankruptcy forty-eight hours after the last link was completed in the transcontinental telegraph system across the United States. The term *killer application* may not have been used back then, but the telegraph certainly killed the Pony Express. Albrecht also noted that Irving Thalberg, business adviser to movie producer Louis B. Mayer, told his client, "No Civil War picture has ever made a nickel." Following Thalberg's advice, Mayer passed up *Gone with the Wind*.[8] The inability to sense changes in the market and a competitor's ability to change the rules of the game have left a number of companies wondering what hit them.

R.M. Narchal, K. Kittappa, and P. Bhattachary, as directors of planning for the National Productivity Council in India, claimed that an environmental-scanning system can be viewed as "a set of radars to monitor important events in the environment which may create opportunities or threats for the organization. These events tend to be visible in the environment in the form of weak signals and generate early warnings for organizations."[9] Environmental scanning reduces the likelihood the company will be blindsided by large and small shock waves. Albrecht noted that environmental scanning is at its best when it identifies the shock waves we must ride, the major trends we can exploit, and the key events we must manage.[10]

Executives need to conduct an environmental audit before they begin the environmental-scanning process. The environmental audit identifies major factors and forces that may affect both the overall environment and the company in the future. The list may include ten to twenty factors. These factors may be sociological, economic, technological, legal, international, political, or competitive in nature. The Quick Environmental Scanning Technique, known as QUEST, offers a systematic way for executives to identify and contemplate future environmental factors that may have critical implications for the strategic positioning of the company. QUEST is a multistep process that enables executives to gain insights into what the future may hold. It is described briefly in Chapter 10. A more detailed description of QUEST can be found in the book *Leaders* by Warren Bennis and Burt Nanus.

Environmental scans need to be run frequently to monitor the state of key factors. The frequency of the scans is contingent on the speed of change, the potential magnitude of the change, and how long it will take the company to adjust to the change in one or more of the key factors. Author Regis McKenna believes that the accelerating rate of change requires executives to keep track of all forces affecting the company in real time. McKenna believes the best companies learn to gauge what they should do next by the smallest shift in the wind.[11] It is for this reason that executives need to be certain that they are monitoring the factors that are at the leading edge of change. Too often, executives get caught up in monitoring things that are not the drivers of success, or they monitor factors that lag behind the wall of real change.

Some organizations have established environmental intelligence units that employ people whose only job is to read the signals and alert leaders about their implications.[12] A number of companies now use the latest information technology and real-time databases to assist in the environmental-scanning process. Wayne Burkan, author of *Wide-Angle Vision*, noted, "One of the nice things about computers is that they are never bored. If you create systems that regularly audit your leading indicators, the computer will do the job of scanning the environment. When a variation occurs, your computer can notify you of what has changed.[13]

STEP THREE: DEVELOPING CONTINGENCY SCENARIOS

Environmental scanning, by itself, is not sufficient to keep the company from being blindsided. When IBM was enjoying market dominance in the 1960s, the sign "THINK" appeared in its corporate offices. It became clear in the two decades that followed for IBM that *unfocused* thought would produce little gain. If you are not thinking about the issues that have the potential to drive the economy, your industry, and your markets, then thinking will be as fruitful as taking flippers into the desert. The lack of focus also applies to environmental scanning. Scanning the horizon is fruitful only when there is a clear sense of what one is looking for. Without a set of parameters to look for on the radar screen, scanning is like turning on a light and then leaving the room.

Strategic management encourages executives to run various scenarios about what the future may hold. Paul Schoemaker, as chairman of Decision Strategies International, Inc., defined scenario planning as "a disciplined method for imagining possible futures that companies have applied to a range of issues."[14] Strategic management relies more on scenario building than on traditional forecasting techniques. Forecasts often have limited value because they tend to be extrapolations from the past. Peter Drucker noted, "In turbulent times, managers cannot assume that tomorrow will be an extension of today."[15]

Most forecasts concentrate on quantitative data. According to Pierre Wack, author of *Scenarios: Uncharted Waters Ahead*, "Sooner or later forecasts will fail where they are needed the most: in anticipating major shifts in the business environment that make whole strategies obsolete."[16] Scenarios try to identify factors that are new and different as well as qualitative in nature. Scenarios are particularly useful in times of ambiguity and discontinuity. By running "What if . . . ?" scenarios, executives direct their thinking toward identifying and exploring a whole range of possibilities.

While it is natural for executives to plan for the most likely event, scenarios encourage executives to prepare for the unexpected and to think the unthinkable. Schoemaker noted that scenario planning "tries to capture the new states that will develop after major shocks or deviations in key variables . . . [scenario planning] attempts to capture the richness and range of possibilities, stimulating decision makers to consider changes they would otherwise ignore . . . above all, scenarios are aimed at challenging the prevailing mindset."[17] He further noted, "Scenario planning requires intellectual courage to reveal evidence that does not fit our current conceptual maps, especially when it threatens our very existence."[18]

Peter Senge, author of *The Dance of Change*, noted that scenarios "force managers to consider how they would manage under different alternative paths into the future. This offsets the tendency for managers to implicitly assume a single future."[19] The use of scenarios in the 1970s forced Shell Oil's managers to realize their assumption that "the oil business would continue as usual" was based on outdated assumptions about the nature of global geopolitics and the oil industry.[20]

Environmental scanning, key factor monitoring, and scenario planning are essential if the company is to become aware of emerging opportunities and threats at the earliest possible moment. The importance of timing, especially having lead time over current and future competitors, cannot be overemphasized. The ability to be at the right place at the right time with the right capabilities can give the company a formidable competitive advantage.

The ability to generate good ideas has always been an important part of corporate strategy. In the years ahead, having sufficient lead time to capitalize on emerging opportunities will be an essential part of visionary leadership. As Kanter indicated, "Staying ahead of change means anticipating the new actions that external events will eventually require and taking them early, before others, before being forced, while there is still time to exercise choice about how and what—and time to influence, shape, or redirect the external events themselves."[21] Executives who have the vision to see things that others don't see, who can think thoughts that others can't think, and who can do things that others can't even dream of doing are destined to lead their companies where no companies have gone before.

Scenario building enables executives to identify various situations that could occur. It may put the company in a position to harvest lucrative opportunities that are not visible to the untrained eye. It may also keep the company from being blindsided. Most executives consider their jobs to be coming up with the answers to various questions. Visionary leaders illustrate the benefits of operating from an anticipatory stance. They go two steps beyond merely coming up with the answers. Visionary leaders realize that higher positions in management involve being able to identify the questions that will need to be answered in the years ahead. They also know that success comes to those who have the answers before anyone else is even aware of the questions.

CONCLUSION: EMBRACE THE FUTURE

As soon as you recognize that change is a fact of corporate life, you will be in a position to develop a corporate culture and commensurate strategy where change is a way of life. The more you think about the future, the more comfortable you will feel about it and the challenges that it will bring. After a short time, strategic thinking will become second nature.

> *"The horizon leans forward, offering you space to place new steps of change."*
> —Maya Angelou, American poet and writer

NOTES

1. James L. Adams, *The Care and Feeding of Ideas* (Reading, Mass.: Addison-Wesley, 1986), p. 2.
2. Ibid., p. 205.
3. Craig R. Hickman and Michael A. Silver, *Creating Excellence* (New York: New American Library, 1984), p. 32.
4. Rosabeth Moss Kanter, *The Change Masters* (New York: Simon & Schuster, 1983), p. 369.
5. Harold Fearon, William Reif, William Ruch, and William Werther, "Management and the Year 2000," *Arizona Business,* April 1981, p. 3.
6. Karl Albrecht, *The Northbound Train* (New York: AMACOM, 1994), p. 72.

7. Ibid., p. 7.
8. Karl Albrecht, *Corporate Radar* (New York: AMACOM, 2000), p. ix.
9. R. M. Narchal, K. Kittappa, and P. Bhattacharya, "An Environmental Scanning System for Business Planning," *Long-Range Planning,* December 1987, p. 97.
10. Ibid., p. 69.
11. Regis McKenna, "Real Time," *Inc.,* September 1997, p. 90.
12. Ibid., p. 72.
13. Wayne C. Burkan, "Developing Your Wide Angle Vision: Skills for Anticipating the Future," *The Futurist,* 1998, p. 38.
14. Paul J. H. Schoemaker, "Scenario Planning: A Tool for Strategic Thinking," *Sloan Management Review,* Winter 1995, p. 25.
15. Peter F. Drucker, *Managing in Turbulent Times* (New York: Harper & Row, 1980), p. 41.
16. Pierre Wack, "Scenarios: Uncharted Waters Ahead," *Harvard Business Review,* September–October 1985, p. 73.
17. Schoemaker, p. 27.
18. Ibid., p. 38.
19. Peter M. Senge, "Mental Models," *Planning Review,* April 1992, p. 8.
20. Ibid., p. 7.
21. Kanter, p. 64.

10

Strategic Learning

"In times of rapid change, the learners will inherit the future."[1]
—Eric Hoffer, author of *The Ordeal of Change*

S trategic learning incorporates the three *I*s of anticipatory management. It encourages executives to do strategic *i*nquiries that lead to strategic *i*nsights that serve as the basis for launching strategic *i*nitiatives. Strategic learning helps top management clarify strategic opportunities and threats that may be looming over the horizon. The first two *I*s help executives to identify possible strategic positions for the company that may enable it to gain temporary legal monopolies.

The need for the company to be a learning organization was addressed in Chapter 3. This chapter focuses on the need to gain insights that could affect the overall nature and success of the company over the next five to ten years. Strategic learning provides the basis for developing a shared and compelling vision for what the company should be in the years ahead. The company's vision must be set in the context of what the future may hold. Strategic learning helps executives gain insights into possible futures. These insights help management identify and evaluate various strategic positions for the company.

GAINING STRATEGIC INSIGHTS

Insights are like an epiphany. They are a sudden realization about the nature of things. When you extend your time horizon, possibilities may become certainties. For example, when electric power companies extended their time horizons, they realized there would come a time when the Nuclear Regulatory Commission would not recertify the nuclear plants. Years ago, most power company executives were not concerned about the recertification of the plants because that situation was so far into the future. The realization by today's executives that there will come a time in the not-too-distant future when the nuclear plants may be shut down has forced them to explore alternative means for providing electricity.

Strategic learning ties in directly with Gary Hamel and C. K. Prahalad's concept of industry foresight. Strategic insights into what the future may hold can serve as the basis for gaining industry foresight. When you have an idea about what might be, you can begin contemplating the corresponding set of factors and forces that will accompany the corresponding changes. Hamel and Prahalad note that there is more to industry foresight than merely gaining one or two insights: "Industry foresight is based on deep insights into trends in technology, demographics, regulations, and lifestyles, which can be harnessed to rewrite industry rules and create new competitive space."[2] Foresight can give a company an edge. Companies that see the future first will have a head start over their competitors, which can provide valuable lead time for the development of products, services, and processes that may put the company at the leading edge.

Creating a forward-focused company would be easy if the future was perfectly clear or merely an extension of the present. Unfortunately, the future will be the result of almost an infinite number of factors and forces interacting with one another. The ever-accelerating rate of change blurs our vision to the point that it is difficult to even focus on the present. The inevitable incidence of discontinuities in the years ahead compounds the challenges associated with trying to gain foresight. While crystal-clear clarity into what the future may hold is not possible, insights may be gained if you look at the future from the correct perspective.

Foreseeing future events is very difficult. It is even more difficult to foresee the exact dates for those events. Trying to foresee today who will be the first female president of the United States, as well as the year she will take office, would be a challenge. Instead, strategic learning encourages you to direct your attention to patterns of forces and factors that could produce the election of the first female president. The same applies to foreseeing the development of a vaccine to prevent AIDS or the commercialization of battery-powered automobiles. Trying to foresee the exact formulation and date would be a formidable challenge. Instead, attention should be directed toward the circumstances that would need to exist for the vaccine to be developed. It is not as critical to know which company will actually introduce the battery-operated car or the quarter during which it will hit the market. It is more important to foresee which companies may be positioned to introduce the car and to be within a year of when it will be introduced on a large scale.

Strategic learning goes well beyond gut feelings about what the future may hold. It is a deliberate attempt to see the possibilities—and to see the future before others see it. Pattern recognition can play an instrumental role in gaining strategic insights and developing industry foresight. The classic question, "What's missing in this picture?" can play a valuable role in strategic learning. Strategic learning looks for gaps that may occur as a result of trends. These gaps may come from the aging of the population or the increase in the Hispanic population in the United States. The gaps may also come from the accelerating speed and power of computers or the ability of software to do what has not been possible before.

Companies that see the potential for gaps may be in a position to capitalize on the opportunities that will come with them. Gaps can also occur within the company. Trends and innovations in telecommunications and changing lifestyles will almost certainly create gaps between how business is being conducted and how it will need to be conducted. The flip side of the "What's missing in this picture?" question also needs to be part of the strategic learning process. Executives also need to ask, "What's in the picture that shouldn't be in the picture?" Executives should also ponder what will no longer be needed. Technological breakthroughs and changing psychographics may create situations where what is commonplace today may be obsolete tomorrow. In a world of innovation, creative destruction, and cannibalization most products, services, processes skills, and facilities will have an even shorter shelf life.

SCENARIOS REVEAL WHAT THE FUTURE MAY HOLD

Chapter 9 concluded with the need to run scenarios. This chapter highlights how scenarios can provide insights that could determine the company's vision and overall strategy. Scenarios explore possible futures and the impact they could have on the company. Scenarios may also provide insights into what could happen with various decisions made by the company. Liam Fahey and Robert M. Randall, editors of *Learning from the Future: Competitive Foresight Scenarios,* view scenarios as "flight simulations to imaginative destinations to test real decisions."[3]

By asking "What if . . . ?" questions and formulating a list of possible scenarios, executives may gain insights into what may be over the horizon. In many cases, executives will recognize certain events or situations are no longer in the "whether or not" category. As you extend your time horizon and consider the possibilities, certain events or situations are almost inevitable. If events or situations are almost certain to happen, executives need to focus their attention on when they are likely to happen, what will be the leading indicators that precede them, and how they can position their companies to benefit from them. The following examples illustrate how running scenarios may provide insights into what the future may hold:

Example #1—A Dying Market Segment

One day, the managing partner of a medium-size engineering company became concerned about the diminishing number of projects that were coming up for bid. He scheduled a retreat for top management to discuss his observation. A consultant served as the facilitator to assist them in breaking away from the present and gaining foresight into the future. The management team looked at the future of their industry and concluded that it was going to wane sooner than they originally had thought. The company had been very successful in designing a specific type of structure for governments throughout the world. Even management's best-case scenario indicated that within five years, few governments would need any more of these structures built. This insight prompted management to realize that if it didn't change its business, it would go bankrupt in only a few years.

Management's insight that its profitable business was about to die was like being hit by a truck. However, it served as the awareness stage that must precede change. Fortunately, management recognized its precarious position early enough to do something about it. It spent the next six months identifying emerging opportunities and reviewing the company's strengths and competencies. Management identified one particular opportunity that had the potential, within ten years, to be as lucrative as its current market had been, but only if the company could be positioned to meet the emerging market's needs. This lead time gave the company a head start over other engineering companies that had not recognized the emerging opportunity.

Within three years, everyone in the company had gone through an extensive training program so they would possess the answers to the questions their "new" clients would ask. As noted earlier, when you have the answers before any one else even knows the questions, you are destined to be ahead of your competition. This example brings up a line from the movie, *The Carpetbaggers*. When the banker asks the entrepreneur how can he get into plastics when he doesn't know anything about plastics, the entrepreneur responds, "I'll be on the first ship to Germany to learn all there is to know about plastics." The entrepreneur wanted to know more about plastics than anyone else in the United States!

Example #2—A Saturated Market

A young sales manager for a company that had a number of retail outlets in the Southeast was concerned that the CEO and vice president of marketing had been taking the market for granted. He believed the market was becoming saturated with competition and that a predatory price war would soon follow. He was frustrated because the marketing vice president believed everything was fine. The vice president pointed to the company's record sales and profits as proof. The young sales manager sought the advice of a friend who was a consultant. The consultant advised him to stop wasting his time trying to convince his boss of the need to change. The consultant cited the words of the famous trumpet player Louis Armstrong, "There are people who don't know and you just can't tell them."

The consultant suggested a different strategy for initiating change. He encouraged his friend to analyze the profit potential, distribution sites, and capital requirements for other geographic markets. The consultant told his friend to be patient; if his friend's prognosis was correct, then there would come a time when his efforts would pay off. Within the year, the CEO frantically called a meeting to inform everyone that while the company's sales had dropped 10 percent as a result of price competition, its profits had disappeared.

The CEO looked around the room and asked if anyone had any ideas about how to turn the situation around. The sales manager followed the consultant's advice and did not automatically volunteer his advice. When it was clear that no one—especially the vice president of marketing—had any ideas, the sales manager stated, "If I could have five minutes of your time, I would like to brief you on . . ." The sales manager then distributed copies of his proposal to enter three different geographic markets that had the potential to restore the company's profitability. A few days after the meeting, he became the vice president of marketing.

SCENARIOS CAN PROVIDE A WAKE-UP CALL

The sooner you realize or accept that something is inevitable, the sooner you can deal constructively with it. As soon as you recognize that "never" *will* happen and that "someday" could be *tomorrow*, the sooner you will stop putting off until tomorrow what should be addressed today!

The funeral business provides an interesting example of how strategic inquiries may provide interesting insights and foresight. A number of owners of funeral businesses met to look into the future of their industry so they could better position their companies to benefit from changes that might be on the horizon. The group was composed of people who had founded their business decades ago, sons and daughters who were second- and third-generation owners, professional managers who had been brought in by the owners to run their companies, as well as consultants and suppliers to funeral businesses. The group spent its time identifying factors and forces that could shape the funeral industry. It highlighted the trend toward consolidation, the likelihood of closer government scrutiny, changing demographics and psychographics, and the impact of the economy on the need for their services.

The group made every effort to extend its mental time horizon beyond the next two or three years. It also tried to incorporate kaleidoscopic thinking so that it could see their industry and the evolving world around it from various vantage points as well as through the eyes of the industry's various stakeholders. The group's inquiries produced a number of insights, with the first one being the most noteworthy. The group concluded that the industry would undergo more dramatic changes in the coming decade than it had experienced in the last two decades. One of the most noteworthy insights was that its industry was not immune from the do-it-yourself trend that was being experienced in various industries.

The do-it-yourself concept ranged from the bereaved family contracting with various service providers separately, rather than going through a funeral home to coordinate the whole process, all the way to the family or friends bypassing the various service providers altogether and burying the deceased by themselves at a place of their choosing—including their own property. When the facilitator proposed running the do-it-yourself scenario, a number of people balked at such a preposterous idea. A few people who had been in the funeral business for a long time quickly exclaimed, "There's no way that people in this country would do such a thing!" Yet it took only a few moments before another group in the room supported the merit of running such a scenario. They exclaimed, "The people out West have been using the do-it-yourself approach to funeral services for over a century!"

The discussion of this trend continued for some time, with numerous points of view being expressed. When the dust settled, most of the group acknowledged that enough people are already doing it and are asking if the trend can be monitored more closely for the group. The group also recognized it would need to explore ways to benefit from the trend rather than be victims of it.

The group developed a list of factors and forces that could affect its businesses in the years ahead. The trend toward cremation was also cited as an area that needed to be monitored closely. The three most noteworthy benefits of the session were that the participants extended their mental time horizons, they did not get caught up in trying to deny the potential for major change, and they started thinking about what they could do differently to position their companies to ride the waves of change rather than have the waves of change crash over them.

QUEST FOR INSIGHTS

The Quick Environmental Scanning Technique (QUEST), presented by Warren Bennis and Burt Nanus in their book *Leaders*, demonstrates the value of running scenarios. They claim that QUEST "permits leaders, managers, and planners in an organization to share views about future external environments that have critical implications for the organization's positioning."[4] This approach is based on the logic used in brainstorming. If you bring together people with different perceptions and create an environment where participants can build on each other's ideas, new insights and ideas may emerge.

With QUEST, executives identify various possible situations such as changes in government regulations, major technological breakthroughs, dramatic shifts in consumer demand, a return to double-digit inflation, or the loss of a key raw material. Bennis and Nanus profiled how an airline ran scenarios to gain insights into what the future may hold. The factors included a surge in airline terrorism, a merger between two major airlines, and a declaration that a major type of aircraft is unsafe.[5] In his book *Visionary Leadership*, Burt Nanus illustrated how a company that makes pet food can use environmental scanning to identify key factors that have the potential to have a significant impact on the company's future.

Retail and service companies can also benefit from running scenarios involving changing economic conditions, the entrance of a major chain or franchise in one's geographic area, the enactment of stiff government regulation, or the impact of a major technological breakthrough. For example, a jewelry chain should run scenarios involving each of the following situations:

- The imposition of a 20 percent luxury tax
- A shift in values away from conspicuous consumption
- A period of sustained economic growth
- The development of a gold substitute
- A massive influx of diamonds from Russia
- A major recession
- A major military call-up of troops in its target markets
- General acceptance of faux jewelry

- Acceptance by males to wear more jewelry
- The merger of two major competitors
- An established Internet company entering the market with speed, price, and selection advantages

While most of these changes may not occur overnight or at all, one or more of them could happen individually or together within a few years. Once the list of key factors, events, or trends has been generated, scenarios can be constructed to reflect a string or cluster of events that could unfold over a period of time.

The major strength of using QUEST lies in the development of a cross-impact matrix, which provides a vehicle for looking at the interrelatedness of possible events and situations. This technique encourages executives to look at each possible event or situation from various angles and in the context of other events and situations. Executives usually gain new insights when they try to place a probability on the likelihood of occurrence for each possible event and try to determine the interrelatedness of the events. When the matrix is completed, it indicates situations that could have a favorable impact on the company as well as those that could have a devastating effect.

Developing scenarios is not very different from the process of running the numbers in financial management. Scenarios and financial analysis help executives develop an understanding of the situation. Harold Geneen, former CEO of IT&T, is acknowledged for running the numbers more than any other CEO in the last few decades. Yet Geneen noted, "The meaning of numbers, like that of words, can only be comprehended in relationship to one another."[6] When you look at a situation from numerous vantage points, you begin to get a real feel for the situation. Geneen indicated that only by running various ratios could he really understand what they meant. Scenarios provide similar insights.

SCENARIOS HELP TO ESTABLISH AN EARLY WARNING SYSTEM FOR INITIATING CONTINGENCY PLANS

It would be nearly impossible to run every possible scenario and to develop a cross-impact matrix to capture the interrelatedness of all major factors, forces, and events. Executives should use the

Pareto 80/20 principle when running scenarios and only identify the factors, forces, or events that would have the greatest influence on the company. Particular attention should be directed toward factors, forces, or events that have the highest probability of occurrence or those that have a low probability but would have a dramatic effect on the company. Most events that have only .02 (one in fifty) probability of occurring this year usually would not be the subject of a scenario. If the event has the potential, however, to blow the company out of the water, then it would be wise to run a scenario for it.

Scenarios not only provide insights into possibilities and probabilities; they also provide the basis for establishing an early warning system. Each scenario depicts a series or sequence of events that could occur. The series of events can be like a line of dominos—where one event leads to another event that prompts another event. An early warning system can be set up that monitors the environment for any indication that the initial events are about to occur. This is similar to the monitoring of leading indicators by economists to note a turn in the economy.

Companies need to run multiple scenarios because there can be multiple futures. Discontinuities can change the world. A breakthrough innovation can make everything in the market obsolete. A war in the Middle East can turn an economy upside down. A new government regulation can stop a company in its tracks. A fire in the production facilities of a major supplier can bring an assembly line to a standstill. The loss of a key staff member can leave a company without the knowledge to get or complete a project. Scenarios should not be restricted only to events that could jeopardize the company. Factors, forces, and events that can have a beneficial effect on the company should also be identified. Scenarios should be run for the ones that have the greatest potential to benefit the company.

Scenarios can play an integral part in establishing a radar and sonar system for the company. Scenarios encourage executives to continuously scan the company's environment. Companies that have an environmental-scanning system that incorporates the features of radar, sonar, and a CAT scan will see the future first. The radar metaphor is appropriate because the company needs to sense what may be over the horizon. Economic and political factors, as well as psychographic shifts, fall into this category. The sonar metaphor is appropriate because the company needs to look beneath the surface for subtle changes that may not appear on radar. Ideas in a competitor's research-and-development laboratory fall into this category. The CAT-scan metaphor is appropriate because the company also needs to look within itself for signs of change. Worker attitudes and satisfaction fall into this category.

Scenarios reduce the likelihood the company will be blindsided. Environmental scanning looks for the earliest clues or cues that something may occur. The earlier the company identifies the first signs that a sequence of events may be unfolding, the earlier the company can reposition itself to capitalize on beneficial events or to reposition itself to minimize the impact of detrimental events.

General Electric benefited from running scenarios when it projected the possibility that the Iron Curtain would be dismantled. It established contacts with key individuals in Poland and other Eastern European countries so it could establish alliances with them when free enterprise was allowed.

Strategic insights are valuable because foresight of new realities can serve as the foundation for developing innovative approaches to deal with them. Insights into the whole range of possible future situations give management the incentive to also develop contingency plans to address various possible futures.

Scenarios should foster serious discussions about what the future may hold. It is easy to contemplate obvious events. Time should be available, however, for people to explore numerous possibilities and probabilities. Scenarios are the most valuable when they encourage people to think the unthinkable. The saying "Hope for the best, but prepare for the worst" captures the beneficial nature of running scenarios.

Two situations illustrate that there may be merit in thinking the unthinkable. Years ago a United Airlines jet lost its hydraulic fluid while in flight. The airplane crashed, but some people survived. Industry officials were amazed that anyone could have survived the flaming crash because it was assumed the loss of hydraulics would make it impossible to control the airplane. Flight simulators did not include that scenario because there was no contingency plan available. Fortunately, the airplane had a veteran crew. Their experience, intuition, judgment, and improvisation saved a number of lives.

A more recent event in the world of electronic commerce

shows that even the most unlikely event may need to be included in scenario analysis. America Online (AOL) was faced with a challenge when it was rumored that Microsoft might provide Internet access for free. AOL was charging its customers about twenty dollars a month for Internet access. This is one of the first times in history that a company considered giving away a major service. Internet service providers like AOL were faced with the possibility of having their primary source of revenue, profits, cash flow, and existence placed in immediate jeopardy.

Contingency plans increase the company's agility. As soon as the company's game plan shows the first sign that it is not in tune with new realities, the company may be able to initiate a plan that is in a better position to meet contingencies. Companies with contingency plans that are in tune with possible futures benefit from a much quicker response than companies that must start from scratch when their plans are derailed.

SIMULATIONS PROVIDE INSIGHTS INTO RELATIONSHIPS AND SENSITIVITIES

Simulations provide useful insights into the interrelatedness of factors that could affect the company in the future. Scenarios raise "What if . . . ?" questions so that executives can prepare "If, then . . ." strategies and contingency plans. Simulations attempt to model reality. They try to capture the relationships among factors and their corresponding cause-and-effect sensitivities. Companies that develop simulations are in a position to test the effect that various changes could have on the company's future performance.

Scenarios usually look for the effect that a single event may have on the company's performance. They tend to be fairly linear, like a line of dominos falling. Simulations try to incorporate the multidimensional nature of the real world and may enable executives to gain insights into what would happen if numerous events, factors, or forces were to occur within a certain period of time. Simulations are like war games because they may be able to provide a systems or *whole-field* perspective. Rekha Balu, senior writer for *Fast Company*, noted, "A good simulation usually tells a good story, letting you explore the consequences of your decisions so you can see how different scenarios unfold."[7] Simulations also enable executives to experiment with numerous simultaneous changes within and outside the company. If the simulation effectively models reality, executives should be able to identify the optimal strategy for positioning their company.

Journalist Peter Carbonara observed that some companies spend several million dollars collecting data and writing the software required to capture their environment so that executives can make smarter decisions. Harris Chemical Group, for example, gathered every piece of data it could about its position, its competitors, and the world market for boron. It put the data into a computer simulation that calculated the financial impact of various strategic moves.[8]

Simulations are a form of virtual reality. They give executives the opportunity to experiment without implementing actual plans. The best simulations are like flight simulators because they let executives take mental journeys before they take physical journeys. They allow executives to experiment without risking resources in an actual trial-and-error format in the real world. They give executives the opportunity to experiment and even try things that they would be hesitant to try. They can also force people out of their existing mind-sets and routines.

John McClellan, CEO of Decision Architects, noted that through the use of simulations, "People should see things and say, 'I never thought of that before. But now that I've seen it, I believe it.'"[9] Simulations may also keep executives from venturing down a path that may place the company in peril. Mercer Management Consulting's John Fay noted that a good simulation can kill bad ideas.[10]

Simulations can help executives grasp the dynamics of a complex world and provide insights into how they can create a forward-focused company. A word of caution needs to be provided here about relying on simulations: They are only as good as the accuracy of the models that are used in them. Simulations that fail to incorporate key factors and their relationships may cause management to adopt a flawed strategy.

Simulations are like an electronic spreadsheet. It would be wonderful if they came with all the factors and formulas already loaded into the software. Unfortunately, companies need to identify the factors and their corresponding relationships before the simulation can be run. The fact that the world is ever-changing makes it even more difficult to identify the factors, model their corresponding relationships, and keep the model up-to-date.

The process for developing a simulation can provide valuable insights. The moral to the simulation story is to learn from the process of building them and experimenting with them, but rely on them only to the extent that they accurately reflect current and future realities.

CLARIFYING STRATEGIC OPPORTUNITIES AND THREATS

Executives with a long-term horizon and mental dexterity are able to develop different perceptions of the future. Scenario building and simulations may not provide them with a crystal-clear picture of what the future will bring, but it will alert them to various possibilities. Executives can also gain insights into potential opportunities and threats. For example, by thinking on a global basis, rather than thinking only about one's domestic markets, executives can identify:

- Emerging wants and needs
- Products and services that should be developed
- Technologies, capabilities, and resources that will be needed
- Organizational designs and managerial approaches that will be appropriate
- Markets that will offer greater price margins
- Candidates for joint ventures or licensing arrangements that will be beneficial
- Funding assistance by the respective governments that will give the company a valuable boost or edge

When the prospects of entering foreign markets or utilizing a radically different technology to serve markets are raised, managers of most companies exclaim, "But I don't know anything about doing business abroad" or "I know very little about that technology!" This is the value of having a strategic orientation and running scenarios. If you identify an emerging opportunity early enough, you can have a head start over everyone else. You have the time to study potential foreign markets and to learn how to sell products in those markets. With lead time, you won't be rushed into anything, which reduces uncertainty and takes much of the anxiety out of doing something that you have never done before. Additional lead time also gives you a chance to get the bugs out and to develop a high level of proficiency before competition enters the scene.

IDENTIFYING POSSIBLE STRATEGIC POSITIONS

Paul Schoemaker, as chairman of Decision Strategies International, noted that executives must decide once they construct scenarios whether they should gamble on one scenario, stay flexible to exploit multiple scenarios, develop exit routes in case things sour, or hedge the risk through strategic partnering or diversification. Scenarios can be used to identify early warning signals, assess the robustness of your core competencies, generate better strategic options, and evaluate the risk/return profile of each option in view of the uncertainties.[11]

The future will offer an almost unlimited number of opportunities. No company, no matter how large, has the capability to meet all the needs of the global marketplace. In the years ahead, the name of the game will be "nichemanship." The companies that thrive will be the ones that identify emerging markets early and develop the ability to meet the market segment's needs to the point that no other company will even consider entering that market.

At this point, executives need to develop a list of possible strategic positions for the company. Unfortunately, many executives use an incremental approach for positioning their companies. Even if they are able to identify where they want their companies to be in three years, their targets tend to be an extrapolation of the last few years' growth. At the end of each year, they simply add another year to their plan. Many corporate strategies are nothing more than minor modifications of existing product lines, efforts to expand sales territories, or attempts to fine-tune operations to improve efficiency.

CONCLUSION: LEARNING-IMPAIRED COMPANIES WON'T SURVIVE

Strategic learning has offensive and defensive dimensions. From an offensive perspective, it enables your company to be a path-maker and to set the rules for how the game will be played. Success will be partly contingent on the extent to which you anticipate potential opportunities and position your company to capitalize on them. From a defensive perspective, strategic learning helps you anticipate potential threats and position your company to minimize their corresponding detrimental effects.

It will be impossible for you or your company to foresee every factor and force. Our ever-accelerating, ever-changing, multidimensional world will challenge the brightest executives and the most extensive databases. No one will be able to anticipate every key event. No scenario or simulation will be able to capture every possibility, every probability, and every potential state of nature. Your company will thrive in the years ahead to the extent to which it sees the future first and learns new ways to do things and new things to do.

"God grant me the serenity to accept the things I cannot change, the courage to change the things I can, and the wisdom to know the difference."
—Dr. Reinhold Niebuhr, American theologian

NOTES

1. Jeff Papows, *In Enterprise.com* (Reading, Mass.: Perseus Books, 1998), p. 105.
2. Gary Hamel and C. K. Prahalad, "Competing in the Future," *Harvard Business Review,* July–August 1994, p. 128.
3. "Using Scenarios in Business," *The Futurist,* June–July 1998, p. 61.
4. Warren Bennis and Burt Nanus, *Leaders* (New York: Harper & Row, 1985), p. 166.
5. Ibid., p. 172.
6. Harold Geneen, *Managing* (New York: Doubleday, 1984), p. 182.
7. Rekha Balu, "The Practice of Change," *Fast Company,* December 1999, p. 408.

8. Peter Carbonara, "Game Over," *Fast Company,* December 1996, p. 131.
9. Ibid., p. 131
10. Ibid., p. 131.
11. Paul J. H. Schoemaker, "Scenario Planning: A Tool for Strategic Thinking," *Sloan Management Review,* Winter 1995, p. 34.

11

Strategic Positioning

"Executives with a clear vision invent excellent futures for their companies; those who lack it set their companies adrift in dangerous waters." [1]

—Craig Hickman and Michael Silva, authors of *Creating Excellence*

Lewis Carroll's classic book *Alice's Adventures in Wonderland* captures the dilemma faced by many executives today. When Alice asks the Cheshire Cat which path to take, the cat asks where she wants to go. When Alice indicates she does not really know where, the cat states, "Then it doesn't matter which way you go." [2] Over the years, the Cheshire Cat's response has been transformed into the popular saying, "When you don't know where you're going, any road will take you there . . . nowhere!"

Success is contingent on the extent to which executives demonstrate bifocal management. Executives need to craft a shared and compelling vision. They also need to ensure that systems are in place that allow few things to fall through the cracks on a daily basis. Some executives relish the opportunity to think on a strategic level. They look forward to running scenarios and contemplating possible competitive strategies. Other executives enjoy developing detailed action plans and monitoring ongoing performance. Few executives have the ability to blend both proficiencies. Fixation on operational matters without a sense for the big picture is like a mechanic tuning the engine of a car that will never leave the garage. Visionary leadership combines strategic orientation with precise operational focus. Executives who want to create a forward-focused company need to be like champion archers, in that they need to identify the bull's-eye of distant targets and have the ability to focus their company's efforts on hitting them.

DEVELOPING A UNIFIED CORPORATE STRATEGIC VISION

The first two steps of the strategic management process are prerequisites for creating a unified corporate vision. When George Bush was president of the United States in the early 1990s, he used to refer to the "vision thing." It was apparent that either he did not understand the importance of having a clearly articulated vision or he did not have a clear vision for the future of the United States. Jimmy Carter also had difficulty with the "vision thing." Although President Carter was considered to be a very intelligent person, his staff indicated that his views about the future were like the back side of a tapestry . . . you could see a general outline but the figures were not very crisp. Many companies operate without a clearly articulated vision of what they are striving to be.

It may be helpful to start the discussion on developing a unified corporate vision by indicating what a vision is not. First of all, the vision should not be confused with a company's mission statement. For years, consultants have encouraged CEOs to develop mission statements for their companies. Although mission statements have merit and every company should have one, they tend to resemble the back side of a tapestry. They may be colorful and may even inspire a few people to strive to new heights, but they tend to be too general to provide a clear sense of direction.

Most mission statements are nothing more than a string of platitudes. They sound like a corporate version of the national anthem, whereby the company expresses its commitment to providing the highest level of quality and service, being innovative, being a conscientious employer, and being a responsible corporate citizen. Let's face it, mission statements are so generic that they all sound alike. You might as well say the company's mission is, "To be the best that it can be!"

The following legend identifies the relationships between—

and trickle-down effect of—the various components of the strategic management process:

mission—A general statement that reflects the company's reason for being.

vision—A statement that identifies specifically what the company wants to be.

strategic position—It targets the company's future competitive, market, and financial position.

objectives and goals—Identify specific targets that will lead to the fulfillment of the vision.

key values—Identify what is sacred to the company. These are areas that will not be compromised.

strategy—The company's basic game plan for fulfilling the vision.

long-term and operational plans—The company's road map. Plans identify the resources, time lines, critical path, and budget.

tactics—Components of the plans that are subject to ongoing modifications.

While a company's mission indicates the type of business the company is striving to become in very general terms, the vision is intended to serve as the front side of the tapestry. It should provide a clear mental picture of where the company should be at a specific time in the next five to ten years. It represents the proverbial x that marks the spot! James Collins and Jerry Porras, authors of *Built to Last*, noted that if the vision is not clear, crisp, and gut grabbing, it will not galvanize people to put forth their best efforts.[3]

President John F. Kennedy illustrated the difference between a mission statement and a unified vision. After the Soviets launched Sputnik in 1957, NASA was created to turn the United States into "the world's leader in space." This mission statement was nice and appealed to our patriotism, but it wasn't until Kennedy's presidency that a true vision was articulated. His vision was "to land a man on the moon and return him safely to Earth before the end of the decade," which provided a sense of direction. It created a sense of urgency and a bias for action because it provided a benchmark to measure progress.

The vision should not be confused with the company's strategy or long-range plan. The vision represents a desired future destination for the company with a date of arrival. It should spell out what markets the company is expected to be in, its anticipated size in terms of employees and assets, and whether it will be a domestic or global enterprise. It should also indicate whether the company will be publicly traded and whether it may acquire other companies.

The vision serves as the North Star in every decision that is to be made by every manager at every level every day. Any time an issue comes up, the question can be asked, "Will this action move us toward the fulfillment of our vision?" All too often, when people are asked what the company wants to be, either no one can articulate the vision or there is a wide range of responses or they quote a mission or vision statement that is nothing more than a string of esoteric platitudes. Each of these three situations may place the future of the company in jeopardy. The first situation resembles Alice's question to the Cheshire Cat. The second situation causes people to travel in different directions, which diffuses valuable energy and resources. The third situation may be the most common. Most mission and vision statements are so general that they seem to have been generated by a fill-in-the-blanks software package. They look like:

> "XYZ Corporation *strives to be the most innovative, highest-quality, employee-empowering, corporate citizen that embraces diversity and customer responsiveness organization in the galaxy.*"

When the vision is stated as a specific destination with a specific date of arrival, decision making becomes easier for everyone in the company. The vision not only clarifies what the company is trying to become; it also states what the company is trying *not* to become. A clear vision minimizes the likelihood the company will be seduced by short-term opportunities.

While leadership has been described as the ability to transform the vision into reality, such a transformation cannot be the result of a one-person show. Organizational transformation takes more than rhetoric; it takes commitment from every person at every level. One of the features that sets an excellent company apart from the crowd is that every person working there has a keen awareness of what his or her company represents and what it is specifically trying to accomplish. Hickman and Silva noted, "Vision joins strategy and corporate culture together to achieve corporate excellence. Without vision to bind them, corporate strategy and culture tend to drift apart."[4]

This is why it was essential for Apple Computer to have John Sculley at the helm when it attempted to make the transition from a group of young mavericks to an established company with staying power. In an industry where products can become obsolete within one year and the average company's life expectancy is less than five years, Apple realized that strategic management was essential if it was to exist in the twenty-first century. Ironically, Apple brought Steven Jobs back in the late 1990s so that it would have the vision, energy, innovation, and attitude needed to compete in the twenty-first century.

All too often, top management is composed of executives who are within a few years of retirement and are tired from their climb to the top. These executives concentrate their attention on ensuring that nothing goes wrong rather than on laying the groundwork for the next decade. They see the retirement light at the end of the tunnel, so they adopt the attitude "If I don't make any mistakes, I'm home free!" or "I won't be around to benefit from a bold initiative, so why should I take the time or the chance?" The same executives also tend to look for quick fixes or cosmetic solutions for problem situations that require far more comprehensive action.

SELECTING THE TARGET STRATEGIC POSITION

The vision provides a basis for navigating the seas of change. It also serves as the basis for selecting the company's target strategic position, which identifies the markets to be served, the technological expertise the company will need to develop or acquire, the resources it will need to have at its disposal, and the comparative advantages it must have over its competition.

The company's target strategic position may place the company in a different industry. Executives must be prepared to reallocate the company's limited resources to reposition the company so that it can capitalize on tomorrow's opportunities. Peter Drucker offers an interesting approach for addressing the appropriateness of the company's current position. He encourages managers to take a long look at what the company is involved in doing and ask, "If we were not committed to this today, would we go into it?" If the answer is no, then the next question should be, "How can we get out—fast?"[5]

The market life-cycle concept has direct application to this step in the strategic management process. Selecting the target strategic position is a deliberate effort to identify the industries or markets the company will be in, where it expects to be in each market life cycle, the geographic territories it will operate in, and the configuration of the company in financial and structural terms.

This approach may explain why Jack Welch recommended that General Electric sell its countertop consumer appliances (toaster ovens, etc.) business to Black and Decker. Quite a few observers thought that Welch was selling out the company's heritage. Welch, however, recognized that GE's resources should be redeployed and invested in emerging industries rather than in trying to squeeze a profit out of a highly saturated mature market. Welch believed his company's future should include medical technology. He used the proceeds from the sale of the countertop appliance division to finance the development of medical technology products that would be major breadwinners for GE in the years to come.

Jack Welch believed that GE must strive to be the leader in each industry it is in—and to be the leader, GE must be number one or number two in everything the company does. According to Welch, companies that refuse to think likewise, who hang on to losing or stagnant operations, won't survive the decade.[6]

IDENTIFYING STRATEGIC INITIATIVES

The targeted strategic position clarifies where the company should be three to ten years into the future. Once the *where* has been targeted, attention can be directed toward *how* to get to the desired destination. If the company plans to initiate a major repositioning effort, merely fine-tuning existing products and processes will not be sufficient. If executives want to move their company from where it is to where it should be, they must establish an atmosphere that encourages innovativeness and unleashes corpreneurial endeavors.

Executives need to pay close attention to efforts that require substantial lead time. If executives want to transform their companies, then new markets need to be researched, new prototypes need to be created and test-marketed, new technologies need to be adopted, new production and distribution capabilities need to be developed, new skills need to be learned, and financial reserves must be set aside.

Most of these efforts require at least two years lead time before they can become commercially viable. Savvy executives acknowledge the need to develop sinking funds for major capital acquisitions or for replacing expensive equipment when it wears out. The same logic needs to be adopted for the company's strategic initiatives. DuPont provides a good example of committing today's resources to tomorrow's markets. The company allocates more than $200 million each year to fuel its efforts to position the company to be a leader in the emerging biotechnology field. This commitment is justified because biotechnology is expected to have at least as revolutionary an impact on the way people live as computer technology has had on the way people work.

Identifying strategic initiatives means that the company will no longer do business as usual. Executives must accept the need to plant the seeds for tomorrow's success rather than focus their attention solely on this year's bottom line. For an organization to be future-oriented, its management systems must be designed to direct everyone's attention toward doing the things that will move the company to its desired strategic position. Goals must be set for new product development, incentives must be established to reward people for being innovative, and performance reviews must focus on the extent to which each person has moved the company closer to its target strategic position.

CRAFTING THE VISION: AN EXAMPLE

Developing the company's vision involves considerable time and thought. The process defies the single afternoon strategic-planning retreat when the executive team brainstorms a few emotionally charged words and then wordsmiths them into an eloquent vision statement. The roller-coaster nature of the vision development process is reflected in the following example. (The example has been modified to provide anonymity. It also represents a simplified and abbreviated version of the actual situation.)

The founder and chief executive of a successful manufacturing company contacted a consultant and asked to meet with him to discuss a dilemma. The chief executive was concerned that the company may not be positioned to capitalize on the opportunities that were on the horizon. The chief executive indicated that the executive team had spent two days in a corporate-planning retreat a few months earlier. The chief executive indicated that the retreat had been worthwhile because he and the other members of the executive team had successfully drafted the company's first mission statement.

The chief executive, however, expressed his growing frustration because the mission statement did not provide the focus, sense of urgency, and bias for action that he had expected and the company needed. The chief executive then handed a copy of the company's mission statement to the consultant.

Mission Statement for Harper Manufacturing

Harper Manufacturing *designs and manufactures fabrication machinery. We are dedicated to identifying customer needs and meeting those needs with innovative and high-quality products backed up with outstanding service.*

While the mission statement put into words what the company did and its business strategy, it did not elicit the energy needed for the company to excel, nor did it provide specific guidance for the multitude of decisions that need to be made. After a few months of trying to use the mission statement as the company's North Star, the chief executive concluded that while it sounded nice, it did not provide the specific sense of direction that he needed. The consultant indicated that the chief executive needed a bridge to connect the company's general, value-laden mission to the various decisions that need to be made in identifying the company's priorities, drafting the company's strategy, and developing the company's critical time line.

The consultant told the chief executive that most chief executives echo the Peggy Lee song "Is That All There Is?" when they try to operationalize their company's mission statement. He suggested that the chief executive develop a specific vision statement. The process for developing the vision began by asking the chief executive about what he thought the company should become as well as his perceptions about the industry's future. The consultant then asked each of the vice presidents the same questions before asking a stratified sample of key employees similar questions. Effort was made to have the sample include veteran employees as well as people who had recently joined the company. The consultant chose to conduct individual interviews because he wanted to learn each person's perceptions while providing confidentiality.

The interviews provided the consultant with perspectives from various vantage points. It was no surprise that there was not a consensus on exactly what the future held or on what the company should become. The usual functional mental silos existed for people in manufacturing, marketing, and finance. The interviews also provided a wide range of attitudes about risk, technology, and the company's human resources. Some of the managers were very optimistic about the future. Other managers believed that the future would be filled with turbulence, more intense competition, and eroding profitability. The interviews also indicated that some of the people were team players while others would rather do their own thing.

The consultant put together a profile that highlighted some of the points that were generated in the interviews. The profile was forwarded to the chief executive so that he could understand how his staff saw the company and the world around it. The first of a series of weekly Friday afternoon meetings was then scheduled for the chief executive and the executive team. The consultant served as the facilitator by ensuring that the meeting's topic was covered and that no individual, including the chief executive, dominated the meeting or adversely affected the views of the other people there.

The first meeting focused on the company's need to operate with a strategic perspective. The consultant presented various models that play an integral role in fostering visionary leadership and strategic management. The second meeting was designed to have the executive team identify key factors for the company's future success. The group went through a strengths, weaknesses, opportunities, and threats (SWOT) analysis for the company. Particular attention was directed toward current SWOT factors as well as SWOT factors in the next five years. The future SWOT analysis was essential because it helped the team to identify factors that may not exist today but could in the next five years. The consultant brought up points from in the profile paper at various times so that the team could see there were varying views of SWOT-related factors.

The second meeting identified some general issues. The third meeting forced the team to be more specific in its discussions of SWOT factors. The team closely scrutinized each SWOT factor. The team members were encouraged to share their thoughts and perceptions. The group continued meeting weekly to analyze the company's future. The team incorporated QUEST and ran scenarios for various possible situations.

The team followed the steps profiled in the strategic management process and moved toward a consensus for what the future represented with each passing week. The strategic *inquiries* about the future led to strategic *insights* into the factors and forces that could have a beneficial or detrimental effect on the company.

The team's attention was then directed to windows of opportunity that would open as well as how the company could harvest current opportunities. The team then identified the resource and capability requirements for each of the current and potential opportunities. At that time, the team decided to modify the company's mission statement so that it would reflect the proactive stance it wanted the company to develop and demonstrate. The original mission statement was changed to:

The Mission for Harper Manufacturing

Harper Manufacturing *is committed to being the premier "value-added" designer and manufacturer of specialized fabrication machinery. We are dedicated to identifying customer needs and meeting those needs with innovative and high-quality products backed up with outstanding service.*

The new mission statement reflected the belief that Harper Manufacturing wanted to be *the* premier value-added company in its field. Although only a few words were added to the mission statement, the new statement captured the distinctiveness the management team wanted to develop for the company. The team wanted the company to evolve from one of the best companies in the field to being the *premier* company in the field. The mission statement was changed to indicate that the company would gain distinction only if it could offer superior value to its target market by doing things that its competition was not able to do.

The team then directed its attention toward developing a vision for where the company should be in five years, with consideration to the favorable opportunities that existed and those that were expected to emerge. The consultant encouraged the team to state the vision as a destination in five years. Attention was directed toward using the long-term backwards rather than the short-term forward approach. The consultant encouraged the team to identify a destination that could be achieved with innovation and stretch rather than simply adding five years to the company's current situation.

The chief executive encouraged the team to pay particular attention to what the stockholders wanted the company to be worth in five years. The team recognized that other stakeholders' interests and expectations would need to be met, but it thought that if the stockholders did not have their investment objectives met, the team may not be around to satisfy the other stakeholders' expectations—especially their own!

When the board of directors was asked where they wanted the company to be in the future, the directors indicated that the principal stockholders wanted it to be worth at least $368,000,000 in five years so they could cash out. The team then estimated the company would have to be able to generate $220,000,000 in sales, with $66,000,000 in pre-tax profit and $46,000,000 in after-tax profit in the fifth year using an eight-to-one price/after-tax earnings ratio, for the company to be worth $368,000,000. The company had generated $97,341,000 in sales with $29,202,300 in pre-tax profit and $19,565,541 in after-tax profit the year that just ended. The eight-to-one price earnings ratio put the company's current worth at $156,524,320.

The management team realized that the five-year valuation and profitability targets were challenging, but it also knew that it had to start somewhere. The overall value and corresponding profit level permitted the team to investigate the conditions that would need to exist for the targets to become a reality. The board's two financial targets provided the basis needed for identifying the company's strategic-planning gap. The strategic-planning gap measured the difference between where the company needed to be in five years and where it would be if it didn't change what it was doing.

The team adopted the "inquiries . . . insights . . . initiatives" format of strategic management. The team ran scenarios that reflected various market conditions. Particular attention was given to economic, competitive, and technological conditions. The team then projected the corresponding level of sales and profits for the company's existing products and services to determine possible levels of sales and profits for those products in the next five years. It soon became apparent that even under the best conditions the company could not fulfill the financial targets with the company's current product and service offerings.

When the team combined the long-term backwards approach with its projections for enhancing sales and profits for the company's three existing products and corresponding services, it concluded that the company needed to develop one or more products or services that would generate at least a $6,000,000 pre-tax profit in the fifth year.

The team was confronted by an interesting dilemma when it realized the company's current products and services—as successful as they had been—would not be able to fulfill the five-year valuation target. The team could either lower the valuation target so that it would conform to the team's projection of what could be achieved with the company's current products and services or it could keep the five-year valuation target and find a way to make it a reality.

Many teams set lower targets when they believe the targets are out of their reach. Instead of rising to the challenge, they settle for doing the best they can with the products they currently have at their disposal. Harper Manufacturing's team realized that if it was to be the premier company in the field, it could not settle for merely doing more of the same. It knew that it had to rely on innovation rather than rationalization. The team recognized that it had to create its future by developing one or more products or services to bridge the strategic-planning gap.

The team devoted its next meeting to scanning the horizon for emerging opportunities. It used the Beyond Customer-Led Matrix and the Future-Positioning Matrix presented in Chapter 6 to identify unexploited and emerging opportunities. The team chose to look for unexploited and emerging opportunities rather than existing markets because these opportunities would offer higher profit potential than existing markets that were saturated with competition. The team also recognized that it had the time needed to develop new products and services if it used a five-year time horizon.

The team then analyzed its current markets to determine if certain needs were either not being met or not being met in a satisfactory manner. The gap analysis was not limited to the company's existing customers. It also included companies that were buying products and services from the company's competitors. The team did not restrict its analysis to the company's current market segments but explored other market segments to see if gaps existed.

If the team had adopted a three-year time horizon, it would have been relegated to developing one or more products that were imitations of products offered by other companies. The team recognized an imitative strategy would not elevate the company to the premier status set in the mission statement nor would it generate the profit margin needed to achieve the company's overall valuation target.

The team then took a mental leap forward and brainstormed a list of emerging markets that might offer lucrative and durable opportunities. Attention was directed toward markets that were near the edge of the company's five-year radar screen. The team did not want to direct its attention to markets where the window of opportunity would not open for at least five years. Instead, they looked for windows that would open in about two years. The two-year window of opportunity was chosen because it would give the company two years to develop the product or service and three years to harvest that opportunity. The team also knew it should not get caught up in sales projections because profit was the bull's-eye of the target if it was to achieve the company's valuation target.

The team's brainstorming session went well beyond the company's current markets, products, processes, services, and technology. The team was even encouraged to test the outer limits of its industry to see if related industries offered opportunities. The openness of the brainstorming sessions encouraged the team to think outside the proverbial box. The executives were encouraged to think thoughts they may have been reluctant to think if they had used traditional shorter-term time horizons.

The team generated a number of emerging market gaps/opportunities and current market gaps/opportunities in the first brainstorming session. The consultant suggested that the team not try to analyze the gaps or rough-out product or service specifics or logistics at that time. Instead, the consultant encouraged the group to stay outside the box for the next week when the team would meet again to continue its brainstorming. The consultant reminded the group that the two principle rules of brainstorming were: (1) It's the quantity not the quality of ideas that counts in the beginning, and (2) criticism or evaluation of ideas is not allowed until the brainstorming session is concluded. The second brainstorming session produced new ideas as well as ideas that piggybacked on some of the ideas generated during the preceding week.

Two things should be noted at this time that reflected the revised mission statement. First, the team decided that it should proactively solicit new product or service ideas from its current and potential customers. The team sought to establish an alliance with potential and existing customers in the development of breakthrough products and services. This would reduce the amount of time, funding, and risk associated with the company's research-and-development efforts. It would also give the company a committed customer. Second, the team decided that the company would not acquire or license the product or service in its effort to bridge the gap. The team was committed to being a developer of fabrication-related machinery or services.

The team's brainstorming sessions were very productive. Everyone was amazed at the number of opportunities they were able to identify. The list of market gaps and customer needs and the team's corresponding product and service ideas was impressive—and well beyond what the company needed to fulfill its vision. The next meetings were devoted to performing reality checks. The team analyzed the various market gaps and their corresponding products and service logistics. Each gap or customer need was subjected to a preliminary analysis to determine whether it had the potential to be a breakthrough opportunity. The team used a screening process similar to the one used by venture-capital firms when they consider funding proposals. Attention was directed toward the ability to develop a proprietary position, the opportunity to dominate the market, lucrative profit margins, and sustained growth. Additional meetings addressed whether the company would be able to enhance sales and profits for its current products and services to meet the target and whether the company had the talent and resources needed to actually develop the products needed to bridge the $6,000,000 fifth-year pre-tax profit gap.

The complete list of product and service ideas was well beyond the company's available resources. The team then projected the financial, human, technological, informational, and infrastructural requirements associated with the most promising opportunities. A number of the opportunities were dropped from consideration because their requirements exceeded the company's available resources and the resources that it would generate in the future. A few of the opportunities were dropped from consideration because they would change the company's size, strategy, and culture to the point that the company would not reflect the revised mission statement.

It turned out that the overall size of the company was one of the primary criteria for screening opportunities. The management team believed that the size of the company played a key role in the management, quality of life, and success of the company. The team wanted total employment not to exceed three hundred people. The management team recognized that the growth necessary to achieve the valuation target would stretch the company's management team and employee base during the next five years.

It was at this time that the team tightened up the company's vision statement so it would reflect the numerous iterations of weekly meetings that had followed the revision in the mission statement. The following statements and tables for Harper Manufacturing are calibrated for a five-year time horizon.

Vision for Harper Manufacturing in the Year 20YZ

By January 1, 20YZ, *Harper Manufacturing is expected to employ three hundred people who will generate $220,000,000 in sales with a pre-tax profit of $66,000,000 and an after-tax profit of $46,000,000. By 20YZ, the company will be positioned so it may be sold*

*to another company, outside investors, or the manage-
ment team for at least $368,000,000.*

The visioning process produced a number of insights. Five
insights were particularly noteworthy. First, there appeared to be
sufficiently lucrative opportunities in the fabrication-machinery
field to ensure that the company would not have to transform itself
into a completely different industry. Second, management realized
that its core competence was identifying customer needs and then
designing and manufacturing fabrication machines that fit the
company's needs. The process reaffirmed the company's mission
statement that Harper Manufacturing should be both a developer
and a manufacturer. Third, the company needed to develop at least
one product or service that could generate at least $6,000,000 in
pre-tax profit by the fifth year.

The fourth insight came as a direct result of the recognition
that the company's current products and services could not sufficiently fulfill the vision. The management team realized that there
was a strategic-planning gap in the company's management team.
The company needed to have a technology director if it was to
develop athe products or services needed to hit the five-year target.
The team realized that if the company's journey for fulfilling its
vision was mapped out on a PERT chart, then hiring a technology
director would be the first activity on the company's critical path.
Fifth, the company would need to hire at least 150 people because
of growth and attrition.

The management team then directed its attention in subsequent weekly sessions toward articulating various factors and issues that would be critical in managing the company so that it
would be positioned to transform its vision into reality. Tables
11-1, 11-2, and 11-3 reflect the outcomes of those sessions.

Table 11-1. Market position for 20YZ.

Product A: The world's leader (in terms of number of contracts)

Product B: In the top three domestically (in terms of number of contracts)

Product C: Top two in the world (in terms of number of contracts)

New Product "D": The "leading-edge" manufacturer of specialized
fabrication machinery in the world in an emerging market (in terms of
number of contracts)

The management team also crafted the following statement of corporate philosophy:

Harper Manufacturing *will approach every aspect of its operations with an opportunistic "We can make it happen" attitude. The company's future will not be determined by economic conditions or by our competitors. Our destiny will be determined by our own ideas, actions, and dedication. For our company to be the premier company in its field, we must seek customers that are also committed to being premier companies. We also recognize that for our company to be the benchmark as the leading-edge developer and producer of fabrication machinery, we cannot focus our attention on our competitors. Instead, we must focus our attention on what our current and potential customers need.*

Table 11-2. Product, sales, and profit mix for 20YZ.

Sales Goal Margin	Stretch 35%	Target 30%	Minimum 20%	% of Sales
Product A	$87,500,000	$70,000,000	$52,500,000	35%
Net	$30,625,000	$21,000,000	$10,500,000	
Product B	$87,500,000	$70,000,000	$52,500,000	35%
Net	$30,625,000	$21,000,000	$10,500,000	
Product C	$50,000,000	$40,000,000	$30,000,000	20%
Net	$17,500,000	$12,000,000	$6,000,000	
New Product "D"	$25,000,000	$20,000,000	$15,000,000	10%
Net	$8,750,000	$6,000,000	$3,000,000	
Total Product Sales	$250,000,000	$200,000,000	$150,000,000	100%
Net	$87,500,000	$60,000,000	$30,000,000	
Additional Revenue	15% of Sales	10% of Sales	5% of Sales	
Parts and Services	$37,500,000	$20,000,000	$7,500,000	
Margin	35%	30%	20%	
Net	$11,250,000	$6,000,000	$1,500,000	
Total Revenue	$287,500,000	$220,000,000	$157,500,000	
Net Income	$100,625,000	$66,000,000	$31,500,000	
Income Tax @ %	$33,492,424	$20,000,000	$9,545,454	
Net Income A.T.	$67,132,576	$46,000,000	$21,954,546	
Valuation @ 8 to 1	$537,060,608	$368,000,000	$175,636,368	

Table 11-3. Geographic territories.

	Domestic North American Sales	**Foreign** Non-North American Sales
Product A	60%	40%
Product B	65%	35%
Product C	70%	30%
New Product "D"	100%	0%

CONCLUSION: VISIONING MUST BE AN ONGOING PROCESS

The visioning process is an ongoing one where management regularly ponders what may be over the horizon, identifies and monitors key factors, conducts environmental scanning sessions, runs various scenarios, and does other activities to remain in tune with what is possible. It encourages you to take an objective look at where the best opportunities may be for your company in the years to come. Only then will you be able to capitalize on the opportunities that lie ahead. It also encourages you to make a deliberate effort to lead the company in such a way that every person, every resource, and every moment in time is directed toward moving the company to its target strategic position.

The visioning process is not something that is done once every five to ten years. When Andy Grove, as chairman of Intel, was asked if it is possible for companies to have a five-year vision when things are changing so quickly, he responded, "It is necessary, but the five-year vision needs to be revised and modified systematically each year or twice a year. We look at our five-year picture and modify the second half of it so it is constantly a five-year plan rather than one that is prepared and then placed on the shelf."[7]

> *"Where there is no vision, the people perish."*
> —Proverbs 29:18

NOTES

1. Craig Hickman and Michael A. Silva, *Creating Excellence* (New York: New American Library, 1984), p. 150.

2. Lewis Carroll, *Alice's Adventures in Wonderland* (London: Oxford University Press, 1971), p. 71.
3. James C. Collins and Jerry Porras, "Organizational Vision and Visionary Organizations," *California Management Review,* Fall 1991, p. 31.
4. Hickman and Silva, p. 156.
5. Peter F. Drucker, *Management* (New York: Harper & Row, 1973), p. 126.
6. Hickman and Silva, p. 162.
7. Interview with author via an America Online chat room, November 17, 1998.

12

Strategic Monitoring and Controlling

"The key to executing your strategy is to have people in your organization understand it—including the crucial but perplexing processes by which intangible assets are converted into tangible outcomes."[1]

—Robert S. Kaplan and David Norton, authors
of *The Balanced Scorecard*

M urphy's Law is based on the principle that whatever can possibly go wrong will. During times of rapid change and uncertainty, no executive can afford to believe that everything will go as planned. This viewpoint doesn't suggest that executives should stop developing plans, nor does it suggest that the process of planning is nothing more than an exercise in futility. It is because of the rapidity of change and the corresponding uncertainty that executives need to develop plans. Planning is essential because it represents the process where management identifies and develops a set of choreographed and sequenced actions to translate the company's vision into reality.

This chapter highlights a number of ideas, concepts, and approaches that foster the development of a mental framework for increasing the odds that the company is doing the right things, in the right way, at the right time, and in the most efficient manner. This chapter provides a set of guidelines for establishing a performance-management system that ensures that the strategic perspective is not lost in the shuffle by the company's ongoing operations.

Off-site strategic visioning retreats are frequently devoted to identifying what the company should be doing—especially what it should be doing differently—to be positioned favorably for the years ahead. Unfortunately, the enthusiasm and energy demonstrated at retreats are usually met with a corresponding lack of action following these strategic sessions. Too often, initiatives that were identified gather dust when executives return to the world of day-to-day management.

Without a clear action plan and identified responsibility for their implementation, strategic initiatives that are needed to fulfill the company's vision are destined to die of neglect. To make matters worse, these initiatives are frequently forgotten by the time the executive team meets again a year later to contemplate the company's strategy. Ironically, subsequent annual strategic-planning sessions have a tendency to raise the same issues that were raised in previous sessions. As Yogi Berra, former baseball player and manager, stated, "It's déjà vu . . . all over again."

Peter Drucker noted decades ago that a plan isn't really a plan unless it degenerates into action. More recently, someone observed that strategic-planning sessions often resemble two elephants mating: While there may be a lot of noise and energy, it takes at least two years until you find out if anything productive came from the "interactive session."

MEASUREMENT AND CONTROL ARE INTEGRAL PARTS OF STRATEGIC MANAGEMENT

Challenging times call for innovative approaches. This is definitely true for developing plans and their corresponding control systems. A study conducted by the Institute for Management Accountants indicates that 64 percent of U.S. companies are experimenting with some type of new performance-measurement system.[2]

The latest approaches for addressing the challenges of planning and control resemble the management by objectives (MBO) systems developed years ago. The MBO system is built on a four-step foundation. Step one involves setting specific objectives. Step two involves developing action plans to achieve the objectives. Step three involves conducting periodic reviews of the factors that affect the achievement of the objectives within their corresponding time lines and budgets. Step four then compares what was actually accomplished with the objectives that were established in step one. The fourth step plays a key role in modifying the plans for the following year so that the company will be on track in fulfilling its longer-term goals. Step four also provides the basis for conducting performance reviews, providing rewards, as well as improving future performance via training and development.

Effective control is only possible when the planning processes provide it with a solid foundation. If the company's planning processes fail to identify specifically what the company is trying to accomplish, the strategy to be used to achieve the objectives, and the time-line and resource requirements for achieving the objectives, then controlling will be like trying to steer a ship without a rudder.

Someone once applied Murphy's Law to military situations by saying, "In combat, plans have to be adjusted as soon as the first shot is fired." Without effective monitoring and controlling processes, management will not know if the company's plans need to be adjusted. Management will keep on going until it is too late to initiate change. The Contextual Change Model that was profiled in the introduction noted that without awareness, there cannot be constructive change.

In its purest form, controlling is actually an ongoing effort to change the company's future. Controlling is most effective when it forces management to look ahead, when there is still time to alter the company's course or strategies. By focusing on the company's current situation, as well as any corresponding trends, controlling identifies the need to change early enough for the company to still operate from a proactive stance. Control processes that take a rearview mirror or "after-the-fact" approach relegate the company to a reactive stance.

BUILDING A STRATEGIC MEASUREMENT AND CONTROL SYSTEM

The company's vision needs to serve as the cornerstone for the company's plans and strategies. The company's plans and strategies, in turn, need to provide parameters for the allocation of resources and serve as the basis for the company's time line. The time line, in turn, must identify and reflect key performance milestones. Monitoring and controlling the company's operations will be effective only to the extent the processes incorporate factors that contribute to the company's success.

Measurement plays an integral role in the strategic management process. The measurement system should ensure that executives are practicing bifocal management. Management needs ensure that the right things are happening in the right way and at the right time. Also, the concern for meeting ongoing operational targets and staying within the period's operating budget should not keep people from addressing strategic issues. The measurement system will be worthwhile only if short-term actions, targets, and milestones lead to the accomplishment of long-term objectives.

The measurement system must measure the right factors. There are two facts of organizational life that need to be considered when developing the performance-measurement system. The first fact of life is, "What gets measured, gets managed!" The second fact of life is, "If management wants something to happen, then it needs to be encouraged, reviewed, and rewarded." If one of these three components is missing, then the desired behavior will not be exhibited or sustained.

Measurement works best when the factor to be managed can be put in quantitative form. Someone once said, "If you can't put it into numbers, then you don't know what you are talking about enough to manage it." Larry Seldon, a professor of finance at Columbia University, stated, "If I don't measure it, I don't understand it."[3] Two notes of caution, however, need to be provided here. First, management needs to be careful that the measurement system is not composed only of factors that are easy to quantify and measure. Second, management also needs to ensure that in its zeal to put together a measurement system, it doesn't merely monitor factors that are already being monitored. If management is truly committed to developing an effective performance-management system, it needs to call a time-out, deliberately step back and release its grip on the company's current system. Then management needs to direct its attention to identifying the factors that are truly important to the company's long-term success.

FOCUS: IDENTIFYING THE DRIVERS OF SUCCESS

Although we might like to live in a world of facts, we must recognize that we live in a world of perceptions and assumptions. Every decision we make is the result of a mental model that reflects our perceptions of the world and our assumptions about what it takes for the company to succeed. Our mental models attempt to identify the factors and forces that affect performance as well as how the factors and forces affect each other.

Mental models reflect one's assumptions about current and future market conditions, how competitors will respond to the company's strategies, how the company's employees will respond to change efforts, and how long it will take to recalibrate the company's internal processes to implement the change efforts. Mental models also reflect assumptions about price elasticity, customer response time in adopting a new product, and the company's cost-effectiveness in improving product or service quality. When the company's strategy has not produced the expected results as indicated by various interim metrics or milestones, management needs to recognize that the assumptions that went into the strategy were inappropriate or the plan was not well executed.

Identification of the factors that contribute to the company's success is essential if management is to be successful in fostering breakthrough performance. Identification of key contributing or causal factors represents the very foundation of a performance-management system. Every moment that management invests in identifying key factors will produce substantial returns in the development of its performance-management system. While a multitude of factors may contribute to the company's success, management must identify the factors that are the true drivers of success. Pareto's 80/20 principle may be helpful here. It states that 80 percent of the gain usually comes from 20 percent of the factors. Management needs to identify which few factors make the greatest difference in the company's long-term performance. Particular emphasis must be placed on identifying causal factors rather than symptom or result factors. John Shank, a professor of accounting at Dartmouth, stated, "At great companies . . . they don't talk about profits, they talk key drivers."[4]

Cash flow is an interesting example of the need to separate

causal from result factors. Cash flow may be crucial to the operation of the company, but it is a result factor more than it is a causal factor. While insufficient cash flow may jeopardize the company, such a condition is the result of numerous factors. If management seeks to maintain a sufficient level of cash, then it has to focus on the factors that ultimately generate positive cash flow rather than just focus on the company's current cash position.

Cash-flow problems are the product of either lower than expected sales receipts or higher than expected cash outlays,

- which can be the result of offering products that are not in tune with market needs and the inability to control expenses
- which can be the result of ineffective new product development programs and poor cost-accounting procedures
- which can be the result of poor market research/intelligence and improperly trained staff
- which can be the result of a lack of commitment to delighting customers and a high turnover rate
- which can be caused by a complacent corporate culture and management's failure to offer compensation packages that attract talent and reward performance.

If management wants to achieve breakthrough performance, it should focus its attention on the identification of emerging markets that offer lucrative growth opportunities and the development of first-to-market products and services that command considerable profit margins by enjoying temporary legal monopolies. The same reasoning applies to the company's human resources. Management needs to recognize that all products, processes, patents, and profits come from people.

Jeffrey Pfeffer, as professor of organizational behavior at Stanford University, noted, "Measurement is a critical component of any management process, and this is true for the process of managing the organization's workforce. . . . It is no accident that companies seriously committed to achieving competitive advantage through people make measurement of their efforts a critical component of the overall process. . . . In a world in which financial results are measured, a failure to measure human resource policy and practice implementation dooms this to second-class status."[5]

The engineering-services company McKim and Creed P.A., which is based in Wilmington, North Carolina, provides an interesting example of how the top management of an emerging business recognized the need to focus its attention on its drivers of success. It would have been natural for the growing engineering and related services business to have one of its founders serve as the chief executive officer and the other to serve as the chief operating officer. Herb McKim and Mike Creed, however, realized that although they were in the consulting services business, they were really in the *people* business. As a service business, future success would depend on the quality of its people. They recognized their business would grow and succeed only to the extent that it had the right number of people in the right place, at the right time, and with the right capabilities. The lack of capable people would have the same devastating consequences as a stock-out for a business that sells tangible products.

Unlike most businesses, however, one of the founders volunteered to oversee the human side of the enterprise. While the other founder directed his attention toward business development and the company's finances, he focused his efforts on ensuring that the company had the ability to staff existing and prospective projects. He also invested considerable time and resources in hiring new specialists and developing the existing staff's capabilities so that the business would have the talent needed to serve emerging markets.

Many companies still consider the human resource function to be a staffing function rather than the very pulse of the enterprise. McKim and Creed recognized that its people were the ultimate drivers of success. McKim and Creed's performance-management system placed a premium on human resources. Top management's commitment to, investment in, and development of its human resources enabled McKim and Creed to become one of the fastest growing engineering-services businesses in its field.

DEVELOPING THE BALANCED SCORECARD

Tom Peters, management consultant and author, observed, "If you are spending 100 percent of your time doing continuous improvement, then you are spending 0 percent of your time on innovation!" The same logic can be applied to management's tendency to be preoccupied with the company's financial dimensions. If management is preoccupied with monitoring cash flow and absorbed in fine-tuning daily operations, it will overlook the company's true drivers of success. In their book *The Balanced Scorecard*, Robert Kaplan and David Norton provide a useful mental framework for managing the overall enterprise. Kaplan and Norton propose that executives use a balanced scorecard that monitors and measures the company's drivers of success.

Executives have always had some sort of scorecard. When management develops the company's performance-management system, it needs to ensure that its corresponding scorecard differentiates the drivers of success from the factors that are the effects of the drivers. For example, should the scorecard focus on employee turnover, productivity, or satisfaction? Which employee factor is the cause and which employee factor is an effect? The same question applies to financial measures. Should management focus on sales (and corresponding cash flow) or monitor the percentage of repeat purchases?

The process of developing the balanced scorecard tends to be very frustrating for most executives because they must identify and articulate the drivers of success. The process of developing the scorecard usually brings different perspectives to the surface. Kaplan and Norton wrote, "In our experience with the design of scorecard programs, we have never encountered a management team that had reached full consensus on the relative importance of its strategic objectives. . . . When executives from different functional perspectives . . . attempt to work together as a team, there are blind spots— areas of relative ignorance around which it is difficult to form teams and create consensus because so little shared understanding exists about overall business objectives and the contribution and integration of different functional units."[6] The balanced scorecard has the potential to create a shared model of the entire business if top management—working as a team—develops it.

The process of identifying the true drivers of success presents another challenge for the members of the executive team. The development of the scorecard forces them to be specific in terms of performance expectations. The scorecard will be of little value if the performance expectations are merely a set of lofty platitudes.

The scorecard needs to be composed of the drivers of success—and the drivers need to be stated in quantitative terms.

Imagine if a thermometer had only six calibrations: hot, warm, tepid, cool, cold, and frigid. It would be difficult for a household thermostat using such general calibrations to provide the ideal temperature for one's home. A similar lack of precision makes monitoring and managing a company very difficult. The first step in developing the balanced scorecard is to translate the company's vision and strategy statements into an integrated set of objectives and measures that describe the long-term drivers of success. Kaplan and Norton noted that, despite the best intentions of those at the top, lofty statements about becoming "best in the class," "the number-one supplier," or "an empowered organization" don't translate easily into operational terms that provide useful guides to action.[7]

The scorecard needs to be viewed as an organizational thermostat. While thermostats incorporate thermometers, it is the thermostat that initiates the changes needed to produce the desired results. The scorecard must do more than monitor the temperature of the company's drivers of success; it must serve as the springboard for modifying the company's operations and, in some instances, altering its strategy in the years ahead.

THE SCORECARD NEEDS TO BE BALANCED AND HOLISTIC

The scorecard will be beneficial only if it is balanced and managers view the company with a holistic perspective. Future financial performance is the result of both financial and nonfinancial decisions. The balanced scorecard does not devalue the role played by financial strategies and the need for financial measures. Instead, Kaplan and Norton emphasize a more holistic perspective by supplementing the financial factors with three sets of nonfinancial factors. They stress the need for executives to use a scorecard that also includes customer factors, internal business-process factors, and learning-and-growth perspectives and measures. These three additional perspectives, like the financial perspectives, are derived from an explicit and rigorous translation of the organization's vision and strategy into tangible objectives and measures.[8]

According to Kaplan and Norton, financial measures tell the story of past events. Financial measures are inadequate for guiding and evaluating the journey that information-age companies must face to create future value through investment in customers, suppliers, employees, processes, and innovation.[9]

Financial indicators are not always the *leading* indicators of organizational performance. Customer and employee satisfaction factors influence cash flow. A drop in the repeat purchase rate is certain to have an adverse effect on cash flow. Cash flow also deteriorates when the company is forced to spend more money on advertising when market share drops. Cash flow is also affected when product quality fluctuates and the company needs to spend more money on process-improvement efforts. In these instances, management may need to take a closer look to determine whether the company's products are in sync with market demands or whether work processes are being properly monitored. Cash flow may also deteriorate if there is a drop in the level of employee commitment, training, and experimentation.

If management wants to improve future cash flow, the company's strategy may need to be altered to attract new customers as well as to foster customer retention. Analog Devices initiated a process to learn what its customers really valued. It surveyed its customers and did benchmarking studies and found that they cared about things like delivery time and improved quality. Analog then built a model that would help its managers track and thus manage such things. Arthur M. Schneiderman, who developed Analog's balanced scorecard, found, "Overall, there were about fifteen nonfinancial measures that we identified as critical to the company's performance."[10]

If customer satisfaction is a driver of financial success, then management may need to direct its attention to establishing customer alliances, boosting new product development, reducing cycle time, improving response time, enhancing quality, reducing costs, and incorporating the latest information technology. The same logic also applies to enhancing employee satisfaction by having a work environment that attracts the best talent, management practices that enable employees at all levels to grow and contribute, and compensation systems that provide benchmark-level rewards when people turn in outstanding performances.

Management must make every effort to ensure that all components of the scorecard and corresponding business strategy are consistent with one another. The scorecard and strategy must reflect the cause-and-effect nature of the overall business. Major omissions or inconsistencies in the scorecard or strategy will undermine the synergistic effect needed to move the company ahead. Kaplan and Norton noted, "Once targets for customer, internal business-processes, and learning-and-growth measures are established, managers can align their strategic quality, response time, and reengineering initiatives for achieving breakthrough objectives."[11]

THE BALANCED SCORECARD CAN FOSTER BIFOCAL MANAGEMENT

The balanced scorecard is noteworthy because it links short-term actions and goal achievement to strategic milestones. The balanced scorecard addresses a serious deficiency in traditional management systems. Traditional management systems place so much emphasis on current financial metrics that the company's overall strategy does not receive sufficient attention.

Kaplan and Norton believe the balanced scorecard has its greatest impact when it is deployed to drive organizational change. They advise senior executives to establish targets for scorecard measures, which, if achieved in three to five years, will transform the company. The targets should represent a discontinuity in business-unit performance. Managers must establish stretch targets for their customer, internal-business-process, and learning-and-growth objectives.[12] Breakthrough performances in the scorecard's nonfinancial dimensions should lead to breakthrough financial performance. The scorecard is instrumental in change efforts because it identifies what the company needs to do well to succeed. Linking compensation to achieving stretch targets for scorecard measures also helps to foster change.

The balanced scorecard's holistic nature enables management to link organizational, departmental, team, and individual goals and actions. The balanced scorecard helps management translate the scorecard into operational measures. The operational measures, in turn, become the focus for improvement activities in local units.

The balanced scorecard can also provide the basis for creating a personal scorecard for everyone in the company. Peter Drucker's statement that a plan is not a plan unless it degenerates into action also applies to the balanced scorecard. The balanced scorecard does not have its full effect unless it degenerates into personal objectives, measures, targets, and initiatives. Once corporate and individual-unit targets are established, each person establishes his or her corresponding goals. Every employee then identifies up to five performance measures and targets for the corresponding goals.[13] Each person's performance is then reviewed according to the extent to which the targets were met and the extent to which that person contributed to the goals of both the unit and the company. The company's compensation system helps reinforce the balanced and bifocal nature of the scorecard. According to Kaplan and Norton, individuals will not earn incentive compensation if performance in any given period falls below the minimum threshold.[14]

THE BALANCED SCORECARD CAN BE CONFIGURED AS AN ORGANIZATIONAL DASHBOARD

The concept of a balanced scorecard has contributed to the development of the organizational dashboard. Executives cannot watch every dimension of the company's operations. The cockpit of an airplane provides an interesting example of the need for executives to translate the balanced scorecard into an organizational dashboard. It is physically impossible for the captain and the crew to watch every gauge during every moment of the flight. The same applies to executives at the helms of today's companies.

Executives need to identify the factors that are essential for enhancing current performance and future success. Executives then need to create an organizational dashboard that includes gauges for the factors that are drivers of success. The dashboard needs to be calibrated so that the gauges reflect the ongoing status of the drivers of success. The gauges must be adequately displayed so that executives can monitor them easily and frequently. Considerable thought goes into the design of aircraft dashboards; the same amount of thought should go into the configuration of the company's dashboard.

Automobile drivers provide an interesting example about how people fail to rely on factors that measure performance. Most drivers spend their time looking through the windshield. They spend very little time looking at the gauges on their dashboard. They only glance occasionally at the speedometer and rarely check the fuel gauge. Few drivers take time to monitor the gauges that measure engine temperature, oil pressure, and the extent that the battery is being charged.

The dashboard works best if its gauges monitor the true drivers of success. It must be configured so that executives focus their attention regularly on a balanced set of gauges rather than just the ongoing financial metrics that tend to be located at the center of most organizational dashboards. The dashboard should include gauges that monitor the rate of new product development, the percentage of sales from proprietary products, the amount of time it takes to introduce new products, the overall cycle time, the on-time delivery ratio, and the customer retention index. Gauges that monitor employee satisfaction and organizational learning help to foster a more balanced perspective.

If new product development is an important driver of success, then goals and strategies need to be developed to enhance new product development. 3M's goal of having 30 percent of its sales four years from now come from products that don't exist today can serve as the basis for a new product development gauge that monitors the company's progress in meeting that goal. The gauges can monitor the rate of development and introduction as well as revenue, profit, and return on investment generated by new products.

If the company's human resources are considered drivers of success, then goals and strategies need to be developed to ensure that the company has the right number of people in place with the necessary capabilities. An Ohio-based company has a goal of always having at least one successor for every manager and other key employees. That company monitors the ratio of key personnel to key personnel with successors to make certain the company has minimized the likelihood of having a management stock-out.

If generating ideas for improvement and experimentation are considered drivers of success, then monitoring the number of employee suggestions may provide an indication of the level of employee involvement and learning. For example, a Wainwright

Industries plant monitors whether it is achieving its target of 1.25 suggestions per week per employee.[15] The average profit or savings per suggestion may also serve as a key indicator.

The organization's dashboard can play an integral role in fostering a shared perspective throughout the company. The dashboard enables people at all levels to read from the same set of gauges, with the same set of metrics that are measured the same way. In many companies, there is little agreement on the metrics or how they are measured. Too often, the metrics are measured differently from one unit to the next. For example, employee productivity may be measured in terms of labor cost per unit while another organizational unit may measure employee productivity in terms of sales per employee.

Information technology can play an important role in making the organizational dashboard operational. Joel Kurtzman, editor of *Strategy and Business*, explained that scorecard software, which is usually distributed throughout the company's computer network, lets managers across the entire organization be certain they are talking about the same thing when they get together. Kurtzman noted that if customer satisfaction is dropping, the people in sales, manufacturing, and research and development can all read the same score, and thus be able to tackle the problem from common ground.[16]

THE QUALITY OF THE COMPANY'S MANAGEMENT INFORMATION SYSTEM IS CRITICAL

The company's performance-management system can only be as good as the company's management information system. The company's balanced scorecard and corresponding dashboard will work only to the extent that executives have the right information, at the right time, and in the right format. Ironically, the term *management information system* may be a misnomer. Management needs more than information; it needs knowledge. Knowledge is information that makes a difference, provides insight, aids in decision making, causes management to initiate change, and enables the company to achieve its objectives.

The company's management information system must be

timely, selective, and efficient. It should measure the status of the company's drivers of success as well as its ongoing performance. The information system should indicate milestones, trends, and variances. If the system is properly designed, it will function as an early warning system. The information will help management build on the company's strengths and capitalize on both current and emerging opportunities. The information will also serve as the basis for correcting deficiencies and preventing problems.

If the system only monitors financial factors, it may be dealing with results or lagging factors. Nonfinancial factors also need to be monitored. Management needs to decide whether market share should be measured and monitored more closely than customer satisfaction. Management must also decide whether it monitors the employee turnover rate or employee satisfaction. The second factor in the preceding sets of factors is more causal than the first factor. If the information system is not able to provide the right information, the company's scorecard and dashboard will be of little benefit.

Measurement frequency also plays a key role in the management information system. If the company is looking for continuous improvement, the system needs to measure performance in those areas on a continuous basis. If continuous improvement depends on the plan-do-check-act cycle, then the *check* component needs to be continuous. Measurement frequency may vary with each factor being monitored. The system must also keep people informed of the level of progress being made for key factors on a regular basis. Fortunately, today's electronic bulletin boards and real-time databases can help keep people informed. Tom Valerio of Cigna Property and Casualty used a version of the balanced scorecard that identified multiple performance measures. It tracked and billboarded these measures along the way. By booting up an electronic version of the scorecard on their desktop computers, senior leaders could get an instant read on whether their unit was hitting its objectives. Because of this simple piece of technology, a manager couldn't hide a bad performance.[17]

The company's management information system should incorporate the practice of management by exception. Management by exception identifies which factors need to be monitored closely. Monitoring systems that focus on identifying exceptional deviations have been around for years. Today's online, real-time information technology, however, makes it possible for people at all levels of the organization to monitor even the smallest variances. This speed is vital because the sooner a variance is recognized, the quicker the company can respond.

MONITORING AND MEASURING ARE NOT THE ENDS . . .

Performance-management systems should be viewed as learning systems that constantly raise questions, test assumptions, probe for the real issues, analyze variances, and provide feedback. The balanced scorecard, organizational dashboard, and management information system should also foster insights, learning, and change. Conventional measurement systems are designed to answer questions such as, "Are we meeting our targets?" "Are we on schedule?" and "Are we within our budget?" Performance-management systems, however, emphasize learning as well as monitoring performance and modifying operations.

Most companies use single-loop learning. With single-loop learning, an adverse variation from expected interim results initiates actions until the variation is corrected. With double-loop learning, however, management deliberately steps back and analyzes the whole situation, including the objectives, strategies, plans, tactics, and time lines. Instead of the typical knee-jerk response of "See a variance, fix the variance," which assumes the overall strategy is still the right path to take, management goes all the way back to ground zero and challenges the assumptions and objectives that served as the basis for the development of the strategy being implemented.[18]

Double-loop learning encourages managers to reexamine their mental models and corresponding cause-and-effect relationships. For example, if monthly sales for a product are falling below expectations, management should go beyond the usual single-loop learning response of increasing advertising or lowering its price. With double-loop learning, management steps back and reexamines the product's position in its life cycle and whether the resources invested in that product could be deployed more favorably in the development of a new product to serve an emerging market.

With double-loop learning, departures are seen as opportunities to learn, not only as things to be fixed. If management embraces the concept of double-loop learning, it will not wait for variances to raise the fundamental questions about whether the company is actually doing what it should be doing. If the company is truly a learning organization, then serious questioning of basic issues will take place on a regular basis. Learning organizations deal with strategic issues on an ongoing basis; they don't save them for annual planning retreats or major crises.

CYPRESS SEMICONDUCTOR: PROFILE OF FOCUS AND CONTROL

Having crucial information on a real-time basis permits real-time adjustments. State-of-the-art management information systems resemble the radar-interfaced flight control systems that enable jet fighters to fly closer to the ground at even faster speeds. Cypress Semiconductor has embraced and operationalized a performance-management system that permits its top management to monitor what is happening throughout the entire organization.

Cypress Semiconductor, under the leadership of T. J. Rogers, has demonstrated a total commitment to identifying performance objectives and monitoring whether they are being accomplished. Rogers stated, "Most companies don't fail for lack of talent or vision. They fail for lack of execution—the mundane blocking and tackling that the great companies consistently do well and strive to do better."[19] Cypress Semiconductor's comprehensive system sets and monitors more than six thousand performance factors on an ongoing basis.[20] While Cypress Semiconductor's system may seem overly tight, it forces each manager to focus on the areas that make a difference. It also provides an early warning system that can activate a quick response.

According to Rogers, "The systems are designed to encourage collective thinking and to force each of us to face reality every day."[21] Rogers further explained, "At Cypress, our management systems track corporate, departmental, and individual performance so regularly and in such detail that no manager, including me, can plausibly claim to be in the dark about critical problems. . . .

Our systems give managers the capacity to monitor what's happening at [all] levels of the organization, to anticipate problems or conflicts, to intervene when appropriate, and to identify the best practices—without creating layers of bureaucracy that bog down decisions and sap morale."[22]

According to Rogers, "At Cypress we collect information in such detail and share it so widely that the company is virtually transparent."[23] The system's emphasis on openness and accessibility has numerous benefits. Rogers explained, "Lots of companies espouse a 'no surprises' philosophy. At Cypress, 'no surprises' is a way of life. . . . Our watchwords are discipline, accountability, and relentless attention to detail—at every level of the organization."[24] Cypress Semiconductor's system reflects the emphasis on employee empowerment and personal accountability that comes with MBO. Rogers noted, "All of Cypress's 1,400 employees have goals, which is no different from employees at most other companies. What does make our people different is that every week they set their own goals, commit to achieving them by a specific date, enter them into the database, and report whether or not they completed prior goals."[25]

Cypress's computerized goal system is a detailed guide to the future and an objective record of the past. In any given week, some six thousand goals in the database come due. Rogers noted that Cypress's ability to meet these goals ultimately determines the company's success or failure. Each month, a completed goal report is issued for every person in the company. At year's end, managers have a dozen such objective reviews to refresh their memories and fight the proximity effect.[26]

It would be easy for someone to conclude that Cypress Semiconductor's system is nothing more than an extremely comprehensive system for ensuring that nothing falls through the cracks. Cypress Semiconductor's system, however, does far more than monitor the operational side of the company. The system is designed to foster learning and achieve long-term performance. The people who are implementing the system are also expected to analyze why performance variations exist and to make recommendations for how performance can be improved.

Cypress Semiconductor's system does not focus exclusively on financial and operating factors. It incorporates the balanced scorecard's emphasis on human resource factors in addition to monitoring yields, costs, and cycle times for each manufacturing operation, and the average outgoing quality level for each of the company's leading product lines. Revenue and productivity per employee are also monitored on an ongoing basis because these metrics are critical to the company's competitiveness. Cypress Semiconductor's system also places a premium on ensuring that its customers are not taken for granted. Every officer at Cypress is a "godfather" to one of the company's strategic customers.[27]

Cypress Semiconductor's performance-management system also fosters management by exception. Rogers said that collecting information, reviewing it regularly, and sharing it widely allows him to practice management by exception in the trust sense. He believes that if people use its systems, the organization will virtually run itself. Rogers intervenes only to solve problems and champion key projects.[28]

Management by exception gives Rogers time to scan the horizon for blips on the screen and to focus on things that truly matter. He views his job to be *anticipating* problems. He does this by sorting through the goal system looking for patterns. He uses the system as a kind of organizational speedometer that not only tells him how fast the company is traveling but helps him to identify what is holding the company back.[29]

Cypress's system also enables Rogers to get a quick sense of reality. With a few keystrokes, he can check on the performance of any one of his vice presidents. Rogers noted that his access to the details means vice presidents can't snow him.[30] The company's performance-management system is also tuned in to factors outside the company. Cypress's system constantly checks the company's performance against its best competitors.[31]

CONCLUSION: PROCEED, BUT PROCEED WITH CAUTION

The performance-management system is intended to foster strategic monitoring and control. However, like most things in business, it can become an organizational nightmare if it is not handled deftly. Every effort should be made to keep the performance-management system from being the fuel that lights the fires for bureaucrats and bean counters. This may be one of those instances when it may be better to have a loosely defined system than to have a system that religiously measures the wrong things.

Effort should also be directed toward ensuring that the system stays in tune with the times. For the system to work, it must be ever-evolving. Changing environments and business conditions frequently necessitate changes in business strategy. Such changes may change the drivers of success as well as their corresponding targets and metrics.

Your company's strategic monitoring and control system must identify what really matters. It must also ensure that everyone knows how those factors affect performance. If properly designed and administered, it will also measure those factors frequently enough so that deviations can be spotted early. This will give your company additional time to determine the cause for the deviation and the opportunity to take corrective action before it is too late or too costly.

> *"Change hurts. But indecision kills. What American business is able to make decisions that might appear to destroy shareholder value for several years before they pay off?"*[32]

—Avram Miller, CEO of the
Avram Miller Company

NOTES

1. Robert S. Kaplan and David P. Norton, "Having Trouble with Your Strategy? Then Map It," *Harvard Business Review,* September–October 2000, p. 167.
2. Joel Kurtzman, "Is Your Company off Course? Now You Can Find out Why," *Fortune,* February 17, 1997, p. 128.
3. Ibid., p. 129.
4. Ibid., p. 129.
5. Jeffrey Pfeffer, "Producing Sustainable Competitive Advantage through the Effective Management of People," *Academy of Management Executives,* February 1995, p. 66.
6. Robert S. Kaplan and David P. Norton, *The Balanced Scorecard* (Boston: Harvard Business School Press, 1996), p. 12.
7. Robert S. Kaplan and David P. Norton, "Using the Balanced Score-

card as a Strategic Measurement System," *Harvard Business Review,* January/February 1996, pp. 75–76.

8. Kaplan and Norton, *The Balanced Scorecard,* p. 18.
9. Ibid., p. 7.
10. Kurtzman, p. 130.
11. Kaplan and Norton, *The Balanced Scorecard,* p. 14.
12. Ibid., p. 13.
13. Kaplan and Norton, "Using the Balanced Scorecard as a Strategic Measurement System," p. 81.
14. Ibid., p. 82.
15. "Using Measurement to Boost Your Unit's Performance," *Harvard Management Update,* October 1998, p. 3.
16. Kurtzman, p. 128.
17. Bill Breen and Cheryl Dahle, "20/20 Change Agent," *Fast Company,* December 1999, p. 404.
18. Kaplan and Norton, *The Balanced Scorecard,* p. 16.
19. T. J. Rogers, "No Excuses Management," *Harvard Business Review,* July/August, 1990, p. 84.
20. Ibid., p. 87.
21. Ibid., p. 85.
22. Ibid., p. 84.
23. Ibid., p. 85.
24. Ibid., p. 84.
25. Ibid., p. 87.
26. Ibid., p. 89.
27. Ibid., p. 90.
28. Ibid., p. 86.
29. Ibid., p. 89.
30. Ibid., p. 90.
31. Ibid., p. 92.
32. Katharine Mieszkowski, "The Power of the Internet Is That You Can Experiment," *Fast Company,* December 1999, p. 162.

Epilogue

Who Ever Said Breakthrough Leadership Would Be Easy?

"Change is the law of life. And those who look only to the past and present are certain to miss the future."
—John F. Kennedy, 35th President of the United States

Moving your company forward and creating its future is not an option. The competitive marketplace is in the middle of a revolution where incremental change will not be good enough. You have a choice: You can play a leading role in the revolution by launching bold initiatives or you can be trampled by companies that are in sync with new realities.

Breakthrough leadership is not for the squeamish. You will have to do things that you have never done before—and possibly no one has done before or thought possible. It is like going through a level-five rapids.

Changing the world both inside and outside of the company will be a messy process. It cannot be choreographed perfectly nor can it be done overnight. Leading change takes persistent patience.

Those who have the energy and skill needed to navigate the whitewater associated with the rapids of ever-accelerating change will stand out in the crowd. Their ability to change the way the game is played, to unleash the ideas of people at all levels, and to take their companies to the next level and beyond will enable them to boldly take their companies where no companies have gone before.

The choice is yours; you can either lead or get blown out of the way!

Appendix 1

One Hundred Ways to Self-Destruct as a Leader

Although the sure-fire formula for managerial success continues to elude us, the search has not been a total loss. Along the way, we have learned that certain behaviors will not lead to high levels of performance and employee satisfaction. This list identifies one hundred behaviors that should be avoided as you encounter the never-ending challenges that you will face in the years ahead.

When It Comes to Planning: Don't!

- Fail to set specific and meaningful objectives for the company and your employees.
- Have no vision for the future.
- Only be concerned with short-term results rather than with what might happen in five to seven years.
- Don't think the unthinkable.
- Don't expect the unexpected.
- Ignore obvious trends.
- Fail to stay abreast of technological developments in your field.
- Expect things to be easy and everything to go as planned.

- Initiate change without recognizing the current corporate culture.
- Wing it when sound planning and organization are essential.
- Pursue all activities as they come up—don't prioritize.
- Spend all your time fighting fires while ignoring those issues that are important to the company's success but are not currently urgent.

When It Comes to Managing Change: Protect the Status Quo!

- Be reactive, not proactive. Respond to change rather than initiate it.
- Be satisfied with today . . . and live in the glory of the past.
- Use yesterday as the benchmark for what should be done tomorrow.
- Put off to tomorrow what should be done today.
- Don't try to anticipate things, don't run scenarios, and don't develop contingency plans.
- Believe that the rate of change is slowing down and that things will return to the past.

When It Comes to Organizing: Always Complicate—Never Simplify!

- Place a higher value on day-to-day efficiency rather than on long-term effectiveness.
- Build huge staffs to solve organizational inefficiency problems.
- Expect employees to complete projects without having enough training, authority, or resources.
- Underestimate the bureaucracy in your company.
- Do not consider other people and departments in the organization to be "internal customers."

When It Comes to Staffing: If an Organization Can Only Be as Good as Its People, Then Automate Everything!

- Hire people who are just like you.
- Surround yourself with yes-people.

- Assume that you are above attending management development seminars.
- Make yourself indispensable by not training anyone else to take your place.
- Hire from outside rather than developing your current employees.
- Do the work yourself rather than developing your employees' abilities.
- Don't help your employees advance.
- Don't check the background of prospective employees.
- Initiate a quality improvement program without training people first.

When It Comes to Making Decisions: Assume the One Who Hesitates Wins!

- Make all important decisions by yourself. Do not involve the people in the organization in decision processes that will directly affect them.
- Don't test or challenge your assumptions.
- Be a yes-man/woman.
- Spend all your time trying to get other people to see your point of view rather than trying to see their points of view.
- Assume there will be economies of scale.
- Focus only on the bottom line.
- Bring in a consultant whenever you can't solve a problem.
- Put off important decisions in hopes that they will resolve themselves.
- Vacillate as long as possible whenever a decision needs to be made.
- Wait until you have 100 percent of the possible information before you make every decision.
- Do not admit that you don't know when you don't.
- Don't take the time to look for innovative solutions to routine problems.
- View everything as a problem rather than as a disguised opportunity.

When It Comes to Leadership: Why Try to Be a Leader When You Already Are the Boss?

- Assume all people are alike.
- Treat hourly personnel as if they are hourly personnel.

- Take employees for granted and treat them like they are expendable. Remind them they are lucky to have jobs.
- Ignore the signals of stress . . . keep pushing yourself and others.
- Regard all ideas from employees with suspicion.
- Let your fear of failure overpower the need to try new approaches.
- Play favorites.
- Don't give people a second chance when they experiment and make a mistake.
- Gossip.
- Make sure that rewards are not given to people who contribute to long-term performance.

When It Comes to Communication: Practice Mushroom Management by Keeping Everyone in the Dark!

- Be secretive about everything. Don't keep your employees informed of what is going on in the company.
- Expect your staff to know what you want without telling them.
- Minimize face-to-face communication.
- Don't acknowledge correspondence—especially from your boss.
- Don't return phone calls—let them call you back.
- Tell people what they want to hear rather than what is really the case.
- Discourage discussion of problems and punish those who bring up bad news.
- Breach confidentiality.
- Don't keep employees informed about areas of concern until performance appraisal time.

When It Comes to Setting the Right Example: Manage by Hypocrisy!

- Constantly remind your employees that you are the boss and that you know what is best.
- Overlook violations of corporate policy by employees . . . and do not follow them yourself.

- Give your employees new work to do at the end of the day that it is due.
- Bring your personal problems to work. Display drastic mood swings while at the office.
- Claim ownership for all good ideas even if they aren't your own. Blame your employees when things don't work out.
- Ask for more resources rather than endeavoring to be more productive with the resources that you already have at your disposal.
- Have a "not invented here" attitude toward other people's ideas.
- Say one thing and then do another. Don't say what you mean and don't do what you say.
- Bring your colleagues' mistakes to your boss's attention.
- Expect to change your employees' behavior without changing your example.
- Forget to thank your staff for a job well done.
- Tell your employees there is not enough money for a cost-of-living increase, and then give management a 10 percent bonus. Then fly first-class to an "Enhancing Employee Relations" seminar at an exclusive resort.
- Treat your employees like children.
- Take your vacation during the busiest time of the year.

When It Comes to Control: It's More Exciting If You Fly without Instruments!

- Don't follow up on what needs to be done.
- Wait until the last minute to finish projects.
- Conduct performance reviews only once a year.
- Assume poor results are always the result of lazy personnel.
- When an employee's performance is substandard, give him or her a reasonable rating because you don't want to ruffle his or her feathers or strain your relationship.
- Discuss the performance of one employee with your other employees.
- Dwell on past mistakes rather than viewing them as avenues for future improvements in performance reviews.
- Evaluate employees according to things over which they have no control.

- Be concerned with inspection of the final product rather than with the entire production process.
- Don't worry about whether you are within your budget until the last two months of the year.
- Try to control everything.

When All Else Fails and You Are Still Looking for Ways to Self-Destruct: Here Are Ten Sure-Fire Ways to Fail as a Manager:

- Assume tomorrow will be the same as today.
- Assume problem situations will take care of themselves.
- Go for quick fixes.
- Be all talk and no action.
- Concentrate on organizational politics rather than on performance.
- Try to look better instead of being better.
- Put off informing your boss that you will be over your budget until the end of the year.
- Assume your employees will be loyal to the company no matter what.
- Violate sexual harassment laws.
- Have an affair with one of your employees or your boss.

Note: These ideas have been submitted by people attending the author's seminars and students enrolled in his classes. I also want to thank Benny Waller, who as a graduate student, helped me compile this list.

Appendix 2

One Hundred Ways to Drive Away Your Customers

It is ironic that at a time when companies are trying to attract new customers they are driving their customers away. Their attitudes, practices, and processes turn off perspective customers and alienate current customers. If you want to expedite your company's demise, then follow these guidelines:

How to Be Totally Customer Unresponsive:

- View customers as interruptions.
- Tell customers, "That's not my job."
- Tell customers, "It has always been done this way and I can't change it."
- Have personnel blame "those people in headquarters" any time a mistake is made.
- Make excuses and do not accept responsibility for your company's product or service. Blame problems on your suppliers. Tell the customer, "That's what our supplier provided us with, so you're stuck with it."
- Assume the customer is the problem.
- Don't view customer complaints as opportunities to learn how to improve.

- Don't view customer complaints as opportunities for customer recovery.
- Give customers bogus information because you do not know the right answer when they ask a question.
- If your customers complain about your product or service, don't respond until they call again. Assume that if it is really important, they'll call you a second time.
- Alienate customers . . . make them feel helpless.
- Do not apologize . . . ever.

The Electronic Side of Unresponsiveness:

- Have a Web site address that takes an IQ over 150 to remember.
- Have a Web site that punishes inquirers by having them navigate page after page or answer question after question to get even the simplest information.

The Phone Side of Unresponsiveness:

- Do not have toll-free customer service numbers.
- Do not allow inquiries to be submitted via phone, fax, or e-mail. Insist they be submitted via regular mail.
- Do not provide quotes for products or services over the telephone.
- Route customer calls through various steps, and then have the phone disconnect.
- Have the phone ring more than five times.
- Have the customer listen to awful music or repeated messages while on hold.
- Ask callers if they can be put on hold and not wait for their answer.
- Have the message "Please wait, we appreciate your business," but don't give customers any idea of how long they are going to have to wait . . . especially if it is not a toll-free call.
- Procrastinate in getting back to customers, especially on crucial product information.
- Never return customer calls.
- Keep calling customers to ask them for suggestions and never incorporate the changes.

- Call customers during meal times or weekends to see if they are satisfied.
- Have telephone solicitors argue with prospective customers when they do not want the product.
- Have your phone salespeople say, "I'm sorry I woke you up, but I have a long list of prospects to call."
- Think the customer is on hold when the phone is still active . . . and have the customer hear, "Somebody take care of this jerk."

Show Your Customers You Don't Want Them:

- Write disparaging comments about a customer on the service sheet and then give the sheet back to the customer as a receipt.
- Have the attitude, "If I ignore the customers' problems, they will go away!"
- Operate with "just-in-time" customer responsiveness.
- When customers ask for a specific date for making monthly payments say, "That is not possible, the computer sets the due dates."
- Fail to explore customer empowerment where customers can help solve problems.
- Have a "You bought it, so it's your problem now!" customer service policy.
- Charge the customer for your time even when you tell the customer you cannot figure out what the problem is or how to fix it.
- Look for major solutions first rather than minor ones that might save a customer money.
- Have a corporate culture that says, "Keep your ass to the customer and face to the CEO."

Make Hollow Commitments:

- Make promises that cannot be kept.
- Guarantee something that is so risk-free that it has no added value.
- Offer a conditional warrantee that has so many conditions and restrictions that it is virtually impossible for the customer to use.

- Make the warrantee statement so difficult to read and understand that customers won't read it.
- Say, "These tires are guaranteed never to puncture." And then indicate that the "road hazard warrantee" is available for an additional fee.
- Have the small print contradict or nullify the large print in the promotional material.
- Make sure customers will be hassled if they try to follow up on the warrantee.
- Have a "no return" policy or one with provisions that make it virtually impossible or punishing for the customer to return products.
- Do not pay out quickly . . . make it difficult for customers to get a refund.
- Have service people say, "I'm sorry that part fell off, but I'm sure it will still work without it."
- Have delivery people say, "Oh, that will be an extra $50 to unload the merchandise."
- Advertise something and not have it available.
- Introduce new products and services without briefing your staff.
- Do not empower salespeople. Make them get approval on even the most minor issue.
- Do not empower employees to fix something that needs to be fixed immediately.
- Have a series of people deal with the same customer, so the customer has to repeat his or her story again and again.
- Let your customers do your quality control. Wait for customers to detect product or service problems or defects.
- Misunderstand the customer recovery paradox. Deliberately screw up products so you will have the opportunity to show you care by fixing them.
- Do not consider the customers' expectations of quality. If customers say your product or service is not up to their standards, spend lots of money to change their perceptions but do not improve the product or service.
- Fail to take adequate precautions when preparing equipment for shipment.
- Fail to provide adequate assembly and installation drawings/manuals.

- Assume the owner's manual is user-friendly.
- Ship and charge products to customers they did not order.

How Retail Businesses Drive Customers Away:

- Lock the door when customers are about to enter your business near closing time.
- Tell customers their needs and wants without asking them first.
- Have checkout clerks talk to each other as they check customers out and never once look at the customer or even acknowledge his or her existence.
- Do not have "roamers" in the store to assist customers.
- Have twenty people wait in three checkout lines when ten checkout counters are closed.
- Have your staff stock merchandise while customers wait for service.
- Fill the aisles with so much merchandise and displays that customer movement is impeded.
- Have staff tell customers to come back in a few minutes because they are about to take a break.
- Accept personal phone calls while carrying out a transaction with a customer.
- Don't provide infant changing stations in male restrooms or at all.
- Don't have enough parking spaces available for customers or charge them for parking.
- Never call other stores in an attempt to help the customer locate a product that is out of stock.
- Turn on and off the lights to signal customers the business is closing.

Here's How a Few Specific Businesses Frustrate Customers:

- Grocery Stores:
    —Pack customer's grocery bags as full as possible, regardless of the weight.
- Restaurants:
    —Place customers in a no-smoking section that is only a half-height partition away from the smoking section

. . . and not understand why the customer is not
happy.

—Offer an all-you-can-eat buffet, and then limit the customers to one plate.

—Don't provide separate checks for diners in the same
party. If they are having problems splitting up the bill,
give them a calculator to figure it out.

—Have the checkout or wait staff ask the customer how
much tip should be put on the credit card.

- Hotels:

—Make customers wait until after 3 P.M. before they
can check in.

- Doctors:

—Have waiting rooms for waiting rooms.

—Comingle sick people with healthy people.

—Wonder why people have such high blood pressure . . .
when they have waited for over an hour.

—Make sure the waiting room temperature is less than
sixty degrees.

—Charge $4,000 for laser eye surgery and then tell the
customer to provide a videotape if he or she wants it
recorded.

If You Still Have Too Many Customers, Then . . .

- Assume you know what is best for the customer.
- Don't find out what your customers want and who they are.
- Don't find out why you lose customers.
- Bend over backwards for prospective customers while tak-
ing existing customers for granted.
- Focus only on your current customers while not focusing
on who should be future customers.
- Consider behind-the-scenes personnel more important
than front-line personnel.
- Make sure that both internal and external operations func-
tion inconsistently.
- Hire anyone, especially employees who know that they
will only be paid the minimum.
- Reprimand employees in front of customers.

- Overwhelm your staff with so many internal activities that they do not have the time or patience to serve customers.
- Live in the past. Continue offering the same products and services.
- Do not cannibalize your current products and services.
- Assume you are a monopoly.
- Confuse repeat business with customer loyalty.
- Think you are doing your customers a favor by being in business.

Note: These ideas have been submitted by people attending the author's seminars and by students enrolled in his classes.

Index

About the Author

Dr. Stephen C. Harper is professor of management at the University of North Carolina at Wilmington and president of Harper and Associates Inc.—a management-consulting company. He has been helping entrepreneurs and executives transform their companies into exceptional enterprises for more than twenty-five years.

Steve is the author of three other books: *The McGraw-Hill Guide to Managing Growth in Your Emerging Business* (1995), *The McGraw-Hill Guide to Starting Your Own Business* (1991), and *Management: Who Ever Said It Would Be Easy?* (1983). He has also written dozens of articles that have appeared in national magazines.

Steve has received numerous teaching and service awards, including the University of North Carolina board of governors' Award for Excellence in Teaching. He has also served on the faculty of Arizona State University, where he earned his Ph.D., and at Duke University as a visiting professor of entrepreneurship.

Steve was the cofounder and president of three economic development enterprises and has served on the board of directors for various organizations. He has also served on the editorial boards of *North Carolina Entrepreneur* magazine and *The Journal of Business and Entrepreneurship*.

As a speaker for professional meetings, Steve conducts seminars on strategic thinking, leadership, entrepreneurship, and the management of change. He has conducted more than three hundred seminars for corporations, not-for-profit enterprises, and government agencies on the federal, state, and municipal levels. Steve has also been a speaker for more than one hundred academic, business, and civic groups in the United States and Canada.

CENTRAL

CENTRAL   AUG   2001

ALEXANDRIA LIBRARY
ALEXANDRIA, VA 22304

DEMCO